Textiles and Dress
of Gujarat

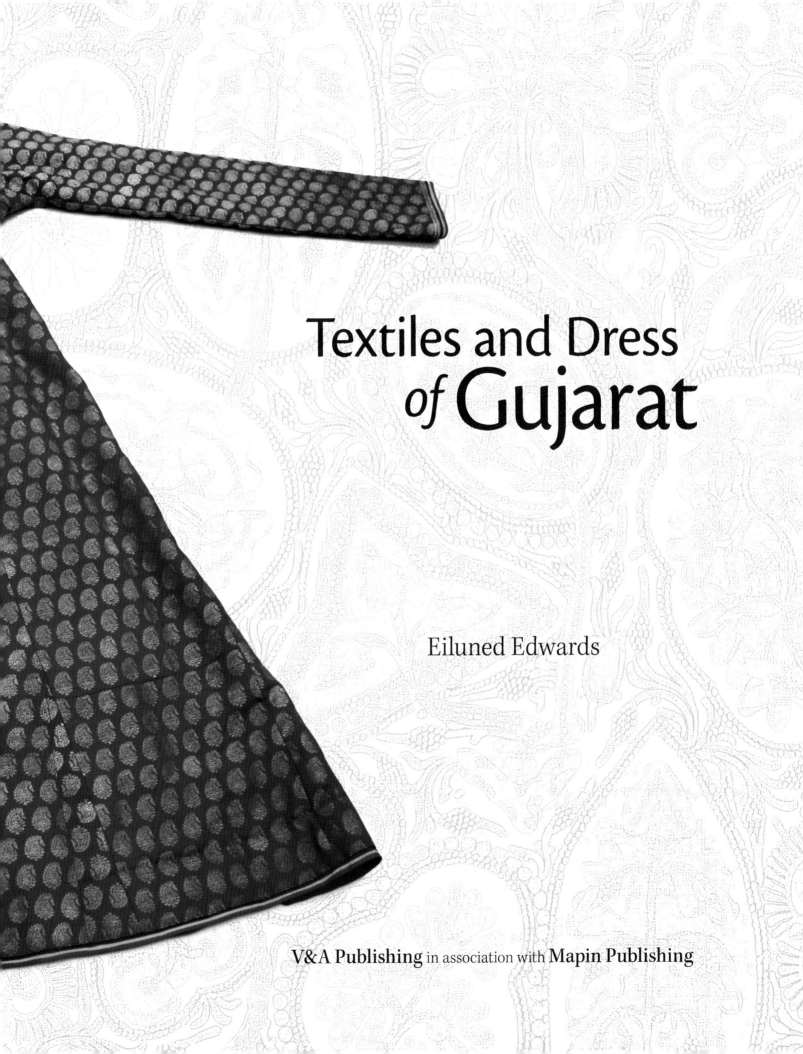

Textiles and Dress *of* Gujarat

Eiluned Edwards

V&A Publishing in association with Mapin Publishing

First published in India in 2011 by
Mapin Publishing Pvt. Ltd
502 Paritosh, Near Darpana Academy
Usmanpura Riverside, Ahmedabad 380013
T: 91 79 40 228 228 • F: 91 79 40 228 201
E: mapin@mapinpub.com • www.mapinpub.com

in association with
V&A Publishing
Victoria and Albert Museum
Cromwell Road
London SW7 2RL
T: 44 (0)20 7942 2000 • www.vandabooks.com

Simultaneously published in the
United States of America in 2011 by
Grantha Corporation
77 Daniele Drive, Hidden Meadows
Ocean Township, NJ 07712
E: mapin@mapinpub.com

Distribution
North America
Antique Collectors' Club, USA
T: 1 800 252 5231 • F: 1 413 529 0862
E: info@antiquecc.com
www.antiquecollectorsclub.com

United Kingdom, Europe, Australia & New Zealand
Macmillan Distribution (MDL)
Brunel Road
Houndmills, Basingstoke
RG21 6XS
T: 44 (0) 1256 302692 • F: 44 (0) 1256 812558
E: orders@macmillan.co.uk
www.macmillandistribution.co.uk

Southeast Asia
Paragon Asia Co. Ltd, Thailand
T: 66 2877 7755 • F: 66 2468 9636
E: info@paragonasia.com

Rest of the world
Mapin Publishing Pvt. Ltd

Text © Eiluned Edwards
Images © author, except as listed

ISBN: 978-81-89995-52-2 (Mapin)
ISBN: 978-1-935677-12-3 (Grantha)
ISBN: 978-1-851776-45-0 (V&A)
LCCN: 2010941951

Editor: Carmen Kagal/Mapin Editorial
Design: Gopal Limbad/Mapin Design Studio

Processed at Reproscan, Mumbai
Printed in Italy

PAGE 1

Detail of *pallav* (draped end of sari) of
a *patolu* woven with gold thread (*jari*)
and featuring a double ikat border

Private collection

PAGES 2−3

Man's robe (*angarkha*) of silk and gold-
wrapped thread (*jari*), lined and quilted,
L 104 x W (across sleeves) 114 cm

See appendix ill. 1 for garment analysis.

V&A: 05648 IS

FACING PAGE

Kachchhi Rabari from Gardo area,
west Kachchh, wearing a white cotton
smock (*kediyun*), an ankle-length
man's garment wrapped around the
hip (*dhoti*) and turban (*pagdi*)

Contents

Contemporary map of Gujarat

PAKISTAN

Rajasthan

Kori Creek

Great Rann

BANASKANTHA

I N D I A

Palanpur

Lakhpat

Kuran
Khavda
Dhordo
Gorewali   Ludiya
Hodko   Bhirindiara
Nirona

KACHCHH

Radhanpur   PATAN   Patan

SABARKANTHA

Visnagar

Mahesana   Himmatnagar

Rapar

Todia
Bhujodi   Lodai
Nakhtrana   Bhuj

Dhamadka
Gagodar
Bhachau

Little
Rann

MAHESANA

Pethapur

DAHOD

Anjar

Viramgam

GANDHINAGAR

KHEDA   PANCHMAHAL

Mandvi   Mundra

Ahmedabad

AHMEDABAD

Dahod

Gulf
of Kachchh

Surendranagar

Nalsarovar

Nadiad

Godhara

MADHYA
PRADESH

G U J A R A T

SURENDRANAGAR

Anand

ANAND   Vadodara

Chota Udaipur

Jamnagar

Khambhat

VADODARA

Sankheda

JAMNAGAR

Rajkot

RAJKOT

BHAVNAGAR

Rajpipla

BHARUCH

NARMADA

PORBANDAR

Bhavnagar

Bharuch

Porbandar

Amreli   Palitana

Junagadh

Shetrunji

SURAT   TAPI

JUNAGADH   AMRELI

Surat   Mandvi   Tapi

Gulf
of
Khambhat

Mangrol

Navsari

DANGS

NAVSARI   Ahwa

Valsad

VALSAD   MAHARASHTRA

Arabian Sea

INDIA

N

INDIAN OCEAN

Boundaries based upon Survey of India map with the permission of Surveyor General of India. ©2011, Government of India.
Responsibility for the correctness of internal details shown on the main map rests with the publisher.

Introduction

This book is about the contemporary production and use of handmade textiles and popular dress in the state of Gujarat, western India. It describes the types of textiles made by the region's artisans whose hereditary occupation as weavers, printers and dyers has been determined by the caste system. Similarly, local usage reflects the caste occupation and faith of local customers; the use of textiles and dress plays a key role in social institutions such as dowry and marriage. The book also tells how the consumption of textiles has changed in the past fifty years, notably with the rise of synthetic fabrics and readymade clothes, and considers the impact of this on craft production. The transformation of cloth into dress is revealed by following the 'social life' of textiles.

Handmade fabrics have played a central role in the formation of the visual identity of the peoples of Gujarat, in carefully regulated dress codes that also encompass jewellery, footwear, and body art in the form of tattoos and *mehendi* (temporary tattoos drawn in henna paste). A coherent aesthetic language is discernible across dress, textiles used in domestic and sacred space, and animal trappings, the symbolism of which is discussed. Distinctive styles of dress and decoration differentiate one community from another; they also reveal the interplay between textiles made by professional artisans, such as tie-dyed fabrics, and decoration like embroidery made by women, which until thirty or forty years ago was widely regarded only as a domestic craft. Contemporary activity is set in historical context and the factors that have influenced the evolution of the state's material culture are delineated. The book concludes with a review of current developments in handmade textiles. It identifies a range of initiatives to preserve the state's craft and textiles heritage, including schemes introduced by state agencies and non-governmental organisations (NGOs); and considers the role of entrepreneurs, educational institutions, including the National Institute of Design (NID) and the National Institute of Fashion Technology (NIFT), and museums, such as the Calico Museum of Textiles, Ahmedabad, and the Tapi Collection at Surat.

PAGE 7

Detail of a ceremonial banner made in Gujarat, radiocarbon-dated 1340 ± 40 years

Resist- and mordant-dyed, block-printed and painted resist cotton.

See fig. 1.12 for larger detail.

V&A: IS 96-1993

FACING PAGE

Embroidered skirt, ivory satin, coloured silk, L 99 x W 77.4 cm, Kachchh, early 20th century

The embroidery is entirely in chain stitch and was made by the Mochi community. The design of flowers, leafy stems and parrots is characteristic of Mochi embroidery for local use.

See appendix ill. 15 for garment analysis.

V&A: IM 246-1920

THE FORMATION OF MODERN GUJARAT

In order to understand the textiles and dress of Gujarat, it is necessary to recall the formation of the modern state. The boundaries of Gujarat in western India were established only in 1960. Prior to India becoming a sovereign nation in 1947, the area of modern Gujarat consisted of numerous smaller princely states. After independence, the national government grouped these into three larger administrative units: Kachchh, Saurashtra and Bombay State. In 1956, Kachchh and Saurashtra were absorbed into Bombay State, along with parts of Hyderabad State and Madhya Pradesh in central India. Linguistically the expanded state divided into a Gujarati-speaking north and a Marathi-speaking south; it lasted only four years. Persistent agitation on the part of Marathi nationalists for a separate state led the national government to split Bombay State into Gujarat and Maharashtra on 1 May 1960.

Considering the emergence of the modern state from older polities, many communities in Gujarat share a greater regional identity with kindred groups in neighbouring Rajasthan to the north, and Sindh province across the border in Pakistan to the west. This is expressed through shared religious practice, occupation, patterns of betrothal and marriage, and dress codes. Thus many of the groups—castes—identified in this book as Gujarati, are also to be found in Rajasthan and Sindh, the region formerly encompassed by Harappan culture—the earliest civilisation on the subcontinent which developed in the Indus Valley in the period 2500–1750 BCE. Clearly there are plural identities, defined variously by caste, gender, occupation, religion, state, country. Partition in 1947 marked the creation of the Dominion of Pakistan on 14 August and the Union of India on 15 August, and the dissolution of the British Indian Empire.

Detail of *mata-ni-pachedi*, ceremonial cloth, dyed, printed and painted

See complete cloth on pp. 138–139.

V&A: IS 6-1967

Detail of veilcloth, cotton, *roghan*
decoration

See complete cloth on p. 151.

Private collection

Many communities were divided by the international border between the two newly established countries which left some family members in Pakistan and others in India. Maintaining cultural and family links has been difficult in the face of on-going tensions between the two countries. Livelihoods were badly affected by Partition: for example, the Rabaris of Kachchh, who are pastoral nomads, lost the western extremity of their old migration routes in Sindh and Baluchistan, areas that offered respite from the recurring droughts of Kachchh. In addition to which they no longer have access to important religious sites such as the shrine of Hinglaj Mata on the Makran coast. The outbreak of hostilities between India and Pakistan in 1965 and 1971 triggered a flood of refugees, mostly Hindu Sodhas from Sindh, to Kachchh (and Rajasthan). They brought with them

FACING PAGE

LEFT

Figure used in the Kanudo ceremony marking the birth of Krishna, near Bhuj, Kachchh

Kachchhi Rabari women fashion the deity's mother in mud and dress the figure in fine clothes and gold jewellery. The infant Krishna is placed in the cavity of his mother's body. The figure is carried through the village to the temple for all-night prayers and hymns.

RIGHT

Vaghari family painting a mordant onto a *mata-ni-pachedi*, Vasna, Ahmedabad

The cloths are predominantly red and a mordant is required to permanently fix the colour to the cloth.

RIGHT

Bharwad boy, Saurashtra, wearing coloured cotton smock and drawstring trousers (*chorni*)

Private collection

FOLLOWING PAGES

Vagadia Rabari women at a wedding, east Kachchh, 1997

These women are wearing dowry items, including embroidered bodices and jewellery. Their jewellery includes necklaces of beadwork (*jermar*) and a torc (*varo*), vambrace (*chud*) of silver and a huge bangle (*baloyun*) stained an auspicious shade of red. *Baloya* were formerly made of ivory but most are now plastic.

only the things they could carry which included exquisite *suf* embroidery with distinctive triangular patterns worked in silk floss, made by the women for dowry. The sale of these embroideries, typified as 'hardship sales' by NGOs, sustained many families during the gruelling period in isolated refugee camps in Kachchh. Nowadays, the skill of Sodha women provides their families with a steady income as many of them work for NGOs making commercial embroidery. Textiles such as these present a compelling narrative, and the use of ethnographic data, drawn from nearly twenty years research in Gujarat, is a particular feature of the book. This material is then allied to the study of historic Gujarati textiles in London's Victoria and Albert Museum which are accessible to visitors to the UK or via the Museum's website. This approach gives deep insights into Gujarat's rich heritage of textiles and dress, and recognises the ingenuity and expertise of the state's craftspeople.

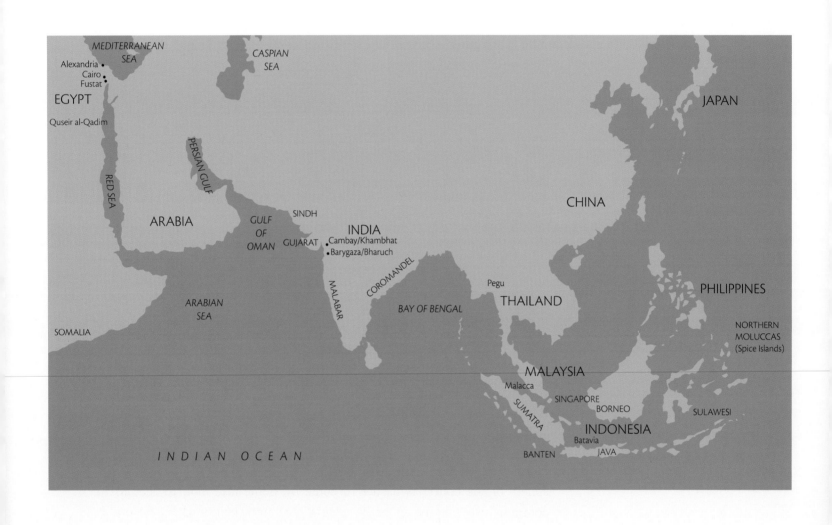

1 Historical Outline of Gujarati Textiles and Dress

TRADE, CONQUEST AND COLONISATION

The textiles and dress of Gujarat are remarkably diverse. They are part of an expansive material culture that is the product of local ingenuity, religious diversity and a long history of cross-cultural influences, the result of international trade, conquest, colonisation and diaspora.

Evidence of textile manufacture in the area that is now Gujarat goes back at least four-and-a-half thousand years to the time of the early civilisations of the Indus Valley. However, textiles and dress are notoriously ephemeral and the oldest surviving examples are only a few hundred years old, dated to the medieval period. Those of earlier epochs were used to destruction or they did not survive storage in the tropical climate of the subcontinent. But information about the region's textiles especially is widespread because of the pivotal role of Gujarat in the maritime trade of the ancient and medieval world, and a good deal has been gleaned from ancient seals, statuary, inscriptions, manuscripts and paintings. The accounts of mariners, traders, and foreign travellers in western India have been a rich source of information on the production, use and circulation of textiles used for royal and court dress. The *Ain-i-Akbari* which chronicles Emperor Akbar's reign (1556–1605) gives a particularly evocative account of the role of cloth and court dress. Precise information on regional dress and what was worn outside the elite sphere of the courts is harder to come by. Some attention to textiles in common usage came in early colonial accounts compiled by European traders and agents, although their focus—not surprisingly—is on trade textiles. An illuminating source for both styles of dress and types of textiles in common use in India is the work of John Forbes Watson (1827–1892); as Reporter for the Products of India he set out to document the full range of textiles used across the subcontinent and published his findings in some eighteen volumes that included fabric swatches. These sources have enhanced our knowledge of what was being made and where it went to, despite the absence, for the most part, of actual fabrics.

FIG 1.1 | FACING PAGE

Map of countries along the ancient maritime routes between South Asia, West Asia and North Africa

INDUS VALLEY CIVILISATION

The first civilisation on the subcontinent, and one of the earliest in the world, evolved in the Indus Valley between 2500 and 1750 BCE and encompassed the contemporary states of Gujarat, Rajasthan and the Punjab in India, and the Punjab and Sindh provinces in Pakistan. Indus or Harappan civilisation (after Harappa in Pakistan, the first site excavated in 1920–21) supported planned cities constructed of burnt brick, a sophisticated material culture and a developed economy.[1] Lothal, in Ahmedabad district, marks the eastern extent of Harappan civilisation, and is the site of the world's earliest dockyard. It connected the city to the ancient course of the Sabarmati River which formed part of the trade route between Sindh and Saurashtra when the salt desert of the Rann of Kachchh was still part of the Arabian Sea. An ancient Akkadian inscription refers to boats from 'Meluhha' (Kachchh or Mohenjodaro) bringing carnelian, ivory, shell, timber, copper and textiles to Mesopotamia (which encompassed parts of modern Iraq and Iran), and examples of Harappan beads, seals and ivory have been reported from sites throughout West Asia, the Persian Gulf and Egypt, which has led to speculation that textiles may have been traded between the Indus Valley settlements and the early civilisations of Bahrain, Sumer (modern Iraq) and Egypt.[2]

Although no textiles survive from this period, archaeological evidence in the form of spindle weights, cotton seeds, the impression of a woven textile found at a grave site, and a fragment of cotton fibre reportedly dyed with madder, confirms that the people of the Indus Valley were cultivating and processing cotton, and using mordants to permanently fix dyes to fabric.[3] The region of Gujarat was a major source of cotton for Harappan civilisation, setting the stage for continued production of the crop in the state down to the present day.[4] Without surviving textiles, precise details about the decoration of cloth and how it was used for dress are hard to come by. But some ideas can be gleaned from figurines excavated at Harappan sites. Of note in this respect is a carved steatite figurine retrieved from Mohenjodaro, dated about 2000 BCE, of a bearded man, possibly a deity or a priest, draped in a mantle decorated with a repeated trefoil design. A similar pattern known as *kakkar* (meaning 'cloud') still features in the contemporary hand embroidery of Kachchh and is also block-printed on *ajrakh*, a textile worn as a shoulder cloth, *lungi* (man's sarong-like garment) and turban by the district's cattle herders. A bronze figure of a dancing girl, also retrieved from Mohenjodaro, but of an earlier date (c. 2700 BCE), imparts valuable information about the body adorned:

FIG 1.2

Steatite male figure, possibly a priest, from Mohenjodaro, c. 2000 BCE

The trefoil pattern on the man's mantle is similar to the *kakkar* or cloud design that is still used in the block-printed and embroidered textiles of Kachchh (see fig. 1.3).

National Museum of Pakistan, Karachi, 50.852.DK 1909

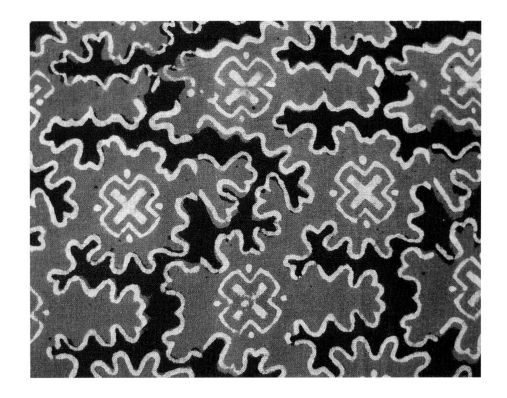

FIG 1.3

Detail of *kakkar* or cloud design

Contemporary block-printed cotton made by the Khatris of Dhamadka and Ajrakhpur in Kachchh district.

FIG 1.4 | BELOW

Bronze figurine of a dancing girl from Mohenjodaro, c. 2700 BCE

The girl's left arm is almost completely covered with bangles; the use of multiple bangles is still evident among women from rural communities in Gujarat today (see fig. 1.5).

National Museum, New Delhi, 5721/195

her hair is elaborately plaited; she wears a bead necklace, similar in type to carnelian and agate bead necklaces discovered at the site; bangles adorn her right wrist and elbow, and cover the entire length of her left arm, a style of ornamentation that prevails in Gujarat today, especially among women in Banni, north Kachchh.

EARLY TRADE TO EAST AND WEST

By the first century CE, India was at the heart of a trading network that extended from the Mediterranean to China. Indian textiles were key commodities of the period, in demand from west to east, travelling both the overland trade routes that linked the Indic world, China and Central Asia to Mediterranean Europe—often conflated into a single route known as the Silk Road—and via significant networks of maritime trade. Gujarati merchants were key figures in that maritime world, exploiting the coastal routes of the Arabian Sea and also the Indian Ocean from their home ports developed along the extensive Gujarat littoral. Boats sailed west to the ports of East Africa and the Middle East carrying goods that reached Egypt via the Red Sea and thence to the markets of the Mediterranean world; others sailed east to the markets of Malaysia, Indonesia and China.

FIG 1.5

Meghwal woman from Banni,
north Kachchh, wearing multiple
plastic bangles

Formerly, they would have been ivory.
Bangles and other ornaments are
included in a woman's dowry.

One of the earliest reports of the maritime trade is *The Periplus of the Erythraean Sea*. An anonymous Greek first century CE account of commercial activities between the ports of Gujarat, southeast India, Bengal and Egypt via the Red Sea ports, it confirms India's thriving trade with Egypt and environs in the first century CE. According to the *Periplus* the west coast was the prime trading area of India and Barygaza (later known as Broach, now Bharuch) on the Gulf of Cambay in Gujarat was not only the leading port of the day but was also a significant production centre. The *Periplus* lists cotton textiles as major trade goods from India, and notes the export of both dress and yardage from Barygaza of 'Indian garments of cotton… and a considerable amount of cloth of ordinary quality'. Indigo is also mentioned as a key export—a product which remains India's most important natural dyestuff.[5]

Although the *Periplus* mentions only the Red Sea trade, merchants from Gujarat, Bengal and the Coromandel Coast also dominated the sea-going trade in Southeast Asia during the first millennium. It is difficult to assess exactly when the Indian textile trade with the east was established but archaeological evidence suggests that Indian merchants were active in Southeast Asia by the first century CE, if not earlier.[6] Later material including statuary, architecture and inscriptions datable to the fifth century CE confirms the influence of Indic culture and the spread of Hindu-Buddhism in the region. Hindu merchant communities gradually settled throughout Indonesia and established trading posts which contributed to the consolidation of aspects of Hindu-Buddhist culture in the archipelago. Within India itself, the courtly sophistication of the first millennium clearly depended on rich and complex fabrics. In the murals at the Ajanta caves, Maharashtra, for instance, ikats and tie-dyed fabrics are clearly depicted in Cave 1 (460–478 CE) and there is a profusion of draped garments worn by both males and females.[7]

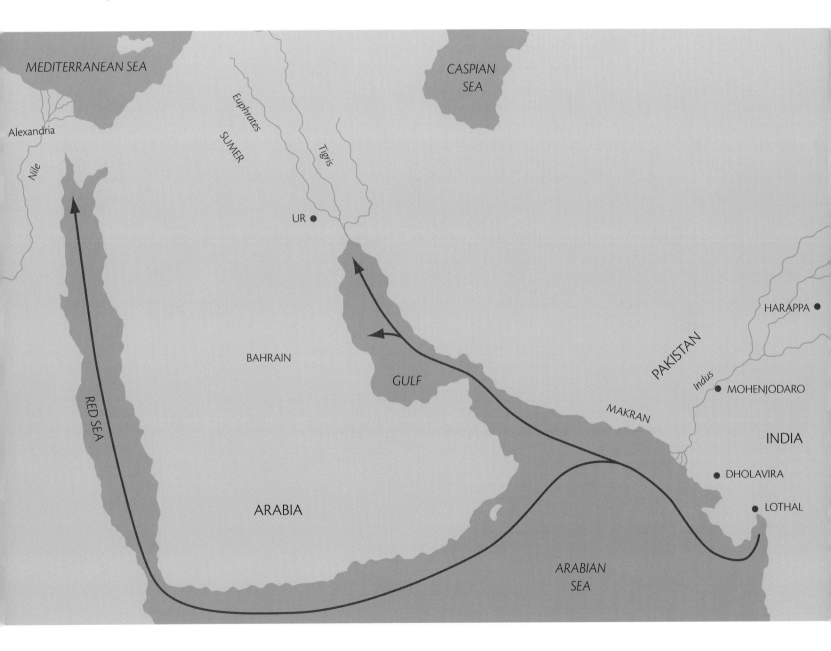

FIG 1.7

**Detail of painting of Ajanta cave 1,
c. 460–478 CE, after a full-scale
painting done in 1820**

The figures in this scene from Ajanta are
wearing wrapped lower garments that
appear to feature stripes of warp ikat.
Another sequence in the same cave (not
illustrated) shows a dancer wearing a
tie-dyed veilcloth and an ikat hip wrap.

V&A: 31-1885 IS

MEDIEVAL PERIOD

By the end of the first millennium, the Hindu Banias (merchants) who had dominated trade in Southeast Asia for several centuries were forced to relinquish their supremacy to Arabs and Indian converts to Islam, many of whom were from the trading and textile-producing communities of Gujarat, notably the Bohras (or Vohras).[8] The first Arabian incursion into the subcontinent was in 643 CE when the ports in Sindh, Saurashtra and along the Gulf of Cambay were raided. As a result of that contact Gujaratis were among the earliest converts to Islam in India. Gujarati trade with Southeast Asia rested on the highly profitable and refined exchange of Indian textiles for Indonesian spices: Gujarati cotton and silk textiles, as well as cottons from the Coromandel coast, for pepper, nutmeg, mace and the most sought after of all the spices—cloves.

It was in this period that the *patolu* of Gujarat, a double ikat silk fabric dyed with natural colours, and the mordant-printed and -painted cottons of Gujarat and the Coromandel coast, became heirlooms of high status throughout Southeast Asia, especially Indonesia. Known as *maa'*, they were credited with talismanic powers and readily became part of existing local textile customs, used for rites of passage, as part of the property transfers of marriage, and as shrouds for those of high status. Transformed from commodities to sacred objects, these funerary cloths have survived intact and have emerged as an important source of information on this aspect of the Gujarati textiles trade. Stylistically, the block-printed and painted cottons reveal the influence of western Indian figurative painting; most obviously, faces have the protruding eye that was prevalent between the twelfth

FIG 1.8

Detail of Jain manuscript painting of a monk resisting the lure of women, *Uttaradhyayana Sutra*, mid-15th century

The monk is depicted wearing diaphanous *bandhani* and the female figures patterned fabrics, the designs of which are still used in block-prints produced in Gujarat today (see fig. 1.9).

V&A: IS 2-1972, f.16b

and the sixteenth centuries, notably in Jain manuscripts. Both *maa'* and manuscripts help reveal information about the fashions of the period, showing the use of draped clothing, dressed hair, jewellery and a variety of types of decorated cloth, including tie-dyes and block-prints similar to those still in production today.

The lure of Gujarat's thriving trade attracted foreign merchants and accounts of those early travellers provide details of business activity in the state, in which the production and export of textiles was prominent. From the Persian scholar Alberuni who visited India in the eleventh century, there is a rare observation on the commonplace dress of the subcontinent, where people 'use turbans for trousers' (presumably a *dhoti*).[9] In the twelfth century, Chau Ju-kua, the inspector of foreign trade in Fu-kien in China, commented that, 'The native products [of Gujarat] comprise great quantities of indigo, myrobalan, and foreign cotton stuffs of every colour. Every year these goods are transported to the Ta-Shi [Arab or Persian] countries for sale'.[10] Marco Polo, one of the first Europeans to visit Gujarat in the late thirteenth century, noted Gujarat's cotton cultivation and indigo production, and was impressed by the quality of its embroidery, observing that, 'In this province of Gozurat... they also work here beautiful mats in red and blue leather, exquisitely inlaid with figures of birds and beasts, and skilfully embroidered with gold and silver wire. These are marvellously beautiful things...'.[11]

FACING PAGE

FIG 1.9 | ABOVE

Detail of contemporary design known as *koyaro* (spider)

Cotton, resist- and mordant-dyed, block-printed by the Khatris of Dhamadka and Ajrakhpur, Kachchh district.

FIG 1.10 | BELOW

Fragment of resist-printed and indigo-dyed cotton from Gujarat, recovered from Fustat, Egypt, L c. 22.5 x W c. 6 cm, c. 15th century

This fragment is block-printed with an imitation tie-dye (*bandhani*) design.

V&A: IS 63-1972

FIG 1.11 | ABOVE RIGHT

Fragment of resist- and mordant-dyed, block-printed cotton from Gujarat recovered from Fustat, Egypt, L 39.5 x W 23 cm; radiocarbon-dated 1340 ± 40 years

This fragment is almost identical to a textile found in Indonesia, held at the V&A (see fig. 1.12).

Ashmolean Museum, Oxford: EA 1990.1129

FIG 1.12 | RIGHT

Detail of ceremonial banner made in Gujarat for the Indonesian market, found in Sulawesi, central Toraja, Indonesia, L 480 x W 100 cm; radiocarbon-dated 1340 ± 40 years

Resist- and mordant-dyed, block-printed and painted resist cotton.

V&A: IS 74-1993

Remarkably, there is material evidence of this trade. The oldest extant textiles from India are cotton fragments that were retrieved from sites in Egypt, notably Fustat and Quseir al-Qadim, remnants of the medieval trade that saw the dispersal of cotton textiles from Gujarati ports via the Red Sea to Egypt and beyond.[12] Technically sophisticated, these textiles were resist- and mordant-printed using engraved wooden blocks; some also feature areas of mordant painting. The simplest are blue and white, resist-printed and dyed with indigo and include imitation tie-dye and designs that show the influence of Indo-Islamic architecture. Many are multi-coloured, which would require several stages of printing and dyeing, comparable with the contemporary production of *ajrakh* and associated block-prints in Kachchh for which they would seem to be the antecedents.[13] Now dispersed to collections worldwide, including the Victoria and Albert Museum in London, and the Calico Museum of Textiles, Ahmedabad, the systematic study of these fragments has been conducted chiefly at the Ashmolean Museum, Oxford, and the Kelsey Museum, University of Michigan, where radio-carbon dating has produced dates ranging from the tenth to the fifteenth century.[14] The site of Fustat is of particular note. As the capital of Egypt between 641 and 969 CE, it had been a commercial centre since Pharaonic times, developing at the meeting point of the riverine and overland trade routes. It was connected to Cairo, the later capital established by the Fatimid dynasty, and the adjoining cities formed a major entrepôt for trade between the Asian markets to the east and those of the Mediterranean to the west. The cotton textiles from Fustat and other sites in Egypt were utility goods rather than luxuries; the evidence of seams and hems indicates that they were used for clothing and furnishings and the use of flax thread (the principal fibre in Egypt at the time) attests to their having been stitched there by local tailors. The discovery of some of the fragments in the burial grounds at Fustat suggests that their end use may have been as funerary shrouds.

The fragments retrieved from sites in Egypt are strikingly similar to textiles found in Southeast Asia of a comparable age which have been preserved whole as *maa'*, discussed earlier. The use of common techniques and designs is apparent; in some cases the textiles are identical, suggesting that Gujarati crafts people were

FIG 1.13
Fragment of resist-printed and mordant-dyed cotton from Gujarat, recovered from Fustat, Egypt,
L 17.8 x W 12.7 cm, c. 15th century
The design is based on the arch-shaped *mihrab* or prayer niche in a mosque that indicates the direction of Mecca.
V&A: IS 62-1972

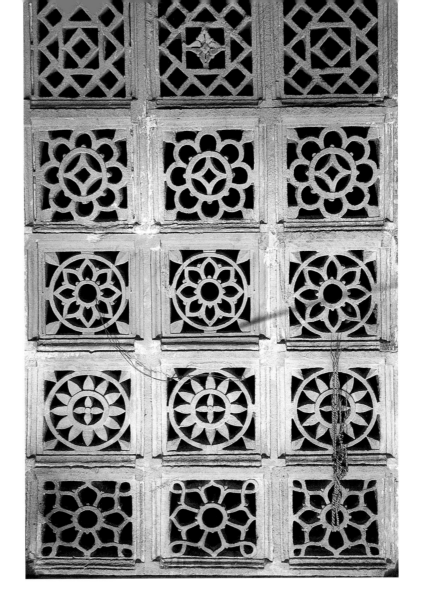

simultaneously supplying cloth and dress to communities thousands of miles
apart, serving a widely dispersed export trade as well as the home market.

If Gujarati artisans were producing their textiles in response to finely calibrated
overseas demand, they were also responding to new design influences within
India—namely the growing presence of Islamic decorative ideals and the
influx of foreign craftsmen, artists and patrons which accompanied the
expansion of Muslim power in north India. Although Gujarat had been subject
to raids by Arabs following the conquest of Sindh in the eighth century, Islam
had been introduced to the region through trade, by which means it had also
spread to Indonesia. Muslim merchants had migrated from the Middle East
and established small settlements in the commercial centres of Bharuch and
Cambay (modern Khambat), which also supported religious renouncers and
teachers. In 936 CE Zoroastrians fleeing religious persecution in Persia, a
consequence of the rise of Islam, sought refuge in Gujarat. They settled in

Sanjan—later becoming known as Parsis—and augmented the state's already diverse culture. In 1298, Gujarat came under Muslim rule after Alauddin Khalji, the sultan of Delhi, defeated Karna, the last Vaghela Rajput ruler. Islam was consolidated in the state during the Delhi Sultanate (1206–1526), during which period a distinctive style of Indo-Islamic architecture started to emerge. The decorative style evident in tombs and mosques permeated other media, notably the textiles of the period. Indeed, it was this stylistic continuity that in the early twentieth century prompted textile scholar R. Pfister to suggest that the provenance of a group of cotton fragments discovered at Fustat in Egypt might be medieval western India.[15] During the thirteenth century, India saw another wave of refugees fleeing the Mongols, princes from Iran, Iraq and Central Asia who settled in Delhi, Lahore and Multan with their retinues and 'many skilled craftsmen came from Khurasaan [Khorasan]'.[16] The period that followed was marked by innovations in textile design as the Sultans set up vast workshops, and India started to gain a reputation for luxury fabrics. The repertoire of stitched clothing also expanded during this time; *jama* (coat), *angarkha* (unlined coat with full skirt), *kurta* (tunic) and *pyjama* (trousers) were introduced for men and *salwar* (baggy drawstring trousers), *kamiz* (long tunic) and *dupatta* (veil) became part of women's dress.

INFLUENCE OF THE MUGHALS (1527–1857)

The independent Sultanate of Gujarat was established in 1403 by Zafar Khan (later Muzaffar Shah I). He was succeeded by his grandson, Ahmad Shah, who abandoned the former Solanki (Rajput) capital of Anhilvada (modern Patan), and established his capital at Ashaval in 1411, which became known as Ahmedabad.[17] The Gujarat Sultanate ended in 1573 when the region was annexed by Mughal Emperor Akbar (1556–1605) and it became a province of the empire. Gujarat was of great commercial importance to the Mughals: its ports linked India to a global trading network and the region was famous for the quality and variety of its textile manufactures. Cotton fabrics were produced in towns along the coast: Bharuch was renowned for bleached calico; Ahmedabad and Surat were famous for silk weaving, including brocade and velvet; and Sarkhej, in Ahmedabad, was the main centre for indigo production in the Mughal empire.

The Mughal empire heralded a flowering of the arts and crafts in northern India under a system of royal patronage. Craftspeople were brought in from

FIG 1.15 | FACING PAGE

Painting of Akbar's triumphant entry into Surat, 1573; ascribed to Farrukh Beg

This event marked the annexation of Gujarat by Emperor Akbar when the region became a province of the Mughal empire.

V&A: IS 2-1986

Persia and a Mughal style evolved that melded Islamic principles of design, Persian decoration and the vernacular styles of the subcontinent that influenced all aspects of material culture. At its height, the Mughal period was marked by great opulence, even profligacy—the prosperity of the empire drew European visitors to India in search of trading opportunities. Accounts by Europeans of this era give some idea of the variety and scale of textile manufactures and how craft production was organised. The French traveller, François Bernier, writing in the mid-seventeenth century, described the imperial workshops, or *karkhanas*, that had been set up in Ahmedabad and other leading cities of the day:

> 'There are besides some large halls which are the 'Kar-kanays' [*karkhanas*], that is to say the places where the craftsmen work. In one of the halls you see embroiderers occupied in their work with the master who supervises them. In another you see the goldsmiths; in yet another, the painters; in another, the lacquer workers; and in others the carpenters, the turners, the tailors, the shoe-makers. In another again, are the workers in silk and brocade and all sorts of fine fabrics of which turbans and girdles are made...'.[18]

Another Frenchman, Jean-Baptiste Tavernier, noted the particulars of indigo dyeing in Gujarat:

> 'The *baftas*, or cotton cloths required to be dyed red, blue, or black, are taken uncoloured to Agra and Ahmadabad because these two towns are near the places where indigo is made, which is used in dyeing. They cost from two rupees the piece up to thirty or forty rupees, according to fineness and the amount of gold on the ends, and in some also at the sides. The Indians know how to pass some of these cloths through a certain water which causes them to appear like a waved camlet [plain weave fabric of silk, wool or hair], and these pieces are the dearest'.[19]

But for the Mughals the power of textiles and dress to embody kingship and transmit 'the substance of authority', transcended their utility or commodity value.[20] Textiles featured in a complex system of imperial gifts known as *khilats* ('robes of honour') given by the emperor as a mark of esteem to a courtier or to visiting dignitaries. Such robes did not merely symbolise the authority of the emperor, they literally *were* authority; thus acceptance of *khilats* indicated the recipient's subservient status. Textiles were also a notable part of the tribute paid to the emperor by provinces under his sovereignty. In Gujarat this meant regular supplies to the court of the renowned Ahmedabadi silk brocades and chain stitched embroideries in silk and gold thread (*jari*).[21] As was the royal custom, all such tributes were stored in special warehouses with the emperor's clothes, arms and jewellery, the contents of which were carefully inventoried and categorised. The *Ain-i-Akbari*—the chronicle of the emperor Akbar's reign, compiled in about 1590 by Abu'l-Fazl—reveals the diversity and value (calculated in gold coins known as *mohur*) of textiles from Gujarat. Within the rich variety of silks, cottons and woollens, it lists under 'Gold stuffs' alone, an astonishing range of brocades including brocaded velvet (10-50 *mohur* per piece), *tas* (1-35 *mohur*), *dara-i-baf* (2-50 *mohur*), *muqayyash*—with silver stripes (1-20 *mohur*), *shirwani* (6-17 *mohur*), and *kurtahwar* (1-20 *mohur*).[22]

It is apparent from the *Ain-i-Akbari* that the emperor took a very close interest in all aspects of cloth production and also intervened in clothing design. Abu'l-Fazl records several pages of innovations. 'The *takauchiya* is a coat without lining, of the Indian form. Formerly it had slits in the skirt and was tied on the left side; His Majesty has ordered it to be made with a round skirt and to be tied on the right side. It requires seven yards and seven *girihs*, and five *girihs* for the binding... '.[23] In a subtle reading of the passage aligned to a study of the paintings of the period, B.N. Goswamy interprets Akbar's intervention as a device to provide a visual distinction between the two religious communities; Hindus were to tie their coats on the left and Muslims on the right—a distinction retained in contemporary *angarkha* and *kediyun* (hip-length smock) worn by several castes of Hindu farmers and herders.[24] Akbar also developed a new terminology for existing garments: 'His Majesty has changed the names of several garments, and invented new and pleasing terms. Instead of *jama* (coat), he says *sarbati*, i.e., covering the whole body; for *izar* (drawers), he says *yar-pirahan* (the companion of the coat); for *nimtana* (a jacket), *tanzeb*...'.[25] Unlike earlier Mughal emperors such as Babur who self-consciously maintained his 'outsider' status by wearing garments of a Central Asian style, Akbar saw dress as a means for the Mughals to merge an alien identity with that of their adopted country. Goswamy suggests that by re-naming garments, Akbar 'planned on overcoming resistances, reaching out in both directions, that of the conquerors and the conquered, the Muslims and the Hindus, in an attempt to narrow down cleavages and introduce a certain uniformity without necessarily destroying separate identities'.[26]

The introduction of garments that reflected the Central Asian heritage of the Mughals (and the Delhi Sultans) as well as Akbar's innovations saw an expansion of the range of garments worn on the subcontinent. This was, however, chiefly confined to the sphere of court dress. Outside the court, dress remained predominantly wrapped and draped cotton, as Chaplain Terry observed during Jehangir's reign (1605–1627):

'The habits both of the men and the women are little different, made for the most part of white cotton-cloth. For the fashion, they are close, straight to the middle, hanging loose downward below the knee. They wear long breeches underneath, made close to their bodies that reach to their ankles, ruffling like boots on the small of their legs. Their feet are bare in their shoes, which most commonly they wear like slippers... The men's heads are covered with a long, thin wreathe of cloth, white or coloured, which goes many times about them; they call it Sash. They uncover not their heads when they shew reverence to their superiors'.[27]

FIG 1.16

Dhebaria Rabari from east Kachchh wearing a smock known as *kediyun*

This style of garment, which fastens asymmetrically with ties, is used by several communities of farmers and herders in rural Gujarat.

Further evidence of everyday dress during Mughal times comes from the Italian adventurer, Nicolas Manucci, who noted, regarding a visit to Surat in 1655–56:

'I was much amused to see the greater number of inhabitants dressed in white clothes, also the many different kinds of people, as well men as women. The latter, mostly Hindus, do not conceal the face as in Persia and Turkey, where women go about with their faces hidden. It is true that the Mahomedan women do not allow their faces to be seen by anyone, it being contrary to their law to allow themselves to be seen with an uncovered face'.[28]

When Europeans first arrived at the trading centres of the Indian Ocean in the early sixteenth century, they discovered a highly organised trading system that was run by Arab, Indian and Chinese merchants. One of the earliest, the Portuguese traveller, Tomé Pires, remarked upon the prevalence of Gujarati merchants: 'There is no doubt that these people have the cream of the trade... There are Gujaratees settled everywhere'.[29] In order to break into the established spice trade, Europeans needed to secure goods that were in demand in the 'Spice Islands' (Moluccas); it was the popularity of Indian textiles throughout Southeast Asia that eventually enabled them to do so. Jan Pietersz Coen, the Director-General of the Dutch East India Company (Vereenigde Oost-Indische Compagnie, or VOC), noted that: 'Piece goods [textiles] we can barter for pepper and gold on the coast of Sumatra; rials and cottons from the [Coromandel] coast for the pepper of Banten—one thing leads to another'.[30] Thus, initially, Indian 'calicoes' were bartered for spices, and these two commodities were to be the foundations of the trade of the East India Companies.

It was initially only as a sideline to the spice trade that Indian cottons were brought to Europe. But by the beginning of the seventeenth century chintz from the Coromandel coast and *baftas*, plain red and blue dyed cottons from Gujarat, had become significant commodities in their own right. Surat superseded Cambay as the chief port of western India. British ships had first docked there in 1608 and after receiving an imperial mandate in 1612, the East India Company established a 'factory' in the port which became the headquarters for much of its export trade. By 1664, textiles accounted for nearly three-quarters of the goods exported from India.[31] From Surat, the East India Company supplied Europe with indigo, printed cloth, quilts and fine chain-stitched embroideries, made by professional male embroiderers from the Mochi, or cobbler's caste, who used an *ari* (a refined version of a cobbler's awl) rather than a needle. Bhuj, the capital of the principality of Kachchh, emerged as a leading production centre for Mochi embroidery; under Maharao Lakhpat (1741–1760) the institutions of a great court were founded at Bhuj, and royal patronage allowed the arts and crafts to flourish.[32]

At its peak in the seventeenth century, the Mughal empire sustained a vibrant and influential material culture and a flourishing export trade, notably of textiles to Europe where Indian textiles became an integral part of European fashions and furnishings of the day. The volume of goods from Gujarat and other parts of India supplied to Britain led to a considerable trade imbalance which had to be redressed with silver bullion. But as Mughal authority weakened in the eighteenth century, the *karkhanas* dispersed and artisans sought employment at the regional courts and other centres of production, and the British East India Company gradually assumed control of the administration of India.

मद्दारावश्रीतिकासिजी

BRITISH POWER IN INDIA: FROM TRADING COMPANY TO THE RAJ

Although trade had brought the British to India, the decline of the Mughal power saw them gradually take control of governance. The process was initiated by the conquest of Bengal by Robert Clive in 1757, and proceeded via direct military action, alliances with native princes, and bureaucratic consolidation. It was only after the Great Revolt of 1857, though, that the East India Company finally gave way to direct rule by the British Crown.[33] Thus it was in 1858 that Queen Victoria launched what became known as the Raj—which lasted until Indian independence in 1947.

During the early years of British rule, little commentary on local dress emerged. One of the rare accounts is provided by Marianna Postans. As the wife of Lieutenant Thomas Postans of the Bombay Native Infantry, who was posted to Kachchh between 1834 and 1839, she wrote a picturesque evocation of the place which gives rare details of specific caste dress. In contrast to earlier travellers' descriptions of popular dress as chiefly composed of draped garments of white cotton, she wrote of the 'peculiarly bright and varied costume' of the inhabitants of Mandvi, and 'the long moustache of the Rajpoot tribe; his arms are a sword, shield and matchlock, and his dress and bearings are marked by an air of mingled haughtiness, foppery and independence.' Her description alludes to the status of Rajputs as members of the warrior caste (Kshatriyas), while its sceptical tone conveys their posturing. She was clearly far more enchanted by the attire of Bania (merchant caste) women which she described thus:

> 'It consists of a satin petticoat with broad horizontal stripes of red, blue and yellow over a bodice tightly covering the bust, and embroidered with various-coloured silks; over the head and shoulders flows the usual "saree", which as it gracefully flutters on the breeze, affords a charming effect of grace and softness to the outlines of their elastic figures, whilst the becoming variety of colours selected for their dress, and the brightness of their numerous ornaments, adds gaiety and animation of no common order to the passing scene'.[34]

Only a few years later, in the 1860s, details of Indian popular dress were assiduously noted for the commercial advantage of the Empire. India was seen as a growth market for the fruits of Britain's industrial revolution. In the UK the mechanisation of cotton spinning—often of raw cotton imported from India—textile dyeing and printing led to large-scale production of

FIG 1.17 | FACING PAGE

Painting of Rao Lakhpatji, c. 1750

This formal portrait makes reference to late Mughal and Rajasthani portraits and shows the Rao in an embroidered coat or *jama*, cummerbund or *patka*, *laheriya* or wave-patterned turban and fine jewellery. He is attended by a Sidi (Muslim of Abyssinian origin) retainer.

Private collection

cheap cotton goods specifically developed for the Indian masses. Design intelligence was supplied by John Forbes Watson, Reporter for the Products of India and Director of the Indian Museum, who recorded in detail the types of textiles used for popular forms of dress in India.[35] Published in eighteen volumes that included samples of textiles collected in India, his work was conceived as portable 'industrial museums' that would enable the Lancashire cotton mills to produce manufactures suitable for the taste of the 'hundreds and millions of lower grades' in India, most of whom wore wrapped garments of unstitched cloth.[36] Commercial ambition also marked British opposition to the mechanisation of the cotton industry in India, which took the form of punitive protectionist legislation sustained until 1925.

Nonetheless, the first mechanised cotton mill was established in Mumbai in 1854. The first in what was to be the second principal centre of the cotton industry in western India, Ahmedabad, came in 1861 through the initiative of Ranchhodlal Chhotalal and a group of local financiers. Indeed, so many mills were set up in Ahmedabad in subsequent years—including the Calico Mill (1880) which became one of the largest corporations in India[37]—that the city earned the sobriquet of 'the Manchester of the East'.[38] Handloom weavers did not fare as well; the influx of cheap British cloth into India combined with the growth of Indian mills undermined the market for indigenous handlooms and left thousands of weavers out of work and starving. From the late nineteenth century onwards, Indian nationalists used the example of the weaving industry to illustrate the negative impact of British commercial domination. Under the leadership of Mahatma Gandhi, a Gujarati Bania from Porbandar in Saurashtra, Indian sensibilities about cloth and dress were harnessed to promote the *swadeshi* (home produce) movement, and *khadi* (handspun handwoven cloth) became 'the cloth of independence'.[39]

AFTER 1947

In the post-colonial period, Gujarat has embraced the policy of industrialisation that was launched by Jawaharlal Nehru (1889–1964), the first prime minister of independent India. It has developed into one of the most heavily industrialised states in the Republic, where the historic culture of entrepreneurship has been supported by nodal agencies that were established in the early days of nationhood. In 1947, the year of independence, the Ahmedabad Textiles and Industrial Research Association (ATIRA) was founded and other key institutions

FIG 1.18 | FACING PAGE

Illustration from John Forbes Watson (1867), *The Textile Manufactures and Costumes of the People of India*, vol. 1, plate III: Male attire, cotton

Forbes Watson compiled 18 volumes of samples of Indian textiles to serve as 'portable industrial museums' that would inspire textile manufacturers in Britain and make them aware of the vast Indian market. He also devoted a volume to explaining how the textiles were worn as clothing in India with illustrations.

V&A: IS 1-2002

MALE ATTIRE. COTTON.

followed, notably the Indian Institute of Management (IIM) in 1961, and the National Institute of Design (NID) and the Centre for Environmental Planning and Technology (CEPT) in 1962. Gujarat was also at the forefront of the mid-twentieth century polyester boom; it is the home state of the late Dhirubhai Ambani (1932–2002), the founding father of the industrial giant, Reliance Industries, which is now the world's largest producer of polyester yarn and fibre, and owner of the famous Vimal brand of saris and suitings. Garden Silk Mills, another of India's leading industrial groups in the field of fashion fabrics, was founded at Surat, and sells high quality synthetics, cottons and silks worldwide. But Gujarat's embrace of modern technology occurs in tandem with ancient 'lo-tech' practices—notably craft—and conservative social customs, especially in the rural areas of the state.

FIG 1.19 | FACING PAGE

Embroidered portrait of Gandhi,
c. 1930

This portrait was embroidered in chain stitch by a professional embroiderer from the Mochi community in Bhuj, Kachchh district, using an *ari* or hook.

Collection of the Shrujan Trust

FIG 1.20 | RIGHT

Garden Silk Mills advert, 2009

Garden Silk Mills based in Surat is one of India's leading textile manufacturers, selling high quality synthetics, cottons and silks worldwide.

Photograph courtesy of Garden Silk Mills

Notes

1 Wheeler, M., *The Indus Civilization*, London: Book Club Associates by arrangement with Cambridge University Press, p. 86.

2 Sharma, D.P. and Madhuri Sharma , *Panorama of Harappan Civilization*, New Delhi: Kaveri Books, pp. 60–64.

3 A fragment of cotton fibre was retrieved from a dyer's workshop at the site of Mohenjodaro and dated to 1760 BCE ± 115. This was reportedly dyed with madder, a natural dye that requires the use of a mordant, or metallic salt, to permanently bond the colour to the fabric. The mordant combines with the dyestuff to create an insoluble substance that coats the fibre. Manipulation of this sophisticated technology at such an early date attests to the skill of dyers from the subcontinent. See Pfister, R., 'Tissus imprimés de l'Inde médiévale', *Revue des Arts Asiatiques*, 10, pp. 161–164 and *Les Toiles imprimées de Fostat et l'Hindoustan*, Paris: Les Editions d'Art et d'Histoire. Also Gittinger, M., *Master Dyers to the World*, Washington D.C.: The Textile Museum, p. 19.

4 The species of cotton at that time was *Gossypium arboreum* which required a long period of cultivation. The export of cotton on a major scale was only possible after the introduction in the sixth or seventh century BCE, of *Gossypium herbaceum*, which could be harvested annually. See Sharma and Sharma, p. 60 and Askari, N. and Rosemary Crill, *Colours of the Indus. Costumes and Textiles of Pakistan*, London: Merrell Holberton in association with V&A Publications, pp. 8–9.

5 Casson, L., *The Periplus Maris Erythraei*, Princeton: Princeton University Press, p. 81.

6 Guy, J., *Woven Cargoes. Indian Textiles in the East*, London: Thames and Hudson, p. 55.

7 Behl, B.K., *The Ajanta Caves. Ancient Paintings of Buddhist India*, London: Thames and Hudson, pp. 84–103.

8 Campbell, J.M., *Muslim and Parsi Castes and Tribes of Gujarat*, Gurgaon: Vintage Books, p. 29.

9 Alberuni (Muhammad ibn Ahmad Bīrūnī), originally from Persia, came to India with the invading forces of Mahmud of Ghazni of Afghanistan. Sultan Mahmud turned the provincial city of Ghazni, now in Afghanistan, into the capital of a prosperous empire that covered much of Afghanistan, Pakistan and north-west India. See Sachau, E.C.,trans., *Alberuni's India*, New Delhi: Low Price Publications.

10 Barnes, R., *Indian Block-Printed Textiles in Egypt. The Newberry Collection in the Ashmolean Museum, Oxford*, vols. I and II, Oxford: Oxford University Press, p. 100.

11 Yule, H. and Henri Cordier, eds., *The Book of Ser Marco Polo*, vol. 2, New Delhi: Munshiram Manoharlal Publishers Pvt Ltd, pp. 393–394.

12 Vogelsang-Eastwood, G., *The Resist Dyed Textiles from Quseir al-Qadim*, Egypt, Paris: A.E.D.T.A.

13 *Ajrakh* is a block-printed textile traditionally resist-dyed with indigo and madder that is made by the Khatri caste of dyers and printers in Kachchh district, Gujarat, Jaisalmer and Barmer in Rajasthan, and Sindh province in Pakistan. It is printed on both sides of the fabric with complex geometric and floral patterns; the overall design features a centre panel framed by a series of borders.

14 Barnes, R., 1997, 2 vols, and Barnes, 1993, *Indian Block-Printed Cotton Fragments in the Kelsey Museum, The University of Michigan*, Ann Arbor: The University of Michigan Press.

15 Pfister, R., 'Tissus imprimés de l'Inde médiévale', in *Revues des Arts Asiatiques*, 10, pp. 161–164 and *Les Toiles Imprimées de Fostat et l'Hindoustan*, Paris: Editions d'Art et d'Histoire. For discussion of Pfister's work, see Barnes, 1997.

16 Isami cit. Alkazi, R., *Medieval Indian Costume*, New Delhi: Art Heritage, p. 14.

17 Burton-Page, J., "Historical Context", in Michell, G. and Snehal Shah, *Ahmadabad*, Mumbai: Marg Publications, pp. 18–20.

18 Bernier cit. Irwin, J. and Margaret Hall, *Indian Embroideries*, Ahmedabad: Calico Museum of Textiles, p. 5. It is believed that the system of *karkhanas* was introduced to India by the emperor Akbar, based on the model of Safavid Persia, although large-scale workshops had been established during the thirteenth century under the Delhi Sultanate, at Delhi, Lahore and Multan.

19 Crooke, W., ed., *Tavernier's Travels in India, 1676*, vols. I and II, trans., Valentine Ball, Oxford: Oxford University Press, p. 5.

20 Cohn, B.S., "Cloth, Clothes and Colonialism. India in the Nineteenth Century", in Annette B. Weiner and Jane Schneider, eds., *Cloth and Human Experience*, Washington and London: Smithsonian Institution Press, p. 313.

21 Bayly, C.A., "The Origins of *Swadeshi* (Home Industry): Cloth and Indian Society, 1700–1930, in Appadurai, A., ed., *The Social Life of Things. Commodities in Cultural Perspective*, Cambridge: Cambridge University Press, p. 299.

22 Abu'l-Fazl Allami, *Ain-i-Akbari*, trans., H. Blochmann, Delhi: Low Price Publications, pp. 98–102.

23 Abu'l-Fazl Allami, p. 94.

24 Goswamy, pp. 15–16.

25 Abu'l-Fazl Allami, p. 96.

26 Goswamy, p. 15.

27 Foster, W., *Early Travels in India, 1583–1619*, London: Humphrey Milford, p. 308.

28 Manucci, N., *A Pepys of Mogul India (1653–1708),* New Delhi: Srishti Publishers, pp. 29–30.

29 Cortesao, Armando, ed., *The Suma Oriental of Tomé Pires*, 2 vols. London: Hakluyt Society, vol. 2, p. 41.

30 The Dutch East India Company, Vereenigde Oost-Indische Compagnie (VOC), was founded in 1619. Coen is quoted by John Guy, p. 15.

31 Crill, R., *Chintz. Indian Textiles for the West*, London: V&A Publishing, p. 15.

32 Goswamy, B.N. and Anna Dallapiccola, *A Place Apart. Painting in Kutch, 1720–1820*, New Delhi: Oxford University Press, pp. 10–13.

33 Dalrymple, W., *The Last Mughal*, London: Bloomsbury Publishing, pp. 11–20.

34 Postans, M., *Cutch; or Random Sketches, Taken During a Residence in One of the Northern Provinces of Western India; Interspersed with Legends and Traditions*, New Delhi: Asian Educational Services, pp. 10–16.

35 The Indian Museum was originally the museum of the East India Company. The collection was managed by the India Office from 1861 to 1879, after which it was handed over to the South Kensington Museum which later became known as the V&A. See Burton, A., *Vision and Accident. The Story of the Victoria and Albert Museum*, London: V&A Publications, pp. 118–120.

36 Forbes Watson, J., *The Textile Manufactures and Costumes of the People of India*, London: Eyre and Spottiswoode, p. 7. A set is held at the V&A. For further details of Forbes Watson's work and distribution of the volumes, see Swallow, D., "The Indian Museum and the British-Indian Textile Trade in the Late Nineteenth Century", in *Textile History*, vol. 30, no. 1, Spring 1999, pp. 29–45.

37 The company's full title is the Ahmedabad Manufacturing and Calico Printing Company Limited.

38 Pandya, Y., ed., *The Ahmedabad Chronicle. Imprints of a Millennium*, Ahmedabad: Vastu-Shilpa Foundation, p. 16.

39 Bean, S.S., "Gandhi and *Khadi*, the Fabric of Indian Independence" in Annette B. Weiner and Jane Schneider, eds., *Cloth and Human Experience*, Washington and London: Smithsonian Institution Press, pp. 355–376.

2 Contemporary Dress

NARRATIVES OF MODERN DRESS

The popular *salwar kamiz*, also known as the 'Punjabi suit', combines *salwar* or *churidar (pyjama)* with a *kamiz* (dress/tunic) and *dupatta* (scarf/veil). It is a practical alternative to a sari for urban women; it is girls' uniform at many Gujarati schools; and is widely worn by 'college girls' throughout the state. For all its practicality, use of this modest ensemble is problematic, especially in rural Gujarat. When Renu, one of the first Vagadia Rabari girls to attend high school in Kachchh in the late 1990s, started to wear standard school uniform—a blue *kamiz* with black *salwar* and *dupatta*—unwittingly, she entered a cultural minefield. She rapidly discovered that adherence to the school dress code brought rejection from her own community, and she was, in effect, ostracised: 'No one recognised me in the village. They didn't offer me food or tea. They said, "She is not Rabari but someone from the village who has come to look". They didn't allow me to enter the house either.'[1] Those reactions were not unique to Rabaris. In rural Saurashtra the *salwar kamiz* had first started to appear in the 1980s but remained confined to 'the educated few'. Some Hindus seemed to fear Islamic influence;[2] others, as Mukulika Banerjee and Daniel Miller have argued, worried that by wearing a *salwar kamiz* girls 'might start to acquire what was perceived as the immodest licence and freedom of city college girls'.[3] The disapproving reception to the *salwar kamiz* in these different contexts reveals how dress provides a medium in which new identities are publicly tested. As such it provides a useful starting point from which to explore ideas of dress in Gujarat.[4]

Contemporary Gujarat presents a rich variety of dress. Surveying the bazaar in any town or city, the sheer diversity

of garments, types of fabrics, methods of textile decoration, forms of adornment, jewellery, *mehendi* and tattoos, defy calculation. The styles and technologies of several millennia are compressed in a single moment and the visual impact is considerable. The experience underlines 'India's notable orientation to the visual', the precedent for which—according to some observers—is the Hindu concept of *darshan*, or 'sacred sight'.[5] In this context, little about dress is random; textiles and clothing are a powerful form of non-verbal communication that has been harnessed into a complex symbolic language. As Christopher Bayly observed, 'Indian society spoke partly in the idiom of cloth'.[6]

Until the development of the polyester industry in the 1950s, people's clothes were made from natural fibres, with cotton the most widely used. Apart from an elite few who had access to imported goods and the wherewithal to buy them, most Gujaratis wore indigenous cotton products from the power looms of Ahmedabad and Mumbai and used handmade textiles such as *khadi, mashru* (satin with a silk warp and a cotton weft), wool and silk. With the emergence of the polyester industry in the 1950s, synthetics fabrics have become an integral part of the narratives of Gujarati dress. Roller-printed polyester copies of popular block-prints, tie-dyes (*bandhani)* and *mashru* abound;[7] they offer cheap alternatives to handmade items. Ersatz versions of brocade and velvet woven in 'art silk' (rayon) and polyester—fabrics previously used by the privileged—have been incorporated into the vibrant ensembles of contemporary dress. Synthetics and industrially manufactured goods are worn alongside textiles that have been woven, block-printed, dyed and embroidered by hand, in a variety of styles including: wrapped and draped garments such as the sari, *dhoti* (man's draped lower garment) and *lungi* (man's sarong-like garment); stitched *salwar kamiz, kurta* and *angarkha;* Western styles like the ubiquitous 'shirt-pants' favoured by men of all ages; and 'fusion' styles such as the combination of jeans and a block-printed *kurta* that is especially popular with students.[8] These fabrics and fashions express the identity of the wearer and demonstrate aspirations of every sort.

As Renu's example suggests, though, not all options were available to people at all times. Numerous factors come together to influence choices of contemporary dress in Gujarat. Here I explore five broad themes: caste and community; modesty; adornment and auspiciousness; purity and pollution; stitched versus unstitched cloth.

FIG 2.1 | FACING PAGE

Vagadia Rabari girl from Kachchh wearing school uniform of *salwar kamiz* and *dupatta*

In conservative areas of Gujarat the use of *salwar kamiz* can be problematic because for some it represents liberal urban mores and the influence of Islam.

FIG 2.2 | FOLLOWING PAGE

Inside section of man's robe (*angarkha*) of silk and gold-wrapped thread (*jari*), lined and quilted

It is decorated with gold *zardozi* embroidery at the neck. Worn as court dress in Sindh, Pakistan, mid-19th century. The fabric was probably made in Ahmedabad which was renowned for its sumptuous figured silks and satins until the decline of the industry in the early 20th century.

See complete garment on pp. 2–3

V&A: 05648 IS

CASTE DRESS

In Gujarat, as in other states, the details of dress have provided a means of differentiating between groups. The use of certain fabrics, a particular style of jewellery and clothing traditionally has identified a person's caste and religious faith. The hereditary system of caste remains a persistent feature of Indian society, despite it having been formally abolished under the Indian Constitution (1950).[9] Although caste is particularly associated with Hinduism, it is apparent across all faiths in India, and is sustained by the custom of arranged marriage, as a glance at the matrimonial pages of the *Times of India* reveals.[10] Although applicants to the service can opt for 'caste no bar', the majority define themselves by caste, region and religion and are seeking a partner whose background is compatible with, if not the same as, their own. Religion still plays a central role in daily life, and few Gujaratis describe themselves as having no faith.[11] Religious tenets underpin many social customs and have a direct influence on the clothing choices of a majority of people. Overt religious identification is evident in the *burqa* worn by some groups of Muslim women, the widespread use of prayer caps by Muslim men, and the saffron robes of members of the Swaminarayan sect, but there is a considerable repertoire of garments common to all religious groups. Nonetheless, in Gujarat, particular styles of dress and ornament have been a means of placing an individual in the social schema.

How dress identifies individuals is subject to interpretation. Despite Forbes Watson's claim, made in the mid-nineteenth century, that 'there is a much greater fixity of fashion in India than in Europe', others have noted innovations over time.[12] Thus, the late nineteenth century scholar Fazalullah Lutfullah noted, 'Among rich Musulmans the fashion of dress is changing. The long full dress robe *jama* and the loose trousers *tammán* of the Delhi court have fallen into disuse... and woollen coats buttoned to the neck and patent leather shoes are coming into use'.[13] Fazalullah Lutfullah's account reveals how richly varied dress was in a single group. A comparable diversity is evident in the sartorial landscape of modern Gujarat, where highly mutable fashion co-exists with a 'fixity' of dress, that is not solely an urban-rural divide, but is also a matter of customs of clothing,

FIG 2.3

Patanwadi Rabari women from north Gujarat wearing the embroidered 'half-sari' that indicates their married status

The draping of the garment and the style of embroidery, which is customarily executed in an interlacing stitch using deep pink thread on a dark background, are associated particularly with the Patanwadi subgroup.

FIG 2.4

Nagar Brahmin woman wearing a double ikat silk sari or *patolu* for her brother's *janoi* (sacred thread) ceremony, Ahmedabad, 1975

Patola were customarily worn by Nagar women for religious ceremonies and weddings. They were also used by Jain and Bohra merchants, particular designs being associated with each community.

Photograph courtesy of Dhruv family

FIG 2.5 | FACING PAGE

Detail of *patolu* featured in fig. 2.4 known as *popat kunjar bhat*

It is particularly associated with Gujarati Brahmins. The pattern features elephants, flowers and red and green parrots arranged within a trellis. The silk threads have been expertly dyed and woven to produce a clearly defined ikat pattern.

Private collection

or worship, even occupation expressing a community's core values. Thus Patanwadi Rabaris who migrated from northern Gujarat to Ahmedabad in the 1960s and have established a niche for themselves in the city's social fabric, have maintained their use of caste dress.[14]

Nonetheless, caste dress has greater prevalence in remote parts of the state among more conservative communities, and is most assiduously worn by the older generation. Despite being one of the most industrialised states in India, much of Gujarat is dominated by agriculture and pastoralism. The use of 'caste dress' has persisted among farmers and herders in parts of Saurashtra and the desert district of Kachchh where change has come slowly because of its remoteness. But not every community can be said to have or have had a 'caste dress' as such. In common with Fazalullah Lutfullah's 'rich Musulmans', the comparative wealth of the urban, educated elite allows them to enjoy a flexibility of dress that is not apparent in other sectors of society. In this social stratum, choice of clothing is largely up to the individual, and women have as much choice as men; personal preference is determined largely by the particular social context and the occasion. But in parallel to the formal rules of conservative pastoral and farming castes which regulate 'age appropriate' styles, there is a marked tendency for Hindu women to wear saris after they marry, and to abandon the daily use of *salwar kamiz*, or jeans and T-shirt, that they wore in their youth. The young especially draw on a wide range of influences, and are as *au fait* with Western fashions as they are with Indian modes of dress.[15]

Some urbanites are aware of the association of their caste with certain fabrics, ways of draping a sari, or methods of tying a turban, but perceive these customs as part of their history, and not as current fashion. For example, the *patolu,* an exquisite double ikat silk sari made in Patan, was formerly worn by Nagar Brahmins, Jains and Bohras (Ismaili Muslim merchants) on ceremonial occasions. These groups were identified by their use of *patola* and were associated with particular patterns, such as the parrot and elephant design known as *popat kunjar bhat* favoured by Nagars, and the non-figurative *Vohra gajji bhat,* preferred

by the Muslim Bohras. Nowadays, old *patola* are perceived as 'museum pieces— beautiful, but we don't wear them'—and are preserved as heirlooms rather than worn as contemporary dress, although synthetic copies of *popat kunjar bhat* have become widely popular.[16]

Even among the most conservative individuals and groups dress codes are not static; they reflect social change and technological developments. The typical village dress of Hindu women throughout Gujarat (and Rajasthan) consists of a three-part ensemble of a gathered, ankle length skirt (*ghaghra*), backless blouse (*kanchali* or *kapadu*) and veilcloth (*odhani*) or half-sari (*sadlo*).[17] Girls' clothes are essentially the same; the chief difference is in the cut of their blouses, the front of which lacks the ruching around the bust that signifies a married woman. Although a good deal of change was evident in urban dress in the late nineteenth century, the three basic components of female dress in this context have been steadfast for many centuries.[18]

But the textiles from which it is made and the manner of its making has undergone radical change in the past fifty years. The production of dress in the rural areas of Gujarat used to rely on a network of castes. The basic fabric was made by weavers, usually locally based; it then passed to the dyers and printers for surface decoration and would be sold from the workshop, in the bazaar, or hawked from village to village, by a system known as *pheriya* which is still the practice among a few Khatris (caste of dyers and block-printers) in west Kachchh.[19] Clients would purchase the cloth and take it to their tailor for stitching; the garment was not finished until distinctive embroidery and mirrorwork had been added after tailoring by the women for their own use which finally transformed it into caste dress. This pattern of production has now largely disappeared; while the orthodox style of caste 'uniform' is still in place, aniline dyes have supplanted natural colours, handmade fabrics have been superseded by polyester and factory-made cloth; braids and sequins are rapidly replacing hand embroidery.[20] These changes reflect technological innovations in the prevalent use of polyester on the one hand, and illustrate the disappearance of handmade fabrics from local usage on the other. This has raised questions about the future of craft and the sustainability of the state's distinctive cultural heritage in the twenty-first century.

As Gujarat modernises and the meaning of caste identity is contested, dress is important as a medium in which change is visibly negotiated, reflecting

FIG 2.6 | FACING PAGE
Patolu sari, silk, double ikat, L 440 x W 110 cm, Gujarat, probably Patan, late 19th or early 20th century

This non-figurative design was popular with Bohras, an Ismaili Muslim merchant community, and is known as *Vohra gajji bhat* ('Vohra-type design').

V&A: IS 190-1960

the influence of social and technological developments. One compelling contemporary example of that negotiation through dress is offered by the Rabaris of Kachchh, a community of pastoral nomads that is currently engaged in a process of change. It is a process that many Gujarati communities have already undergone. The modernising agenda of successive governments since independence in 1947 has gradually reached even the most remote rural outposts of the state, rendering many of the occupational categories of caste redundant. The hereditary caste occupation of Rabaris is camel breeding although they are better known as shepherds, who are seen occasionally crossing the state highways with herds of sheep and goats en route to their next camp. Camels were valuable draught animals and there was always a camel corps in the private armies of India's princes.

But the demise of princely India and the development of road haulage have made camels and Rabaris redundant. In addition to this, the decline of pastoral nomadism, deemed archaic in modern India, has forced many Rabari families to settle, which has then given Rabari children the opportunity to attend school. A by-product of settlement and education has been that educated Rabaris (predominantly men) have abandoned their hereditary occupation of herding, taken up new occupations and ceased to wear caste dress. The chief reason for giving up their traditional *dhoti*, embroidered smock (*kediyun*) or tunic (*kamiz*), turban (*rumal* or *pagdi*) and shoulder cloth (*khesado* or *dhablo*) is that this attire is associated with illiteracy by urban communities. A similar pattern is evident among the few Rabari women who have studied to college level; they have forsaken the typical gathered skirt (*ghaghra*), backless blouse (*kapadu* or *kanchali*) and veilcloth (*ludi* or *ludaki*), and wear saris. As access to television, films and the internet becomes increasingly widespread, young Rabaris are exposed to a far greater range of influences than their elders. Their aspirations and dress are different to those of the older generation and there have been discernible changes in the rules of the dress code.[21]

Negotiating change remains complex, as the experience of Prabhat Rabari, a primary school teacher from Kachchh, reveals. For his wedding in December 1997, he had ordered a tailor-made suit; conscious that his caste is officially classified as SEBC (Socially and Educationally Backward Classes), he wanted to wear it as a proclamation of educated status and to signal his aspirations. As he put it: 'Now educated Rabaris are thinking they want change in the community; they want suits and boots; they want girls to be educated...' However, the proposal

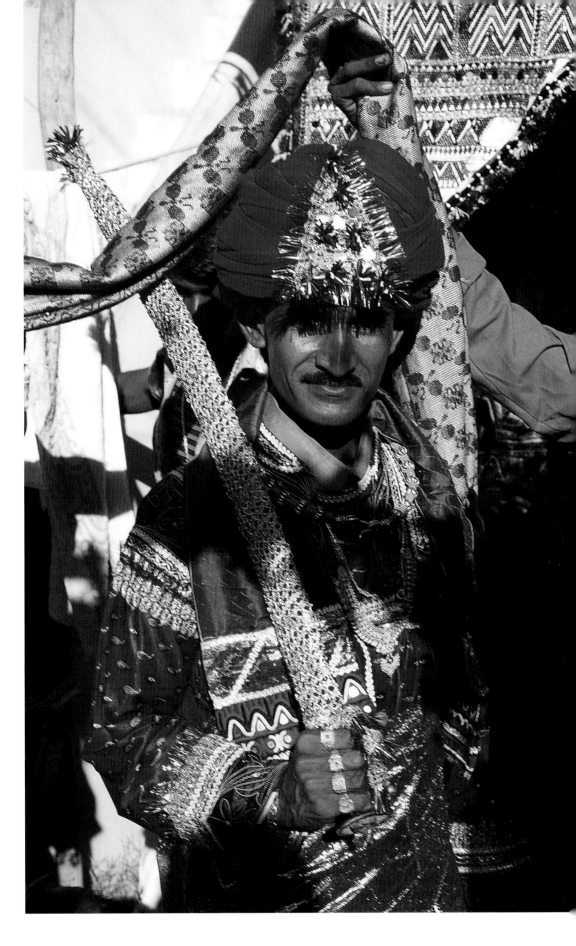

FACING PAGE

FIG 2.7 | ABOVE

Vagadia Rabari *dhang* (migratory group) on the high road near Bhachau, east Kachchh

Rabaris use their camels for haulage and migrate with herds of sheep and goats in search of pasture and water.

FIG 2.8 | BELOW

Dhebaria Rabari man in caste dress wearing an ankle-length man's garment wrapped around the hip (*dhoti*), smock (*kediyun*) and turban (*pagdi*), holding a shoulder cloth (*khesado*) in his lap

All his garments are made of cotton although many Rabaris now wear synthetic fabrics as well as or instead of cotton and wool.

FIG 2.9 | RIGHT

Vagadia Rabari school teacher in borrowed caste dress performing the rituals leading up to the wedding ceremony

He wears a wedding smock (*adano lado*), a turban decoration (*mod*) and carries a ceremonial sword in a beadwork sheath (*talwar miyan*). A small shield (not visible) is slung across his back.

upset his entire clan; a tailored suit did not conform to Rabari rules of purity and modesty. It was deemed 'not Rabari' and inappropriate dress for such an important rite of passage. Sanctions were threatened. Eventually a compromise was found. Prabhat, who as an adult had worn only 'shirt-pants', donned borrowed caste dress for all the rituals leading up to the marriage ceremony but wore his statement suit with the customary red turban of a Rabari groom for the *phera* (circumambulation of the sacred flame). His wife, Laxmi, wore caste dress and was heavily veiled throughout the proceedings for the first time in her adult life. Unusually for a Rabari woman, she was college-educated, taught at a local school, and wore a sari on a daily basis. Prabhat and Laxmi's wedding was the first, and so far only, 'suits and boots' wedding, as he termed it, in the Vagadia Rabari community.[22]

In view of these experiences, what does caste dress signify today? The heavily embellished dress associated with Rabaris and other communities of farmers and herders is replete with symbolism that identifies group membership, gender, religion, occupation, age, marital status and economic standing. For

FIG 2.10 | FAR LEFT

The first "suits and boots" wedding in the Vagadia Rabari community, 1997

The event was so called by the groom because he wore a tailor-made two-piece suit and brogues. However, the bride wore caste dress. They are both primary school teachers and the groom especially wanted to make a statement about his educated status.

FIG 2.11 | CENTRE

Meghwal woman from Banni area of Kachchh in caste dress

Her heavily embroidered tunic, worn over a gathered skirt and dowry jewellery indicate that she is married. Use of a veilcloth is integral to local modesty codes for women.

Dhanetah Jat girl from west Kachchh

*Her red cotton dress (*churi*) denotes her youth—older women tend to dress in maroon or black. It is embroidered with geometric designs that are preferred by these Muslim herders. She wears a veilcloth and a silver necklace known as* hansali.

FIG 2.13 | RIGHT

Muslim women in a bazaar at Jamnagar

The use of the burqa *by Muslim women is more prevalent in the urban areas of Gujarat. Like the veilcloths worn by many Gujarati Hindu women, this enveloping garment embodies female modesty and also manifests the women's religious identity.*

FIG 2.14 | FAR RIGHT

Leva Patel woman from east Kachchh wearing a backless blouse and cotton 'half-sari' (*sadlo*)

The fabric, block-printed and dyed by local Khatris, is gathered into a skirt and one end is draped over the woman's head as a veilcloth. Only older women now wear the sadlo, *the younger generation prefers saris or* salwar kamiz.

caste members it has been a source of pride and an expression of their culture, although as Gujarat urbanises, attitudes are diversifying. To many people, notably foreign visitors and Indian tourists, it has the stamp of authenticity and appears intensely picturesque, a fact that has been exploited in the promotional literature of Gujarat Tourism. To others, including members of castes renowned for their 'timeless' dress, such as Bharwads, Ahirs, Rabaris, Meghwals and Jats, it is simply old-fashioned, and is interpreted as backward, a sign of resistance to change.

Modesty and Veiling

Another significant factor influencing choices in dress in many communities is the concept of *mariyada* (modesty). Interpretation of this varies and is locally determined but it is most obviously demonstrated through veiling, or *laj* (lit. 'shame'). *Mariyada* applies to men and women alike but it is more exacting for women who are perceived as the guardians of family honour. Some degree of veiling is apparent throughout India; even in the urban milieu of the educated elite most women habitually wear a draped *dupatta* or scarf, although few cover their faces. It is an explicit requirement among most rural communities and particular caste and religious groups, varying from the all-enveloping *burqa* worn by Muslim women, to the *pallav* (loose end of a sari or half-sari) draped

FIG 2.15 | LEFT

Ahir woman at a religious fair in Kachchh adjusting her veilcloth

Maintaining *laj* (veiling) requires constant vigilance; one manifestation of this is women repeatedly adjusting their veilcloths as carrying children, fetching water and other tasks threaten to compromise their modesty.

over the head, to the adjustable veilcloth or *dupatta* used by a majority of women, to confinement in the family compound (*ojjal* or *purdah*). The use of a veilcloth varies among young girls but traditionally becomes de rigueur with the onset of menarche. It provides a flexible response to prevailing circumstances; some castes require a woman to cover her face and torso in her father-in-law's presence but in other circumstances, she may expose her face. Whatever form it takes, veiling is an integral part of caste and religious identity for married women, embodying modesty, honour and respect for divine power or human authority.

Men's use of turbans, prayer caps and hats is comparable to veiling. At a mundane level, these head-coverings are also a simple, practical way of shielding the head from extreme heat. The custom in northern India of 'placing one's turban at the feet of those from whom favour or compassion is desired' survives[23] and Rabaris say that 'a man's fate is in his turban'.[24] Covering the head signals conformity to established modes of behaviour. For women especially, failure to comply with

FIG 2.16–2.18 | BELOW LEFT

Kachhi Rabari man tying his turban

Turbans are widely used in Gujarat as a practical protection against the heat but also as a sign of respect to divine authority and conformity to local modesty codes. Rabaris have a saying that 'a man's fate is in his turban'.

FIG 2.19 | BELOW

Shaikh merchant in Ahmedabad wearing a prayer cap

Like the use of turbans among other groups, for Muslim men wearing a prayer cap denotes respect for divine authority as well as modesty. Some Muslim men wear one at all times, others only for prayers at the mosque.

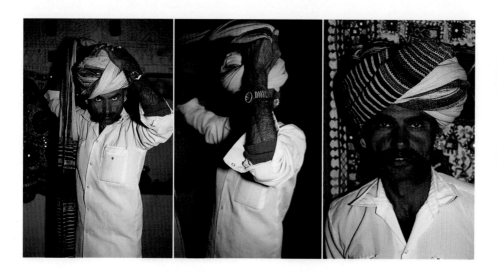

caste rules in this respect provokes censure and in extreme cases, dishonour and out-casting. In this context, modesty is embodied in the prevailing forms of clothing.

ADORNMENT AND AUSPICIOUSNESS

Adornment is another essential component of dress which is manifested through the extensive use of decorated cloth, jewellery, tattoos, coiffured hair, and cosmetics. While it is seen increasingly in terms of fashion, as modern technologies expand the influence of soap operas, films and advertisements to previously remote towns and villages, adornment is intrinsically linked to auspiciousness. Although auspiciousness is alien to Western culture, it is fundamental to life on the subcontinent. Art authority Vidya Dehejia notes: 'One cannot overstate the all-encompassing and pervasive nature of the concept of auspiciousness in the Indian context; it is an underlying perception that permeates everyday life, infusing it with marked significance'.[25] In homes auspiciousness is invoked by, in effect, 'dressing' them with textiles decorated

FIG 2.20

Toran (hanging) at the entrance to a home in east Kachchh

A *toran* is decorative but it also serves a protective purpose. Usually placed over the threshold, it is embellished with auspicious motifs and is designed to deflect evil and preserve the sanctity of the home.

with motifs to deflect the malign and avert disaster. Among herders, livestock is tattooed for identification and protection, and draught animals are richly caparisoned. So powerful is the connection between adornment and auspiciousness that the body unadorned courts danger, and dress without decoration is inauspicious; it signals loss or renunciation. Thus Jain mendicants wear a simple white shift and it was the custom for orthodox Hindu widows to wear a plain white sari and to desist from wearing ornaments.[26] On a daily basis, men, women and children wear clothes and jewellery that are designed to deflect the malign and to signal prosperity. In rural areas, a baby has a protective amulet tied about its neck shortly after birth, and bangles, earrings and anklets are worn from a young age. Tattoos, the use of *kajal*, and highly ornate clothing are also a feature of children's dress; all deemed to be protective, these are seen as precautions against notoriously high infant mortality in the absence of accessible and affordable health care.

FACING PAGE

FIG 2.21 | ABOVE LEFT

Racing camel at Dhrang fair, Kachchh

The saddle cloths are quilts embellished with embroidery and appliqué and the camel's neck is festooned with beads. Used for haulage, camels are valuable livestock in the desert areas of India and their owners protect them by adorning them with auspicious trappings and tattoos.

FIG 2.22 | RIGHT

Vagadia Rabari children on migration riding a camel

The camel's saddle cloth (*atariyun*) is laden with auspicious motifs worked in appliqué and embroidery. It is decorated further with mirrors and tassels—all protective devices against the hardships encountered during migration.

FIG 2.23 | BELOW LEFT

Satwara (Vaghari) wedding party, Saurashtra

To mark the auspiciousness of the event, the oxen hauling the wedding party are caparisoned with elaborately appliquéd *jhul*.

Private collection

FIG 2.24 | RIGHT

Meghwal woman in dowry jewellery, Banni area, north Kachchh

In this context, jewellery is an integral part of dress; it signals prosperity and can be sold in times of hardship.

FIG 2.25 | LEFT

Vagadia Rabari girl on migration, east Kachchh

She is wearing beadwork jewellery, including necklace (*jermar*), matching discs at her temples (*dhabak*) and forehead decoration. Many Rabaris wear amulets and other items of jewellery from birth in the belief that they offer protection from malign influences.

FIG 2.26 | BELOW

Shrine to the horseman-hero Ramdev, north-east Kachchh

The shrine is maintained by local followers of Ramdev who redecorate it and dress the idols in fresh clothing each year.

FIG 2.27–2.29 | RIGHT

Kanudo ceremony marking the birth
of Krishna, near Bhuj, Kachchh

Kachchhi Rabari women fashion the
deity's mother in mud and dress the
figure in fine clothes and gold jewellery.
The infant Krishna is placed in the
cavity of his mother's body. The figure
is carried through the village to the
temple for all-night prayers and hymns.

Most religious festivals are marked by the use of new clothes and an extensive display of jewellery. New clothes harbour no pollution. Ornaments of precious metal, preferably of gold, are associated with purity, demonstrate wealth, and augment the overall sense of auspiciousness. Renewal and decoration are essential both for humans and for deities; horseman heroes such as Ramdev pir and Pabuji, whose images are worshipped in Gujarat and Rajasthan, are given fresh turbans and re-painted, and their shrines are bedecked with new decorations.[27] In the annual Kanudo ceremony that marks the birth of Krishna, the deity's mother is created from mud and dressed in fine clothes and gold jewellery by Rabari and Ahir women in Kachchh. A small baby Krishna, also fashioned from mud, is placed in the cavity of her body and the figure is paraded through the village to a site of worship and an extended programme of *puja* (prayer) and *bhajans* (religious songs) is organised.

But in terms of adornment, a Hindu wedding is unsurpassed. Ornate dress and the use of particular jewellery confers special status on the bride and groom. On their wedding day they are transformed, albeit temporarily, into idealised beings and elevated to the status of royalty. They embody perfection, representing ideals in much the same way that temple statuary offers devotees a template of the idealised body. Their separation from mundane routine is maintained by attendants who manage every stage of their preparation for the *phera* ceremony when they circumambulate the sacred flame, directed by a Brahmin priest. Elaborate textiles, dress and jewellery play a significant role in the property transfers of marriage, enacted through the customs of dowry and bride price which can leave families in debt for many years.[28] The conspicuous

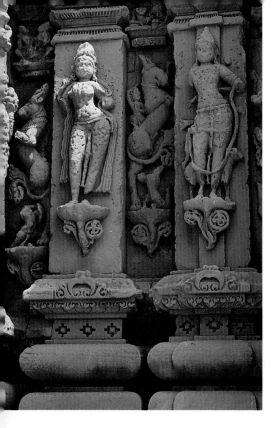

FIG 2.30 | LEFT

Sun temple at Kotai, Kachchh,
c. 10th century

Temple statuary embodies perfection
and offers devotees a template of the
idealised body.

FIG 2.31 | RIGHT

Statuary at Khajuraho temple complex,
Madhya Pradesh, c. 950–1150 CE

This detail shows a woman applying
kajal to her eyes. The stylisation of her
body represents an ideal form.

consumption of a wedding gives kudos to the families of the bride and groom
and is believed to augur well for the future. Indeed a wedding is the supreme
opportunity for display: all wear their finest clothes; gold and silver ornaments
are worn in abundance; hair is dressed with oil and elaborately coiffed; eyes are
protected and enhanced by the application of *kajal; mehendi* is applied, varying
from simple staining to elaborate designs drawn on the brow, hands and feet
of urban brides; and bridegrooms undergo *pithi,* a daily massage by the local
barber who burnishes their skin with sandal paste and *ghee* in the weeks prior
to the wedding to render it fragrant and golden. Among Hindus, maintenance of
personal appearance, dress and adornment are not simply aspects of well-being;
they are details that complete the body, and signal prosperity and fertility.

PURITY: UNCUT CLOTH AND UNSTITCHED CLOTHES

Harappan statuary from Mohenjodaro, notably the male figurine wearing a
mantle and coronet (see fig. 1.2), illustrates another feature of dress in South Asia:
the use of uncut cloth for garments formed by folding, wrapping, tucking, pleating
and draping. The belief prevails in India (and other parts of Asia) that uncut cloth
is ritually pure; in its completeness, it is unpenetrated by pollution. Congruent
with this belief, the use of unstitched garments, fashioned by wrapping and
draping uncut cloth about the body, is widespread throughout Gujarati society
where the sari, *dhoti, lungi,* turban, veilcloth, *dupatta* and shawl are popular forms
of daily dress. The perceived purity of uncut cloth is an aspect of Indian clothing

FACING PAGE

FIG 2.32 AND 2.33 | ABOVE

Vagadia Rabari groom being
prepared for his wedding ceremony,
east Kachchh

His older sister carefully lines his eyes
with *kajal* both to enhance and protect
them. He is dressed in his wedding
attire by his uncles. Among Rabaris, the
custom prevails that a groom does not
utter a word throughout his wedding
day and everything is done for him by
close male relatives and friends.

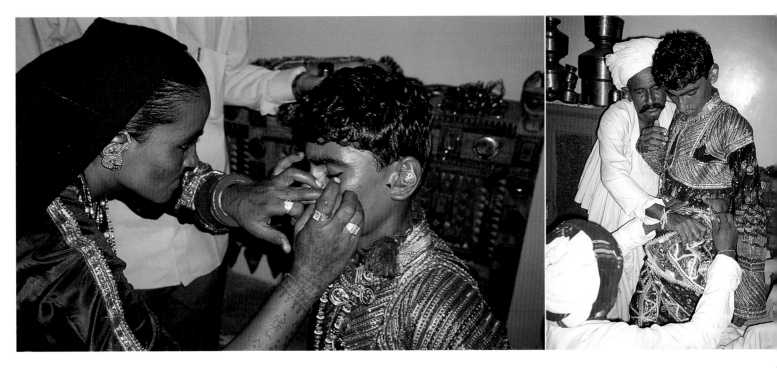

FIG 2.34 | RIGHT

Vagadia Rabari groom in wedding jewellery, east Kachchh

Vagadia grooms are said to be transformed into princes for the day by their fine clothes and extravagant jewellery which includes three pairs of golden earrings (*bhungri*, *toriya* and *oganiya*) and torc (*varo*), necklaces, bangles and anklets of silver (*kadla*).

FIG 2.35 | FAR RIGHT

Handmade shoes (*mojdi*) worn by Vagadia groom, east Kachchh

Like every other item of his dress, the groom's shoes are highly embellished with embroidery, beadwork and in this case, a small set of flashing lights, powered by a battery pack concealed under the decoration.

FIG 2.36 | LEFT

Vagadia Rabari wedding ceremony, east Kachchh

During the *phera*, the bride and groom circle the sacred flame directed by the officiating Brahmin priest. They are symbolically linked by a skein of thread (*varmala*) and their union is signalled by the bride's veilcloth being tied to the groom's cummerbund.

FIG 2.37 | CENTRE

Vagadia Rabari women at a wedding, east Kachchh

Group of women (see pp. 14–15) at a wedding wear dowry items, including embroidered blouses and jewellery. Prominent on arm of woman in foreground is the *baloyun*, a very broad bangle stained an auspicious red.

FIG 2.38 | BELOW LEFT

Jat groom, Banni, Kachchh

Preparing for the formal wedding ceremony (*nikanama*), this Muslim groom wears a beadwork head-covering and has had henna paste applied to his hands.

FIG 2.39 | BELOW RIGHT

Vagadia Rabari groom undergoing massage (*pithi*) in preparation for his wedding ceremony

A Rabari groom undergoes several days of purification and is massaged daily by the local barber with ghee and sandal paste or turmeric so that his skin has a golden glow on the day of the wedding.

that was skilfully manipulated by Gandhi during the struggle for independence. The 'deep deliberation' that determined his adopted garb of loin cloth and shawl from 1921 onwards harnessed the perceived purity of uncut cloth to the moral imperatives of the *swadeshi* campaign.[29]

Unstitched clothing is preferred for religious ceremonies particularly for rites of passage such as marriage, the sacred thread (*janoi*) ceremony which marks the coming of age of Brahmin males, and also for *vaastu puja*, the blessing and purification of a new home. It is worn both by devotees and ritual specialists such as Brahmin priests, although its use extends across all faiths. Male pilgrims making the Hajj don two pieces of unstitched white cloth known as *ihram* to circumambulate the Kaaba. Hindu renouncers and *sadhus* wear simple wrapped garments, often dyed saffron. And Jain mendicants are distinguished by their use of draped white cotton. The symbolism of uncut cloth has transferred from the religious to the secular sphere and the custom of gifting a shawl as a mark of respect, also as a sign of achievement, is widespread at civic events. Under the Government of India's National Crafts Award scheme, the winning artisans not only receive a cash prize and a plaque, they also receive an *angavastram* (shawl or stole) at the ceremony in New Delhi. Colour and the type of fibre from which it is woven can enhance the properties of uncut cloth. According to the

FIG 2.40

Master craftsman Abduljabbar Khatri of Dhamadka being honoured by former President Abdul Kalam as part of the National Craft Awards ceremony, 2003

In recognition of his skills he is given a bronze plaque and a shawl (*angavastram*). The gift of a shawl is a mark of respect which is underpinned by the widespread belief in India in the ritual purity of uncut cloth.

Photograph courtesy of AJM Khatri

Hindu schema of the *Dharmashastras* (Sanskrit, 'religious law books') particular colours were prescribed for each *varna* (four main occupational divisions of caste): Brahmins should dress in white (also widely associated with widows), Kshatriyas in red, Vaishyas in yellow, and Shudras in dark colours.[30] For Muslims, green as the colour of the Prophet is attributed a particular sanctity, and the use of a green *chaddar* (shawl or wrap) to dress the tombs of the dead is common throughout the Islamic world.

In India the belief in a hierarchy of ritual purity evident in the caste system extends to the material world, so textile fibres, like metals, are in effect graded according to purity. For Hindus, silk is the purest of fibres and is worn by Brahmins and officiating priests, and is extensively used for saris. It is, however, proscribed for Muslim men in the Quran. But this does not mean that Muslims wore no silk. Some ignored the ban, hence the popularity of Ahmedabadi brocades in the Mughal courts; others circumvented the proscription via the development of *mashru* satin which has a silk warp and a cotton weft, and is still produced in Patan and a few villages in Kachchh. It has the appearance of silk but is permitted because of its cotton content.[31] A number of groups have sanctified wool as possessing innate purity. Among these, Sufis, the influential mystics of Islam, much venerated in Gujarat, were identified by their use of wool; their name derives from *suf,* the Arabic for wool. Enthoven, writing in 1920, notes the use of wool by Bharwad shepherds, describing their dress as 'three woollen blankets of undyed wool, one wound in broad bands around the head, a second tied around the waist reaching the knee, and a third thrown across the shoulder'.[32] For Bharwads and their *dhabali bhai*, the Rabaris, wool is holy, gifted to them by Krishna, and as a divine gift it is the purest of fibres: 'Wool is very pure, it protects you from pollution and has many properties. If someone were to enter a cremation ground or something like that, it would protect them from pollution'.[33]

The structure of a fabric can also influence its purity. In comparison with silk, most cottons are coarser woven and are, therefore, more permeable to pollution, and thus of a lower status. But the example of *khadi* reveals the layers of meaning that accrue to different fibres. Gandhi's emphasis on the 'moral fibre' of *khadi* elevated this coarse weave to the status of exemplary purity. That symbolism however, has been subverted in the post-colonial era; as the favoured dress of politicians, *khadi* has become tainted by its association with the sometimes murky world of politics. Ever-evolving, it has also been re-branded of late as a

FIG 2.41

Mausoleum at Rani-no-Hajiro, Ahmedabad, mid-15th century

A green *chaddar* (shawl or wrap) covers each of the tombs of Sultan Ahmed Shah's queens and other female royalty. The dressing of tombs is common throughout the Islamic world. For Muslims, green is attributed with particular sanctity as it is the colour of the Prophet.

fashion item featured on the catwalks of Mumbai and New Delhi, where the term *khadi* has ceased to refer only to fabric. It now covers a range of products, including textiles, readymade clothing, handmade soaps, organic herbs and spices which are sold in 'lifestyle stores' in Ahmedabad and other major metropolitan centres. Clever marketing has not only married *khadi*'s essential 'Indian-ness' to contemporary environmental and ethical concerns, it has also harnessed *khadi* to stylish design and good quality. The sense of sacrifice and duty that marked the wearing of *khadi* during the *swadeshi* era—it is said that even Nehru baulked at its coarseness and his sister, Vijayalakshmi, complained of its drabness, having been persuaded to wear it for her wedding—has gone.[34] Refined, re-designed, and in a wide spectrum of colours, *khadi* is fashionable, desirable and now has the added cachet of 'cool'. When synthetic fabrics were first introduced to Gujarat, they were held in similar regard; brought back from the Gulf countries by migrant workers, they were novelties whose rarity and foreignness lent them prestige.[35] But local mass-production has subsequently made them a routine part of the state's material culture. They are widely worn on a daily basis because of their cheapness and functionality which tends to override the question of their purity, although they have been eschewed for ritual occasions when the symbolic power of silk and wool is preferred by those who can afford it.

Tailored Clothing: 'Traps for Impurity'

It has been suggested that tailored clothing was introduced to India by Muslims. Consequent upon this idea was the division between 'Hindu dress', composed of unstitched garments fashioned by wrapping and draping, and 'Muslim dress' which features tailored garments. Forbes Watson stated that, 'It would appear that before the invasion of India by the Mahomedans, the art of sewing was not practised there'.[36] The scholarship of G.S. Ghurye, Moti Chandra and B.N. Goswamy, amongst others, has dispelled this misconception.[37] But a philosophical divergence is evident which accounts for prevailing attitudes to clothing. Hindu orthodoxy had it that stitched clothes were 'traps for impurity'; and Muslims, whom the Quran instructs to cover all parts of the body, necessitating tailored garments, regarded India's unstitched clothing as 'barbaric'.[38] It is apparent that a plethora of new garments and fabric innovations were introduced during the Sultanate and Mughal eras. For some, there might have been an element of coercion to their uptake by Indians under the Mughals who required government employees to wear Mughal styles of dress.

But the vocabulary of Indian dress was expanded, not eradicated, by the influx of styles from the Islamic world of Central Asia and Persia. In the fourteenth and fifteenth centuries, the association of Islamic dress with a powerful cosmopolitan culture not bounded by regional or even national borders prompted many outside Mughal control to adopt stitched clothes too. Thus the Hindu rulers of Vijayanagara replaced traditional South Indian modes of court dress with a new set of garments that originated in the Islamic world as part of a political strategy by an indigenous elite, which Phillip Wagoner suggests was designed to 'enhance their status and authority through participation in the more "universal" culture of Islam... [which] had nothing to do with religious conversion or syncretism'.[39]

TYPES OF DRESS

Many ensembles of contemporary Indian dress combine draped garments of uncut cloth with tailored clothing. Typical in this respect is the widely popular *salwar kamiz* and *dupatta*, the *ghaghra* and backless blouse or bodice (*kapadu*, *kanchali*), and *odhani*, and of course, the sari and *choli* (short blouse). Men's *dhoti* and *lungi* are commonly worn with tailored smocks (*kediyun*, pl. *kediya*), tunics (*kamiz* or *kurta*) and coats (*angarkha* and *sherwani*). Many of the tailored garments for the upper and lower body worn in Gujarat allude to broader regional customs, and are common to other parts of India and South Asia, notably Pakistan. Some of these generic styles are rendered specific to a Gujarati community, or area of the state, by the use of particular fabrics, colours and styles of decoration, and in the case of the sari, by distinctive ways of pleating and draping.

Western style became part of the mix during the colonial period, although there was no compulsion for Indians to adopt it; indeed, the British actively discouraged imitation. Nonetheless, some Indian men did, combining Indian and Western clothing styles, or wearing garments that fused elements of both. The response to Western styles varied and, in part, reflected the degree of contact with Europeans; where it was minimal, Western clothes were little in evidence. A further crucial consideration for understanding Indian responses to European clothes, as Emma Tarlo suggests, was that, 'Western clothes did not fit into the existing classifications of appropriate caste, regional and religious style'.[40]

In the post-colonial period the adoption of Western fashions by men and women has become widespread, although they by no means dominate the sartorial scene and their styling has a local inflection. Western-style trousers and shirts

FACING PAGE
FIG 2.42 | LEFT
Woman wearing sari draped in typical Gujarati style
Photo by Anand Patel

FIG 2.43 | RIGHT
Young man in 'shirt-pants' made for him at a local tailor's workshop specialising in menswear

worn by men throughout India are a good example. In Western countries these are sold as separate items, off-the-peg. In Gujarat, as in other parts of India, they are often consolidated into a single item referred to as 'shirt-pants', and sold as a set. This can be in the form of either readymade clothing, or more commonly—much clothing is still made to order by local tailors—as two pieces of co-ordinating fabric. This is comparable with the production of other sets of clothing such as *salwar kamiz* and *kurta pyjama*. The cut and shape of 'shirt-pants' differs from contemporary European styles. The emphasis is on modesty; the garments should cover but not emphasise the shape of the body. Shirts tend to be cut long and although shaped are rarely tight-fitting. They are often worn loose over trousers (cooler in a hot climate) and are usually open-necked; ties are very little in evidence. 'Pants' tend to be fairly loose-fitting with a high set waistband, front pleats and wide legs.[41]

The following sections identify the main types of garments worn in Gujarat. Constraints of space preclude inclusion of every minor variation of each garment and there is only limited mention of Western styles; although they are a part of the spectrum of contemporary Indian dress, they are not the focus of the book.

MENSWEAR

Forbes Watson characterised indigenous styles of wrapped and draped garments as 'articles which leave the loom in a state ready to be worn'.[42] Most of these items are made from a complete textile often with decorative borders on all sides, rather than a piece cut from running yardage. In this category are *dhotis*, *lungis*, sashes (*patka*), turban wraps (*bukani*) and shawls. The heavy shawls known as *dhablo* and *kambali* used by Rabari men in the cold season, and the turbans they wear for weddings and festivals are typical of these engineered cloths. They feature deep borders with extra weft detail, worked in geometric patterns with stylised camels, village shrines known as *dero*, and girls carrying water pots. Several communities in Gujarat (also Rajasthan) wear a smock with long, tight-fitting sleeves known as *kediyun*, with variations in the length, fit and surface decoration depending on the caste, age and status of the wearer.[43] Bharwads, Ahirs, Dhebaria and Vagadia Rabaris wear a short, white smock with asymmetrical ties that are secured on the left of the yoke (which conforms with Akbar's decree that the Hindus should tie their

FIG 2.44

Kachhi Rabari from Gardo area, west Kachchh, wearing a white cotton smock (*kediyun*), an ankle-length man's garment wrapped around the hip (*dhoti*) and turban (*pagdi*)

Older Gardo Rabaris wear a longer length smock that stops mid-thigh. The sleeves are overlong to compensate for their extremely tight fit; the excess length is gathered at the elbow joint to allow the wearer to flex his arms.

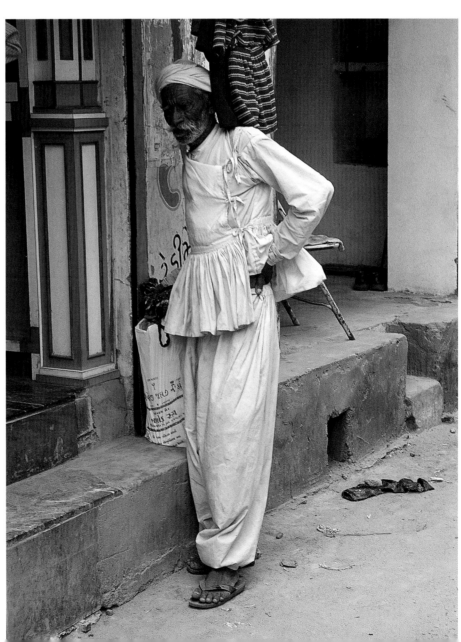

FIG 2.45 | ABOVE RIGHT

Bharwad boy, Saurashtra

His short smock stops above the waist and is made of white cotton. His carefully wrapped turban, covered with an embroidered textile known as a *bukani* (lit. 'two ears') suggests that he is dressed for a special occasion, possibly a wedding.

Private collection

FIG 2.46 | ABOVE LEFT

Bharwad boy, Saurashtra, wearing coloured cotton smock and drawstring trousers (*chorni*)

Private collection

FIG 2.47

Patel farmer, east Kachchh, wearing white cotton smock and drawstring trousers coats to the left). The festival smocks of Dhebaris and Vagadias are decorated with embroidery and bridegrooms wear the same style of garment but in a longer length, essentially an *angarkha*, which is known by these Rabaris as *adano lado*. It is often made of *mashru,* nowadays the synthetic version, and is heavily decorated. A style more associated with urban castes is the *sherwani,* a long, fitted, A-line coat that reaches to below the knee, or longer, with a high round neck and a central front opening that is fastened with buttons; Goswamy notes that it bears a 'marked European influence'.[44] It is popular for formal and festive wear, and made in silk and brocade, it is favoured by urban bridegrooms in Gujarat.

The *kurta* and *kamiz* are loose shirts or tunics, that vary in length from just below the hip to mid-calf, which have a round neck and placket with button-fastening, usually in the centre of the neck. Goswamy notes of the *kurta* that 'it turned into an article of great elegance in the Nawab circles of nineteenth century Lucknow and attained simultaneously a measure of popularity in other centres like Delhi'.[45] It is now a universally popular item of menswear throughout India that has also been adopted by women of the urban elite, notably students. Kachhi Rabaris wear a hip length *kamiz* in white, which they fasten with sets of silver buttons. A calf length version is popular among the cattle herders (*maldharis*) of Banni, north Kachchh, including Muslim clans such as Mutwa, Jat, Node, Raisiputra, Haliputra, Hingorja, Baluch, Sameja and Sumra, and a few nearby groups of Hindu Meghwals.

The shirts and smocks described above are worn with wrapped garments or with trousers, often in a recognised set such as *kurta pyjama* or *salwar kamiz.* Western-style trousers have a fitted waistband and are shaped to the body with darts and pleats; Asian-style trousers, such as *pyjama* and *salwar,* have a drawstring and tend to be baggy, relying on volume of fabric for movement at the hips and knees. *Pyjama* are cut with straight, close-fitting legs, and a wide, flared crotch which is sometimes widened with the insertion of a gusset. The slot for the drawstring is created by turning a deep hem, or by stitching a band of fabric to the waist edge. Made of silk or fine cotton and worn with a *kurta* and shawl, they are popular with middle and upper class Gujaratis for weddings and other religious and cultural events. They continue to be a feature of rural dress. A style of *pyjama* known as *chorni* is still used by Kanbi Patels, Bharwads and Bhopa Rabaris of Saurashtra, usually in white; Vagadia Rabari bridegrooms wear *mashru chorni* with embroidered cuffs at the ankle; and Ahirs wear the same

FIG 2.48 | ABOVE

Dhebaria Rabari smock embellished with *bukiyo* (backstitch) embroidery

Embroidery strengthens seams and joins but its use is underpinned by the belief that auspicious motifs prevent cut cloth from being penetrated by evil.

See appendix ill. 2 for garment analysis.

V&A: IS 145-2007

FIG 2.49 | FAR RIGHT

Vagadia Rabari boy, east Kachchh

Dressed for a wedding, his smock (*jhuli*) is made of brightly coloured polyester, decorated with hand embroidery and fancy braids.

FIG 2.50 | RIGHT

Vagadia Rabari bridegroom, east Kachchh

This young groom is dressed in a long wedding coat known as *adano lado* made from polyester brocade, decorated with hand embroidery and fancy braids.

FIG 2.51 | ABOVE LEFT

Urban bridegroom wearing a *sherwani*

Photograph courtesy of Mayank Prajapati

FIG 2.52 | ABOVE RIGHT

Man wearing a *kurta*

This garment is a popular item of menswear worn throughout India. It has also been adopted by young women of the urban elite, especially students.

Photograph courtesy of Divyesh Shah

FIG 2.53 | BELOW LEFT

Detail of drawstring trousers (*chorni*) worn by Vagadia Rabari boy, east Kachchh

These are made of *mashru* (silk/ cotton satin) and decorated with hand embroidery.

FIG 2.54 | BELOW RIGHT

Ahir men dancing a *dandia ras*, east Kachchh

This group of men, all from the same village, are wearing matching blue tunics (*kamiz*) of shiny synthetic fabric and baggy, white cotton drawstring trousers (*vajani*).

garment but refer to it as *vajani*. In comparison to *pyjama*, *salwar* are far wider in the leg, stitched so that they drape, gradually shaping into a cuff at the ankle. They are a generic north Indian style. Made of fine silks and cottons, they are worn by urban Gujaratis (both men and women) under *kurta* and *kamiz*, as well as by members of rural communities. Among the *maldharis* of Banni, they are worn with a calf length *kamiz* of the same colour of fabric, a vivid floral design scarf imported from Pakistan, and an *ajrakh* turban.

WOMENSWEAR

There is a degree of overlap between menswear and womenswear. As mentioned earlier, garments such as *kurta* and *kamiz* are worn by both men and women and combined with *salwar* or *churidar or pyjama* and a *dupatta*. The convenience of the *salwar kamiz* has seen an increase in the number of women wearing it, but other forms of dress are more widely worn. In the privacy of their own homes, many urban women wear a house-dress resembling a long nightgown, with a sari petticoat beneath it, to perform domestic chores; it has become a popular item of informal wear but is rarely seen in the street, deemed inappropriate for the public domain. Worn by women of all ages in public and in private space, the sari is another example of a garment that leaves the loom ready to be worn. In the case of luxury silk saris, such as the Ahmedabadi brocades and *patola*, the body design and borders are specifically engineered to take into account the pleating of the textile around the body and the fall of the *pallav* which often features *jari*. *Jari* not only adds a sumptuous lustre to the garment, its weight enhances the drape of the sari.

FIG 2.55

Muslim cattle herders, Banni, north Kachchh

In this region, Muslim men favour a longer style of tunic (*kamiz*) made of cotton, polycotton, or synthetic fabric worn over matching, loose-fitting trousers (*salwar*).

FIG 2.56 | FACING PAGE

Fragment of Ashavali (?) sari, silk,
L 630 (including blouse piece) x W 102 cm

A precise definition of what constitutes
an 'Ashavali sari' has proved elusive; the
term is commonly applied to heavy silk
saris with brocaded borders, possibly
woven with *jari*, and produced in
Ahmedabad. The name is derived from
Ashaval, the ancient town on which site
Ahmedabad developed.

V&A: IS 70-1995

FIG 2.57 | RIGHT

Detail of *pallav* (draped end of sari) of
a *patolu* woven with gold thread (*jari*)
and featuring a double ikat border

Private collection

Saris are worn throughout the state with a colour-co-ordinated petticoat and a
choli but are in greater evidence in urban areas than in the villages. Although other
forms of attire are more common in rural Gujarat, in this context polyester saris
have become a sign of social aspiration, adopted by communities such as Kanbi
Patels, whose economic power is due in part to their role in the Gujarati diaspora.
They allow the upwardly mobile to adopt a largely caste-less form of attire and to
separate themselves from the traditions of rustic dress which consists typically

FIG 2.58 | LEFT

Meghwal woman, Banni, north Kachchh

Her three-part ensemble includes a long, backless blouse made of polyester decorated with hand embroidery (*kanchali*), worn over a tie-dyed drawstring skirt of cotton, and a veilcloth of synthetic fabric edged with braid.

FIG 2.59 | ABOVE

Node women, Pachcham, north Kachchh

Belonging to a Muslim community of cattle herders, these women show different styles of dress: one wears a long frock over wide-legged trousers known as *ejar*, the other wears a backless blouse over a drawstring skirt. Both use a veilcloth in accordance with the customs of the area.

of a backless blouse known variously as *kapadu, kanchali* and *kamkho*, worn with either a wrap-round skirt or a drawstring skirt, and a veilcloth. Among the Banni Muslims, women wear a longer *kanchali* over *salwar* or *ejar* (drawstring trousers with straight, wide legs), with a veilcloth. Other garments used specifically by women from Muslim communities such as the Khatris, Shaikhs (merchants), and Memons (Lohana merchants from Sindh who converted to Islam), include a long frock worn with *ejar* and a *dupatta,* and various pan-Islamic styles such as the *burqa* (long loose enveloping garment), *jilbab* (long coat) and *niqab* (face veil).

Although veilcloths appear to be in the category of unstitched clothing, many in common use are actually stitched. The looms on which handwoven veilcloths are made do not produce a stable fabric if the weft is wider than about eighteen inches. In order to produce a garment that gives sufficient cover in terms of utility and modesty, two matching lengths are woven and then stitched together. Since these joins and seams are perceived as vulnerable to pollution, many groups reinforce them with embroidery featuring auspicious motifs and colours in order to deflect malign influences. The central seam has become such a feature of the garment that the manufacturers of synthetic veilcloths also produce them in two matching lengths when they could be easily produced as a single piece. This is also true of synthetic versions of men's shoulder cloths such as *ajrakh*.

FROM CLOTH TO DRESS: THE ROLE OF THE TAILOR

Much of the clothing worn in Gujarat is still made for individual clients by specialist tailors, or *darjis*, whose small workshops line the bazaar in every town and city. In contrast to other artisans such as weavers, who were perceived as creators by Hindus, the tailor 'was a cutter, a destroyer', whose practices were regarded as impure.[46] Tailoring is highly specialised. As well as an obvious gender division whereby a tailor works for either 'ladies' or 'gents', there are those who specialise in ladies' Western dress, others who make only sari blouses, and others still who specialise in dress for Muslim women, making *burqas*, frocks and *ejar*. 'Gents' tailors make either Western dress or Indian dress, typically *kurta, salwar kamiz* or *kurta pyjama*. In areas where the use of caste dress is particularly strong, there are tailors for Ahirs, Bharwads, Rabaris, Kharaks, Patels, and so on, who specialise in making the particular garments worn by their client castes. The most versatile tailors are those who serve the NRI (non-resident Indian) or NRG (non-resident Gujarati) market, as they are called upon to make both *desi*

FIG 2.60 | FACING PAGE

Woollen veilcloth with mirrorwork embroidery known as *phulakiyun* ('floral design') worn by Vagadia Rabari women

Woven in two pieces, Rabari women embroider the centre seam and end borders with auspicious motifs which they believe deflect malign influences. Protection is amplified by the use of fragrant spices packed into embroidered discs (*tigudi*) at intervals along the seam.

FIG 2.61 | FAR RIGHT

Ladies' tailor, Bhachau, east Kachchh

This tailor who specialises in Rabari women's dress, is marking out a blouse using the traditional system of measurements based on cubits, spans and finger widths.

FIG 2.62 | RIGHT

Memsaab Ladies' Tailor, Bhuj, Kachchh

This workshop specialises in dress for NRIs (non-resident Indians). The tailor makes Western-style clothes as well as Indian garments such as sari blouses and *salwar kamiz*.

(of the country, Indian) garments and Western style clothing by an exacting clientele who come armed with fashion and film magazines and mail order catalogues. A noticeable trait among members of the diaspora is to return to Gujarat either for the local marriage season which runs from Diwali to Makar Sankranti, or when a wedding is in the offing in their adopted country.[47] They commission gold jewellery, select saris, buy fabric for other clothes and then have numerous *cholis*, *salwar kamiz* and Western garments stitched by an NRI specialist.[48] Indian craftsmanship in this respect is unmatched. Although readymade clothes are sold throughout Gujarat, the affordability of tailored garments means that most people still wear custom-made dress. Gujarati dress in all its incarnations is a result of the cumulative input of many skilled technicians; in the network of production that goes from handmade cloth to dress, the tailoring skills of the *darji* are allied to the craft skills of weavers, dyers, printers and embroiderers whose production is discussed in the chapters that follow.

Notes

1 Personal communication, Renu Arjanbhai Rabari, June 1997.

2 Tarlo, E., *Clothing Matters. Dress and Identity in India*, London: Hurst and Company, p. 133, note 7.

3 Banerjee, M. and Daniel Miller, *The Sari*, Oxford and New York: Berg, p. 240.

4 Edwards, E.M., 'Textiles and Dress Among the Rabari of Kutch', in Simpson, E. and Aparna Kapadia, eds., *The Idea of Gujarat. History, Ethnography and Text*, London: Routledge.

5 Shukla, P., *The Grace of the Four Moons. Dress, Adornment, and the Art of the Body in Modern India*, Bloomington: Indiana University Press, p. 4.

6 Bayly, C.A., 'The Origins of *Swadeshi* (Home Industry): Cloth and Indian Society, 1700–1930', in Appadurai, A., ed., *The Social Life of Things. Commodities in Cultural Perspective*, Cambridge: Cambridge University Press, p. 302.

7 *Mashru* is a warp-faced fabric woven with a silk warp and a cotton weft. It was devised in order to circumvent the Quranic proscription against men wearing pure silk. The name literally means 'permitted' in Persian. For a discussion of the fabric, see Watt, G., *Indian Art at Delhi 1903*, Delhi: Motilal Banarsidass, pp. 255–256.

8 The term 'Western' is used to describe a range of clothes that originate in the countries of the West.

9 Caste is a hierarchical system that divides Indian society into four classes (*varna*): Brahmins (priests), Kshatriyas (warriors), Vaishyas (merchants), Shudras (service classes). It represents an ideal religious model of Hindu society in which each class is a necessary and interdependent part of the whole. An underlying principle of caste is a ritual notion of purity and pollution which is allied to a system of hereditary occupation. The complexities of caste are explored in many publications; the classic text is Louis Dumont's *Homo Hierarchicus*, first published in French in 1966. The following is helpful and accessible: Bayly, S., *Caste, Society and Politics in India*, Cambridge: Cambridge University Press.

10 The *Times of India* website (http://timesofindia.indiatimes.com) now offers an online matrimonial service, SimplyMarry.com.

11 According to the 2001 Census of India, only 0.1% of the total population of India has no declared religion. See: http://censusindia.gov.in/Census_Data_2001

12 Forbes Watson, J. (1866), *The Textile Manufactures and the Costumes of the People of India*, London: W.H. Allen and Co., p. 3.

13 I am grateful to Abby McGowan for drawing my attention to Fazalullah Lutfullah's commentary on Muslim dress in late nineteenth century Gujarat which goes into detail about the changing fashions. See Campbell, J.M., ed., *Muslim and Parsi Castes and Tribes of Gujarat*, Gurgaon: Vintage Books, pp. 100–108.

14 Chhaya, T.M., *Rural Pockets in the Urban Structure*, unpublished diploma thesis, Ahmedabad: School of Architecture.

15 For a perceptive account of the nuances of dress worn by different castes and age groups in a village in Saurashtra, see Tarlo, pp. 168–283.

16 Personal communication, Padmajaben Dhruv and Manjariben Divangi, December 2008.

17 Many Muslim women wear an ankle length frock, wide legged trousers known as *ejar*, and a veilcloth. Among the Banni Muslims of Kachchh, some women wear a long backless tunic over *ejar* or a long, gathered skirt, and a veilcloth. Hindu women belonging to upwardly mobile groups such as the Kanbi Patels, whose occupation is farming, tend to wear polyester saris.

18 See: Campbell, pp. 100–108.

19 Personal communication, Husainbhai Khatri, March 1997.

20 Aniline dyes became available in India in the late nineteenth and early twentieth century. Their use in Ahmedabad was rapid but more gradual in other parts of the state. It was not until the 1950s that they had almost entirely replaced natural dyes. Personal communication, Khatri Mohammad Siddik, Dhamadka, September 1997.

21 Edwards, E.M., 'Textiles and Dress Among the Rabari of Kutch', in Simpson, E. and Aparna Kapadia, eds., *The Idea of Gujarat. History, Ethnography and Text*, London: Routledge.

22 Personal communication, Prabhat Raja Rabari, December 1997.

23 Srivastava, V.K., *Religious Renunciation of a Pastoral People*, New Delhi: Oxford University Press, p. 49.

24 Personal communication, Vanka Kana Rabari, April 1997.

25 Dehejia, V., *The Body Adorned. Dissolving Boundaries Between Sacred and Profane in India's Art*, New York and

Chichester: Columbia University Press, p. 14.

26 Personal communication, Mrs J Sejpal, Lohana community, Bhuj, March 1994.

27 Smith, J.D., *The Epic of Pabuji*, New Delhi: Katha, pp. 9–17.

28 Edwards, E.M., 'Marriage and Dowry Customs of the Rabari of Kutch: Evolving Traditions', in Foster, H.B. and Donald C. Johnson, *Wedding Dress Across Cultures*, Oxford and New York: Berg, pp. 67–84.

29 cit. Templewood, Viscount, *Nine Troubled Years*, London: Collins, p. 54.

30 Bayly, p. 291.

31 *Mashru* is material with a silk warp and cotton weft (See note no. 7)

32 Enthoven, *The Tribes and Castes of Bombay*, vol. 1, Bombay: Government of Bombay, p. 119.

33 *Dhabali bhai* literally means 'blanket brothers'. It refers to members of thirteen castes in western India that are commensal (also known as *ter tansali*, lit. 'thirteen bowls') and includes Bharwads and Rabaris. Personal communication, Vanka Kana Rabari, June 1997.

34 Bean, S., 'Gandhi and *Khadi*: The Fabric of Independence', in Weiner, A. and Jane Schneider,eds., *Cloth and Human Experience*, Washington and London: Smithsonian Institution Press, p. 372.

35 Frater, J., *Threads of Identity*, Ahmedabad: Mapin Publishing Pvt Ltd, p. 20.

36 Forbes Watson, p. 11.

37 Ghurye, G.S., *Indian Costume*, Bombay: Popular Prakashan Pvt Ltd. Goswamy, B.N., *Indian Costumes*, Ahmedabad: Calico Museum of Textiles.

38 Bayly, p. 295.

39 Wagoner, P., '"Sultan Among Hindu Kings": Dress, Titles and the Islamicization of Hindu Culture at Vijayanagara', in *The Journal of Asian Studies*, vol. 55, no. 4, pp. 851–880.

40 Tarlo, p. 44.

41 Personal communication, Atul Tailor, 1996–2009.

42 Forbes Watson, p. 4.

43 Dhebaria and Vagadia Rabaris wear a *kediyun* with extremely tight-fitting, apparently overlong sleeves. The excess length of the sleeves is pushed up the forearm to gather at the elbow which allows the joint to flex.

44 Goswamy, p. 110.

45 Goswamy, p. 20.

46 Bayly, pp. 295–296.

47 Diwali is the Hindu New Year which falls in October or November, the exact date being determined by the lunar calendar. Makar Sankranti, also known as Uttarayan is the kite festival which takes place on January 14.

48 Personal communication, Haribhai Dabhi, NRI tailor, 1993–2008.

3 Constructed Textiles

FABRIC OF THE GODS

In the Rig Veda and the Upanishads, the ancient texts of Hinduism, the universe is imagined as a cloth woven by the gods and the passage of day and night as a weaver throwing a shuttle across the loom.[1] The mythical status of woven cloth in Indian life has been matched by its enduring significance in the history of the subcontinent. It was with good reason that Nehru commented that 'the history of India may well be written with textiles as its leading motif'.[2] The production of woven textiles in western India, notably cotton, goes back to the early civilizations of the Indus Valley. By the first century CE cotton textiles were an integral part of the sea-going trade via the Indian Ocean which finally petered out in the mid-twentieth century. The Gujarati ports were pivotal in the movement of cotton cloth which went west to the Arab world and the Mediterranean region and east to Southeast Asia.

Although not produced on the scale of cottons, Gujarat has also been the source of some of India's most highly prized handloom silk textiles, some of which, such as brocade and *patola,* also featured in external trade. Ahmedabad was renowned for velvets, brocades, *kinkhab* and *mashru.*[3] Surat was known for figured silks including Chinese-influenced *tanchoi* as well as for the manufacture of *jari,* the metallic thread used in many Gujarati brocades and embroideries. From Patan came *patola,* double ikat silk textiles that are still made there by Salvi weavers. Production of many of these silk textiles has dwindled; *mashru,* for example, is now woven on a small scale only in Patan and one or two villages near Mandvi in Kachchh, and other types of woven silks, such as brocades, are produced in other parts of India following migrations of weavers from Gujarat. Nonetheless, the state has an abiding reputation for handloom silks.

Cotton weaving on the other hand, with a few exceptions, was overtaken by mechanisation in the mid-nineteenth century when textile mills were established in Ahmedabad and Mumbai. This and the influx of cheap British

FIG 3.1

Length of undyed *khadi* (handspun handwoven cloth), cotton, L 138 x W 102 cm, mid-19th century. The attached label reads 'Guzerat. Manufactured in the town of Edur in the Mahee Kantha and retailed at 6¾ pence per yard.'

In the early 20th century, *khadi* became a symbol of the struggle for Indian independence and its association with national identity still resonates today.

V&A: 0122 IS

mill cloth left thousands of weavers without work. The plight of Indian weavers became a leading motif of the nationalists' *swadeshi* campaign—Indians were called upon to abjure using imported cloth in favour of home-produced textiles. In the early twentieth century with Gandhi at the helm of the *swadeshi* movement, the use of *khadi* (handspun handwoven cloth), notably cotton, became a moral imperative for all Indians. Handmade cloth became an enduring symbol of the struggle for independence and the association of *khadi* with an independent national identity still resonates today.

Apart from cotton and silk, the state has a well-developed tradition of wool weaving—usually piece goods—which formerly included shawls, veilcloths, blankets and skirts worn by many rustic communities. Since the decline of this local market, enterprising weavers have developed what has become known as the "shawl business", weaving lightweight shawls made from imported wool, polyester and occasionally silk and *desi* (local) wool which are popular wear in India during the cold season. They have established a lucrative nationwide market and have also penetrated the export market. In addition to woven fabrics Gujarat also sustains, although barely, two other forms of constructed textiles: felt, which is made from unspun wool; and ply-split braiding, for which goat and camel hair are used. This chapter outlines Gujarati traditions of weaving cotton, silk and wool and describes the contemporary production of handlooms, felt and braids.

WEAVING

Cotton

The primacy of woven cotton in the material culture of India has led to it being described as 'the fabric of India'.[4] The earliest evidence of cotton on the subcontinent is seeds from a Neolithic site near Mehrgarh in northern Baluchistan, dated c. 4000 BCE. The domestication of cotton (*Gossypium arboreum*) occurred somewhat later in the Indus Valley region during the Harappan era (2500–1750 BCE) and cotton cultivation in Gujarat developed at this time. Traces of cotton cloth, spindles and spindle whorls found at the Harappan site of Mohenjodaro (1760 BCE) confirm that the Harappans were processing and weaving cotton. However, there is nothing to indicate what type of looms were in use at the time but it seems likely that they were pit looms with a treadle, technology still in use in many parts of India.[5] Other evidence in the form of inscriptions and seals suggests textiles were part of external trade with Mesopotamia and West Asia during the Harappan period.[6] Indian cottons were known in the Mediterranean world from a very early date. The Greek historian Herodotus, writing in c. 440 BCE, refers to 'trees which grow wild, the fruit of which is a wool exceeding in beauty and goodness that of a sheep. The Indians make their clothes of this tree wool'.[7] Certainly by the first century CE, Indian cotton textiles were an integral part of maritime trade via the Indian Ocean, a trade in which Gujarat played a prominent role. Evidence of this is to be found in the *Periplus* which describes cottons of various qualities being exported from the Gujarati port of Bharuch—also a production centre—to the Red Sea ports whence they were traded to other parts of Egypt, East Africa and the Mediterranean.[8] This trade continued for many centuries during which time Gujarati textiles also went east to Southeast Asia and China. During the medieval period commerce was monopolized by goods from Khambat, the main port of western India at the time whose hinterland supported a vast industry. The sheer volume of production is indicated by the observations of visiting Europeans such as the Italian, Ludovico Varthema, who in the early sixteenth century noted that: 'An immense quantity of cotton is produced here, so that every year forty or fifty vessels are laden with cotton and silk stuffs, which stuffs are carried into different countries.'[9] The traces of this extensive trade are to be found in the fragments of block-printed cottons retrieved from Egyptian sites and whole textiles preserved as funerary goods in Southeast Asia. While other regions—notably Bengal—became known for exquisite finely woven cottons whose sheerness prompted poetic names such as *abrawan* (running water) and *shabnam* (morning dew), Gujarati cottons were better known for their surface decoration; they provided a base on which the state's dyers, block-printers and embroiderers wrought their craft.

Ahmedabad became the leading city of western India during the period of the independent Sultanate of Gujarat (1407–1573). In 1573 the emperor Akbar annexed Gujarat, bringing it under direct Mughal control and Ahmedabad became the centre of Mughal administration for the state. Cloth production in Gujarat flourished under the Mughals; textiles were a lucrative source of revenue for the empire and the variety and quality available there attracted foreign merchants. Indeed, it was trade that encouraged the British and Dutch East India Companies to establish their 'factories' in Surat in the early seventeenth century. By then Surat had become the main entrepôt for western India whence considerable quantities of cotton textiles were exported to Europe. In comparison to the European wools and linens of the day, cottons were easy to maintain and the appeal of painted and dyed chintzes especially saw them become all the rage. Cottons were produced in many towns along the coast as well as in Ahmedabad which was the leading centre not only for dyed and printed cottons but for silks, brocades and velvets as well. Under Mughal patronage craft production was organised through a system of ateliers (*karkhanas*) which had been established in the empire's leading cities and in Ahmedabad weavers, block-printers, dyers and embroiderers laboured in vast workshops. However, after the death of the emperor Aurangzeb in 1707 Mughal power waned and with it imperial patronage, the *karkhanas* dispersed and artisans sought work elsewhere.

FIG 3.2 | FOLLOWING PAGE

A page from John Forbes Watson's 18-volume *Textile Manufactures of India*, London 1867 (Ill. no. 116)

It shows a sample of *khes* from Sindh. Forbes Watson's work documented the production and use of textiles in the subcontinent. *Khes* is closely related to *khesado*, the shoulder cloth used by the Rabaris of Kachchh district.

INDIAN FABRICS.

MAN'S GARMENT.

Cotton Scarf; called Kass in Sind.

Length 2 yards 34 inches ; width 26 inches ; weight 2 lbs. 1 oz. ; price 9s. 9d.

From NURRAPORE, SIND.

Prov. No. 346.

EACH END
SAME PATTERN.

The manufacture of cotton fabrics by artisans persisted until the mid-nineteenth century when the first textile mills in India which launched the mechanisation of the cloth industry were set up in Mumbai and Ahmedabad. At the same time the British deluged India with cheap cloth from the Lancashire mills, much of which had been purpose-designed for Indian modes of dress based on data collected in India by John Forbes Watson. His magnum opus, *Textile Manufactures and Costumes of the People of India*, was published in 1867 with the express intention 'to apprise British manufacturers of Indian taste and styles'.[10] Throughout India, village weavers found there was no market for their goods; local consumers who had previously worn handwoven *dhotis*, *lungis*, turbans, shoulder cloths and veilcloths were buying the cheaper, imported products. In the early 1920s Gandhi's orchestration of the *swadeshi* campaign placed handmade cloth centre stage—it was to be a means of regaining economic and political autonomy and *khadi* became a potent symbol for the nationalists. Nowadays, a dwindling number of cotton goods are made by hand in Gujarat: in Saurashtra and north Gujarat white *lungis* with longitudinal borders and brocaded end borders in red known as *pachedi* are still woven which are worn by local herders, and red, blue and green *pachedi* are woven for use by Bharwad shepherds; in the tribal area of Chhota Udaipur, highly decorative loin cloths are produced for the Rathwa community; in Kachchh a distinctive black and white shoulder cloth known as *khesado* which is closely related to the *khes* of Sindh (an item of dress documented by Forbes Watson) has continued in use. Worn mostly by older Rabaris, it has deep end borders of extra weft detail but is rapidly losing ground to industrially-produced alternatives in polyester.

Silk

Hindu belief in the ritual purity of silk has endowed silk textiles in India with a special status quite apart from their aesthetic and economic value. Textile writer Yashodara Agrawal asserts that silk

FIG 3.3 | BELOW

Dhebaria Rabaris, Anjar bazaar, east Kachchh

The man at the centre of this group has a *khesado* draped over his right shoulder. Made of white cotton with extra weft detail in black, orange, blue and green synthetic yarn, a shoulder cloth is part of caste dress for Rabari men.

was in use in India as early as the fifteenth century BCE, based on evidence from the excavations at Nevasa in the western state of Maharashtra.[11] Terms for silken fabric and textiles woven or embroidered with gold occur in Vedic literature and silk weaving is mentioned in the third century BCE.[12] The earliest examples of woven silk in India are silk bags found in a stone relic box excavated at Devni Mori in Gujarat, a site that has been dated to c. 375 CE; these are awaiting further analysis.[13] Although indigenous types of wild silk were known prior to the Common Era, chiefly in eastern India, most of the silk subsequently used in the weaving industry of western India was cultivated 'mulberry silk' imported from China, much of which passed through the Gujarati ports.[14] The *Periplus* provides a reference to the import of silk in the first century CE, noting that raw silk, silk yarn and woven silk were sent overland through Bactria to Bharuch.[15] Silk textiles from Anhilwada (modern Patan)—the capital of Gujarat until 1411—are listed in the *Manasollasa*, a twelfth century treatise on Indian art and craft written by the Chalukya king, Bhulokamalla Someshwara in 1130–1131 CE.[16] There are regular references to *patola* in Gujarati literature from the twelfth century onward; although production is now confined to Patan, it is evident that they were once more widely produced at Ahmedabad, Surat, Khambat, Bharuch and Vadodara.[17]

During the Sultanate period (1206–1526) silk weaving was carried out in huge ateliers similar to the *karkhana* system later developed by the Mughals. Witnessing the vast workshops of Mohammed Tughluq in the early fourteenth century, the Moroccan traveller Ibn Battuta noted that, 'The Sultan of Delhi has a *tiraz* factory in which there are four thousand manufacturers of silk'.[18] It was during the Tughluq dynasty that the drawloom which features a double harness was introduced to India—one provides the weave structure, the other the figured pattern. It was this technology that allowed the development of brocade weaving on a large scale, the *tiraz* (Arabic for 'factory') production of Ibn Battuta's account. Although Ahmedabad's reputation for figured silks was established during the period of the independent Sultanate of Gujarat (1407–1573), it reached its zenith under the Mughals. But the association of imperial power with silk was not without its tensions—the Quran proscribes the wearing of pure silk because its luxuriousness might engender vanity which would impede proper submission to Allah. During the Sultanate some sovereigns, notably Firoz Shah Tughluq (reigned 1351–1388) banned its use altogether; later rulers compromised—silk was forbidden in the mosque but allowed outside and the belief prevailed that it deflected

FIG 3.4

Vagadia Rabari woman, east Kachchh

Dressed for a wedding celebration taking place at the festival of Janmashtami (Lord Krishna's birthday), this young woman is wearing a new blouse of synthetic brocade made from polyester and plastic *jari*.

sword cuts; thus it was used, even encouraged, on the battlefield.[19] Despite these issues, Ahmedabad and Surat became famous for a variety of figured silks woven for furnishings and dress which were in great demand at the imperial and regional courts. Examples are listed in the catalogue of textiles and dress at the City Palace, Jaipur, and the import of Gujarati brocades 'for royal use at Jaipur' is noted.[20] They were also exported to Europe and Southeast Asia and the influence of Gujarati brocades has been remarked upon in the *songket* tradition of Malaysia and Indonesia.[21] Tent panels and floor coverings were woven with gold in the *lampas* technique;[22] velvets were used for tents, floorspreads and curtains; *mashru* and *kinkhab* were used for different items of apparel; and exquisite sashes or *patka* were made with end borders worked in double cloth or tapestry technique, heavy with *jari*. Abu'l-Fazl, chronicler of the emperor Akbar's reign, not only describes the sheer variety of silk and golden textiles being manufactured, he also notes the introduction of foreign expertise—silk weavers from Safavid Persia and Central Asia—to enhance local production: 'Skilful masters and workmen have settled in this country to teach people an improved system of manufacture'.[23] For the Mughals the sumptuous textiles used at court and in their tents whilst on tour around the empire were symbols of royalty and silk was the fabric of choice among royalty and the aristocracy.

But as central Mughal authority collapsed during the eighteenth century, the production of patterned silks disappeared from the imperial centres and the artisans found patrons in the regional courts. By the early nineteenth century, Varanasi in Uttar Pradesh had become the primary centre of patterned silk manufacture in India, its repertoire enhanced by the influx of expert brocade weavers from Gujarat. This migration of skilled weavers repeated an established pattern—artisans driven by famine, natural disaster or regime change were intermittently forced to seek new patrons. In terms of silk weaving specifically, this resulted in a discernible Gujarati influence at silk centres in other parts of India. As Jasleen Dhamija has noted: 'The majority of silk weavers trace their origins to Gujarat. Some of the most important weavers of southern India working in silk were originally known as Sorathis and trace their origins to Saurashtra'.[24]

Despite the exodus of skilled artisans, Ahmedabad and Surat continued to produce *kinkhabs*, saris of silk satin, and elaborate silk fabrics often with metallic thread on a reduced scale until the early twentieth century. Similarly,

FIG 3.5 | RIGHT

Piece of velvet, silk, L 107 x W 49.4 cm, late 19th century

Ahmedabad and Lahore were the leading centres for the production of velvet from the 16th century onwards. Velvet was the most expensive fabric to produce and its production dwindled in tandem with the decline of the Mughal Empire.

V&A: 664A-1883

production of *mashru* and *gajji* silk persisted at Patan and Mandvi. The main categories of Gujarati handloom silk textiles are explored briefly below, although few are currently in production in the state—some are now made in Varanasi and most have their synthetic imitations.

Velvet

Exactly how and when velvet reached India is unknown but its name in Hindi and Urdu, *makhmal,* is derived from Arabic, and it therefore seems likely that it was introduced by Arab traders.[25] Although velvet can be made of any fibre, the Mughals preferred silk which they used to create sumptuous interiors not only for their palaces but also for the tents used when touring their dominions, or on military campaigns. The upholstery of thrones, bolsters, cushions and canopies were all made of velvet and it was also used for *farman*—covers for royal correspondence—books, small gifts and even coats. The sheer luxury of the imperial dwellings was captured by William Hawkins, a British visitor at the emperor Jahangir's mobile court in 1616: 'This tent is curiously wrought and hath many *Seminans* [awnings] joining round about it of most curiously wrought velvet, embroidered with gold, and many of them are of Cloth of Gold and Silver... I may say it is at least two acres of ground, but so richly spread with silks and gold carpets and hangings in the principal places, rich as velvet embroidered with gold, pearl, and precious stone can make it'.[26] By the sixteenth century, Ahmedabad and Lahore were the leading centres in India of velvet production where velvets were woven with a gold ground as well as those made of plain silk. Velvet was the most expensive fabric to produce; laborious to weave and using costly materials, above all other fabrics it captured the excess of the Mughals and its production dwindled in tandem with imperial decline.

Brocade

The city of Ashaval, modern Ahmedabad, was known as a centre for silk and golden fabrics before the fifteenth century. During the Sultanate period the Ahmedabadi silk weavers benefited from royal patronage but under the *karkhana* system of the Mughals, the reputation of both Ahmedabad and Surat for silk brocades soared, bringing international acclaim. Giovanni Careri, an Italian visitor to Ahmedabad in 1693, described the abundance of luxury textiles in the city: 'I may say without enlarging that all the rich silks and gold stuffs curiously wrought with birds and flowers; all the brocades, velvets, taffetas and other sorts made in Ahmedabat [*sic*], are conveyed to Surat, I say those of Ahmedabat, which is the greatest city in India, and nothing inferior to Venice for this trade'.[27] Brocade was painstakingly woven on *naksha* drawlooms that had originated in Persia; traditionally the design was first drawn on paper after which a specialist known as a *naksha bandha* transferred the design onto cotton threads on the *naksha* (also known as a *jala* in Gujarati) which was an indigenous form of early jacquard.[28] The Ahmedabadi and Surti brocades were known for the use of *jari* and a plethora of gold and silver textiles developed. There is a good deal of ambiguity about the precise distinction between the varieties of brocade produced which employed different techniques and designs and the confusion has been compounded by the admix of Persian and local names. As Steven Cohen has observed, they 'still remain to be precisely determined by linguists and historians'.[29] Bearing that in mind, a few key types of brocade and other silk textiles are included in the following sections.

Ashavali Saris

Ashavali saris took their name from the ancient town of Ashaval on which site Ahmedabad developed. Although they have a considerable reputation, an exact definition of what exactly constituted an 'Ashavali sari' has proved elusive. Earlier scholars mention a number of characteristics which are discussed below but, as Steven Cohen observes, 'there seems to be no agreement as to what specific technical characteristics or design features that term originally encompassed'.[30] Yashodhara Agrawal applies the term *Ashavali* to heavy silk saris woven in rich plain colours, noting that gold, green and deep red were especially popular, with longitudinal borders and draped end panel (*pallav*) of brocade. The plain coloured ground featured fine gold stripes, small checks, or tiny *butis* (small floral motifs); later examples were richer, woven with additional trellis or *jali* designs. Like other Gujarati silk textiles, the brocaded areas of *Ashavali* saris—the borders and *pallav*—were woven with mixed cotton and silk yarn and *jari*. Radhika Lalbhai, who has been involved in reviving the weaving of *Ashavali* saris in Ahmedabad, noted that in order to maximise the effect of the gold, the areas of *jari* were woven in a twill known locally as *desi vana* which resulted in the 'enamelled effect' of the patterns worked in gold and silk.[31] The tenets of Islam meant that few textiles produced during the Sultanate and Mughal periods used figurative designs. *Ashavali* saris were an exception—they embraced the folk traditions of Gujarat and featured stylised animals, birds and human figures. These characteristics were later absorbed into the repertoire of Varanasi, introduced in the early nineteenth century by the migration of weavers from Gujarat.[32] Loss of royal patronage, the exodus of silk weavers and the introduction of the jacquard loom to Gujarat in the late nineteenth century eventually led to the disappearance of handloom *Ashavali* saris in Ahmedabad; nonetheless the term is still used in the city, applied to fancy saris woven with rayon 'art silk' and plastic *jari*.

Kinkhab

One of the most widely known Gujarati brocades was *kinkhab*, now produced chiefly in Varanasi. The derivation of the term is unclear but *kinkhab* was technically related to textiles produced in the Ottoman Empire known as *kemha* and *serenk*, and *lampas* and *samite* in western Europe.[33] *Kinkhab*, often anglicized as *kincob*, was woven with silk and gold or silver *jari*, made in such a way that the face of the fabric was almost entirely covered by *jari*; some textiles combined both gold and silver and were known as *ganga-yamuna*, named for the two great rivers of northern India—the Ganga and the Yamuna. A somewhat coarser silk known as *mukta* was used for *kinkhab* as it had to withstand the weight of the gold and silver thread and the process of brocading. Other *jari* brocades were lighter in weight and showed more silk on the surface of the cloth, such as *muqayyash* (with silver stripes) and *kurtahwar* (patterned or striped with gold). Such was the value of the precious metals in these textiles that as the cloth perished with use, people would take their *jari* textiles to reclaiming ovens where the fabric was burnt away leaving the gold and silver. This practice is still in evidence in the Chandla Ol area of Ahmedabad.

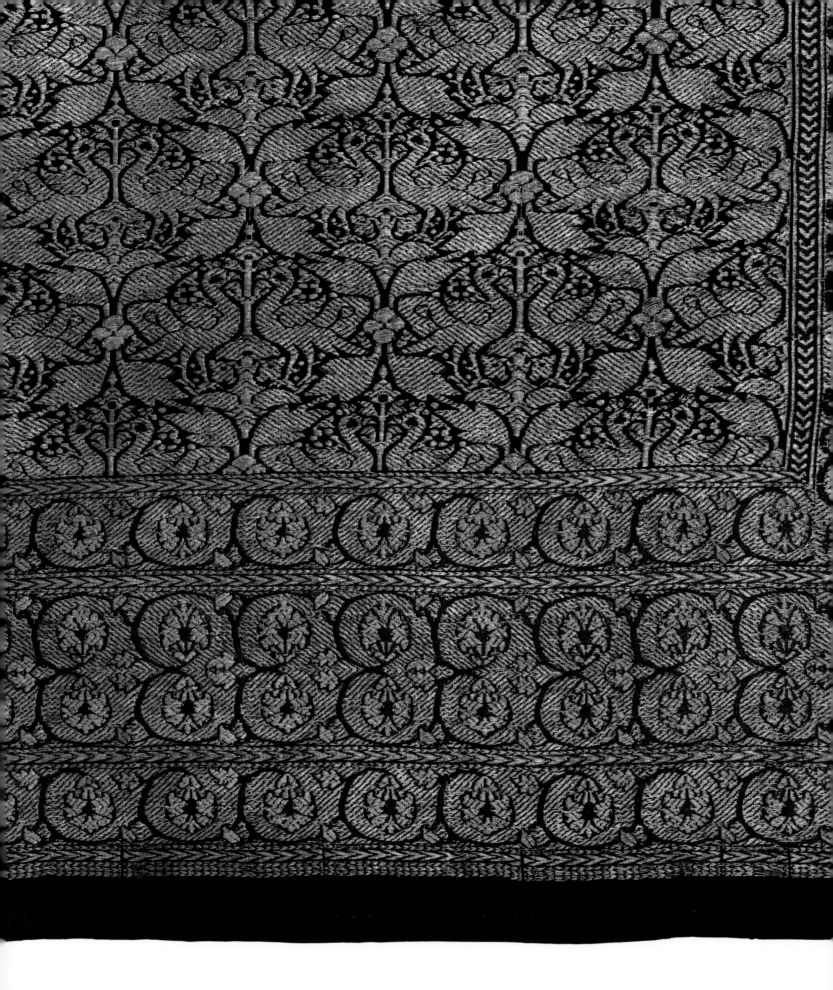

FIG 3.6

Kinkhab, silk with gold and silver *jari*,
L 151.5 x W 83.5 cm, c. 1851, made in
Ahmedabad

Ahmedabad was famous for this type
of brocade which is known as *ganga-yamuna*, so-called because it is made
with gold and silver thread; the name
refers to the two great rivers of northern
India—the Ganga and the Yamuna.

V&A: 784-52

Although much of the silk used was imported through Khambat, the other component in *kinkhab, jari,* was locally produced at Surat. In the thirteenth century, Marco Polo had complimented the gold and silver embroidery of Gujarat which implies *jari* was being produced in the state during the medieval period. During the Mughal era Surat was established as the centre of *jari* production in India—a position it holds to this day. The modern trade is run by Patel entrepreneurs originally from Saurashtra who have taken up the *jari* business as well as diamond cutting and polishing for which Surat is also noted. In small workshops gold and gilded silver wire is drawn by hired workers who then run it through rollers to flatten it, after which the flattened thread is wound around a silk core. *Jari* comes in a range of qualities which now includes plastic *jari,* and is supplied to weavers and embroiderers throughout India.

FIG 3.7—3.10

Workshop for reclaiming precious metals, Chandla Ol, Ahmedabad

Gold and silver are reclaimed from fabrics woven with *jari*, such as brocade saris, by burning away the silk and other materials. The silver or gold is collected by the client; if there is sufficient metal, it can be re-fashioned into jewellery, or sold by weight to a Soni (goldsmith). The number of workshops that provide this service is diminishing as the use of synthetic brocades and plastic *jari* has become widespread.

FIG 3.11–3.13

Jari manufacturing workshop, Surat

ABOVE | A worker draws a length of copper wire; it will then be electroplated with silver.

BELOW LEFT | The electroplated wire is run through rollers to flatten it into a fine silver ribbon. This is later wrapped around an art silk core to form *jari* thread.

BELOW RIGHT | *Jari* is wound onto reels known as *data*. There are four different qualities of *jari* from 'pure *jari*' for which only real silk and pure silver or gold are used; 'imitation *jari*' which has a core of cotton, art silk or polyester and silver is electroplated onto copper wire and chemical gilding is used for a golden appearance; 'half fine' or 'tested *jari*' which is the same as imitation *jari* except that the gilding is with pure gold; 'metallic *jari*' for which metallised polyester film is cut into fine strips and wrapped around a core of cotton, art silk or polyester.

Tanchoi

Tanchoi was thought to have been imported to Surat from China. Lotika Varadarajan and Krishna Amin-Patel assert that the weaving technique used 'is of Chinese origin'. They identify a number of technical characteristics, chief amongst these is 'the exclusive use of silk extra weft ornamentation on a silk ground of plain or satin weave' and they note that the ornamentation is 'dense and well-packed'.[34] Other scholars have also attempted to pinpoint exactly what the term originally encompassed but a definition remains elusive and as Steven Cohen has observed, 'Today, *tanchoi* is a name applied to almost any satin weave with a small scale dense repeating pattern'.[35] The origin of the term *tanchoi* is equally unclear. According to oral history it is said to be derived from 'tran Chhoi', named for the three (Gujarati *tran*) Chhoi brothers who mastered the weaving technique and started to produce this type of textile in Surat, possibly in the nineteenth century. Information on the use of *tanchoi* is more secure; *tanchoi* saris were popular with Parsi women in Surat and Bombay and were used especially for wedding dress; the Chinese influence was also evident in other aspects of Parsi dress, notably in *chinai* embroidery applied to sari borders, skirts and blouses. Manufacture ceased in Surat in the 1950s when weavers in Varanasi undercut the price of Surti *tanchoi;* production continues in Varanasi where the jacquard has replaced the original *jala* except for occasional special orders.

Mashru

Unlike many of the silk textiles discussed above, *mashru* is still produced in Patan and a few villages near Mandvi in Kachchh. *Mashru*, as we now know, has a silk warp and a cotton weft and is a warp-faced fabric, or sateen, which means that the face of the cloth is predominantly silk and the reverse is cotton. It was developed to circumvent the Quranic proscription against the use of pure silk and the term means 'permitted'. The woven patterning

FIG 3.14

Fragment of *tanchoi* (?) silk, L 202 x W 72 cm, Surat (?), mid-19th century

The satin weave of this textile and dense, small scale repeating pattern suggest that it may be a fragment of *tanchoi*, a sari that was popular with Parsi women in Surat and Bombay (Mumbai).

V&A: T 245-1920

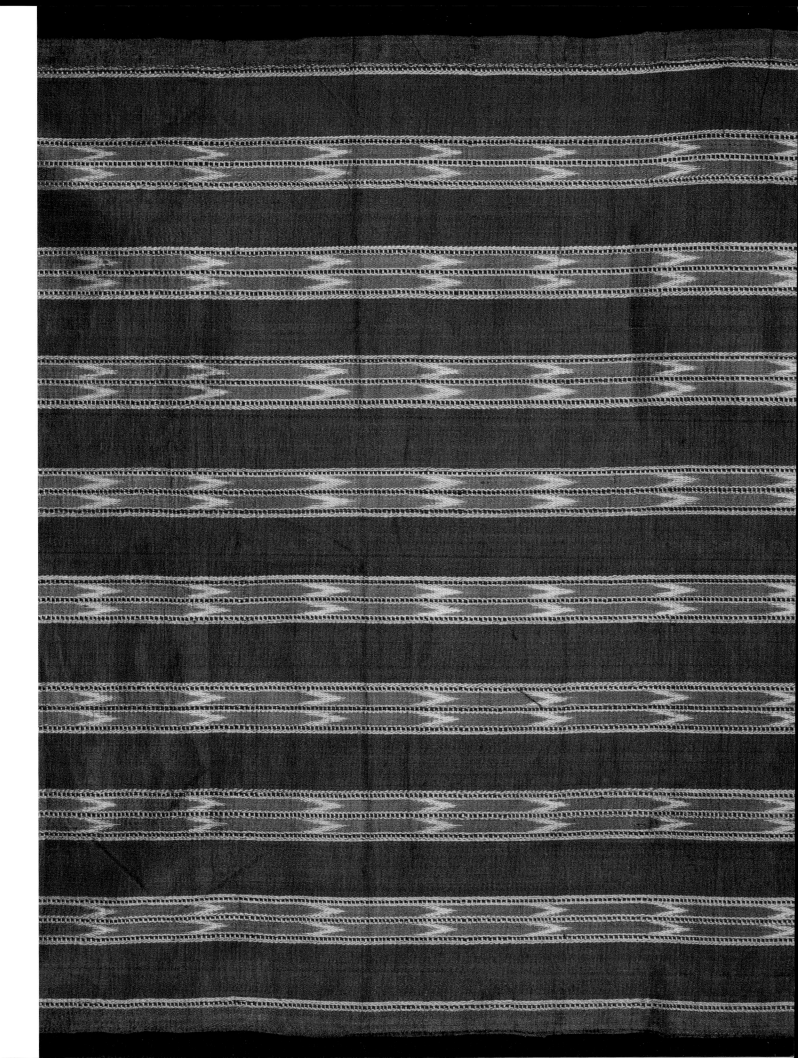

conformed to Islamic aesthetics and were typically lengthwise stripes that often included small chevrons and ikat.[36] *Mashru* was popular for furnishings, hangings, quilts and robes, and was often used as a lining fabric—its cotton content not only enabled the faithful to avoid transgression of religious law, it was also robust enough to withstand wear. During the Mughal period *mashru*

FIG 3.15 | PREVIOUS PAGE

Piece of *mashru*, silk warp, cotton weft, satin weave, warp ikat, W 49.5 cm, Surat, c. 1855

Made of silk and cotton, *mashru* is said to have been devised because wearing pure silk is proscribed for Muslim men. Formerly woven throughout Gujarat, production is now confined to Patan and Mandvi.

V&A: 0301 IS

FIG 3.16 | LEFT

Meghwal women wearing striped *mashru*, Khavda, north Kachchh

These women are in their best dress to celebrate a profit-sharing event run by the NGO for which they make embroidery. *Mashru* is a valued cloth in many communities, used for festival dress and weddings; most is now made of polyester.

FIG 3.17 | LEFT

Vagadia Rabari wedding, east Kachchh

The groom's attendants are both wearing turban wraps of red and black striped polyester *mashru*.

FIG 3.18 | RIGHT

Vagadia Rabari wedding, east Kachchh

The groom is resplendent in red synthetic brocade over which he wears a dhoti of red and black striped polyester *mashru*. Mashru is extensively used for the dress of both bride and groom, and auspicious red dominates the colour palette.

was woven throughout India and was widely used by wealthy Muslims. By the nineteenth and twentieth centuries, it had been adopted by many Hindu communities in Gujarat, a fact revealed in Marianna Postans' account of her residency in Kachchh, 1834–1839. She described women's attire in Mandvi and noted they wore a 'satin petticoat with broad horizontal stripes of red, blue and yellow'.[37] More recently polyester *mashru* has become a staple of caste dress among many rural communities. In Kachchh it is used by women from farming and herding groups for blouses and skirts and Rabari men reserve it for ceremonial occasions such as weddings when red *mashru* turbans, *angarkha* and ceremonial wraps are worn. Kachchh is one of the few places where handloom *mashru* is still woven. Mahajan weavers, who are Hindus, work on simple pit looms using rayon 'art silk' which has replaced mulberry silk. Little of their production is sold in the district—compared to polyester

mashru it is expensive although there are regular commissions from non-governmental organisations (NGOs) working in the craft sector who use the fabric for the purses and bags embroidered by local women that are sold as part of income-generation schemes. *Mashru* production also survives in Patan where a majority of the weavers are Muslims. Like the Kachchhi weavers they use rayon instead of real silk and they have lately developed a pure cotton *mashru*—using cotton for both warp and weft. Most of their production is commissioned by cloth merchants in Ahmedabad.

Wool

Unlike silk weaving in Gujarat which has a history of royal patronage, wool weaving is rooted in rural traditions of dress. The weavers who are from Dalit (lit. 'oppressed', formerly known as 'untouchables') communities used to rely on *desi,* or local, wool spun from fleeces supplied by Rabaris and Bharwads. Until quite recently shearing was carried out by the shepherds themselves or by itinerant Muslim shearers known as *khatroda* from Rajasthan. Fine merino wool is preferred now to the coarse *desi* variety, much of which is imported from New Zealand and Australia. Most fleeces used are bought through agents in Deesa and Rajkot in Gujarat, and Bikaner in Rajasthan. Polyester yarn has become popular, too.[38] In Kachchh and parts of Saurashtra, weavers, who are known locally as Vankars, used to produce woollen veilcloths, skirts and blankets for Rabaris and Bharwads; they also made the flatweaves used for saddle bags and rugs. The last vestiges of the trade linger in Kachchh, chiefly because Rabari caste rules still dictate the use of a woollen veilcloth by Rabari

FIG 3.19 | LEFT

Mahajan weaver, near Mandvi, south Kachchh

Handmade *mashru* is produced on a wooden loom with multiple shafts operated by foot pedals. The pedals are set below ground level and the weaver sits in a pit and manipulates them with his feet to produce the required pattern. The silk warp extends before him into the family compound. Rayon 'art silk' has now replaced mulberry silk.

FIG 3.20 | CENTRE

Detail of *mashru* being woven by hand

The weaver is holding a shuttle which contains a bobbin wound with the cotton yarn of the weft. Preparation of bobbins is often done by female members of the family.

Mashru workshop, Patan, north Gujarat

The weaver works at a pit loom with the warp tethered to a post at the end of the workshop. Patan is now the main centre for handmade *mashru* in Gujarat. This family business provides regular employment for six weavers and also supports several outworkers.

FIG 3.22 | RIGHT

Mashru weaver, Patan, north Gujarat

The shafts of the loom are attached to pulleys operated by foot pedals and the shuttle is thrown across the warp by means of another pulley system. Like the *mashru* woven in Kachchh, that of Patan is made from rayon 'art silk' and cotton.

FIG 3.23 | ABOVE LEFT

Kachchhi Rabaris at Bhujodi, Kachchh, shearing their sheep

FIG 3.24 | ABOVE RIGHT

Vankar at Bhujodi weaving a Rabari veilcloth using *desi* (local) wool

The number of weavers still making these heavy woollen veilcloths has dwindled to a handful as many Rabari women now use cheaper synthetic veilcloths for daily wear.

FIG 3.25 | LEFT

Kachchhi Rabari women at Bhujodi, Kachchh

Many Kachchhi women in the village do mirrorwork embroidery on shawls for local Vankars which provides them with a small but regular income.

women, based on their belief in the ritual purity of wool which surpasses that of silk. But the cost of a woollen veilcloth which represents several days of labour to most Rabaris and the ready availability of cheaper synthetic alternatives (which many now prefer), foretell the end of the custom.

The relationship between the Vankars and Rabaris has evolved. Since the 1970s, entrepreneurial weavers have developed a lucrative business making shawls for the national market and they now employ hundreds of Rabari women to embellish the basic shawls with embroidery and mirrorwork. The work although tedious can be done at home and accommodates domestic responsibilities, providing a reliable source of income for Rabari women. The shawls are popular wear in India in the cold season; they are compatible with Indian styles of draped dress such as the sari and conform to Asian sensibilities about uncut cloth. They have also found favour with tourists and have penetrated the export market.

FELT-MAKING

Apart from its use by local weavers in Kachchh, wool has also been used for the most basic manufactured textile—felt. The craft of felt-making which is better known in the colder climes of Kashmir is practised by the Pinjara

FIG 3.26

Dhrang *melo* (religious fair), Kachchh

Horse caparisoned in handmade felt saddle cloth (*daddi*) and bridle embellished with tassels and beadwork.

and Mansuri communities who produce *namda*, felt rugs and floor coverings, and saddle cloths, known as *daddi*, for camels and horses used by Darbars and other Rajput clans in Kachchh and Saurashtra. Simpler pieces are made using the natural colours of the wool but vivid shades of red, orange and black are favoured for saddle cloths which are finished with felted tassels and pompoms along the edges. Although men lead the construction of each felt piece, they are helped at every stage by women and even children. The pattern areas of coloured wool are laid on to a cotton sheet and loose rolls of wool are fashioned by the women that are passed to the craftsman. Once the pattern has been completed the ground is fused on top. The unspun wool is subject to the application of water, soap and friction which mats the fibres together to produce felt. As motorised vehicles have taken over from animal transport the call for felted animal trappings has all but disappeared. Recent interventions by professional designers have seen the development of fashionable items such as slippers, bags and small rugs which are aimed at the urban market.

PLY-SPLIT BRAIDING

Ply-split braiding like felt-making was used to make a variety of trappings, mainly for camels. Once the main form of haulage in the desert areas of India, including areas such as the Rann of Kachchh, camels were dressed with decorative girths known as *tang*, accoutrements about their necks known as *gorbandh* as well as bridles (*moorka*), ankle (*godiya*) and knee bands (*sariya*); bags known as *khurji* were suspended from the saddle—all were made by ply-split braiding. Unlike the felt-makers who are professional artisans, ply-split braiding in Gujarat is produced by Rabari herders entirely for their own needs and not as a commercial craft. Such discrete usage may account for the

FIG 3.27–3.29 | ABOVE LEFT

Namdawala (felt-maker), Mundra, south Kachchh, making a saddle cloth

Using unspun wool that has been carded and dyed, the felt-maker lays out the geometric design of a saddle cloth on a cotton sheet. A thick layer of undyed wool is then laid over the completed pattern. The whole piece is carefully rolled up in a cotton sheet, soaked with water and rolled repeatedly; the friction felts the wool.

FIG 3.30 | ABOVE

Detail of felt saddle cloth produced by Yusuf Mansuri, Mundra, south Kachchh

FIG 3.31 | FACING PAGE

Contemporary miniature painting from Udaipur, Rajasthan

The painting depicts the popular folk tale of Dhola and Maru, the lovers who eloped on a camel. The artist has carefully rendered the zig-zag pattern of the camel's harness which is typical of ply-split braiding.

Private collection

sparseness of the written record on camel girths and other trappings, although they are mentioned by Abu'l-Fazl among the objects in the imperial storehouses of Emperor Akbar. They are represented in the miniature paintings of western India; the typical zig-zag pattern of braided harnesses and girths is notably evident in depictions of the popular Rajasthani folk tale of Dhola and Maru, the lovers who eloped on a camel. Although Rabaris are not professional craftsmen, their skilfully-made braids are both serviceable and decorative, featuring complex 'op-art' geometrics and small stylised camels and human figures. Additional embellishment in the form of buttons and cowry shells is evident on *gorbandh*, *godiya* and *sariya* especially. The technique requires little equipment—usually just a wooden needle known as *gunthaniya* for passing the working cord through the cord being split.[39] Older examples of *tang* and *gorbandh* are made from light brown camel hair and contrasting dark brown goat hair. In later versions, the use of goat hair persists but camel hair has been replaced by ready-to-use cotton—an oblique sign of the diminishing use of camels for haulage in Gujarat. Also reflecting the disappearance of the camel from the rural landscape, there are now very few girth makers in Gujarat and the craft survives in a few isolated pockets in Kachchh. As the formerly nomadic Rabaris settle and cease to herd animals, it is a craft that has little relevance to their lives in the twenty-first century.[40]

The constructed textiles of Gujarat offer considerable variety in terms of technique, use and circulation. Examination of the production and consumption of woven fabrics of all types, felts and braids not only reveals the influence of the changing fortunes of empires such as that of the Mughals and the British Raj, it also shows how technological advances and social change have affected fashion, taste and local usage. These textiles embody a rich history. Although the textiles discussed in this chapter are highly decorative in their own right, many of the fabrics woven in Gujarat, especially cottons and silks, have provided a base for further decoration be it dyed, printed or embroidered.

FIG 3.32

Kana Bhima, Dhebaria Rabari, east Kachchh, plying yarn

Using a drop spindle, Rabaris used to spin yarn from the wool of their sheep and the hair of their goats and camels while on migration. The practice has all but died out as Rabaris have given up their vocation as nomadic herders.

FIG 3.33 AND 3.34 | ABOVE

Soma Sava, Dhebaria Rabari, east Kachchh, ply-split braiding a camel girth (*tang*) using white cotton and goat hair

He uses a wooden needle (*gunthani*) to split the yarn. Rabaris used to fashion harnesses and storage bags for their camels when they were on migration. Few Rabari men still know the technique; Soma Sava and Kana Bhima (fig. 3.32), now both deceased, were masters of the craft.

FIG 3.35 | RIGHT

Camel girths made by Soma Sava and Kana Bhima

These examples show different materials used for braiding, including traditional yarns made from goat hair (dark brown), camel hair (mid brown) and sheep's wool (dyed orange). Industrially-spun white cotton became popular because it did not attract moths which left many girths in tatters.

Notes

1   Sardar, Z., 'History of Indian Textiles', in Hatanaka, K., *Textile Arts of India*, San Francisco: Chronicle Books, p. 309.

2   Quoted in Kumar, R., *Costumes and Textiles of Royal India*, London: Christie's Books, p. 81.

3   Some technical definitions of these textiles may assist the reader. Although the term brocade is widely used to cover many types of elaborate textiles, especially silks, it is a fabric constructed by means of 'discontinuous supplementary wefts introduced in specific areas to produce a special effect or pattern. Unlike embroidery, brocading is incorporated during the weaving process while the textile or carpet is still on the loom'. See Walker, D., *Flowers Underfoot. Indian Carpets of the Mughal Era*, London: Thames and Hudson, p. 181

   Kinkhab, also anglicized to *kincob*, is a silk brocade woven with gold or silver *jari* (metallic thread of gold or silver wrapped around a silken core). It is woven so that the *jari* is predominant on the face of the textile, giving the appearance of a golden or silver cloth.

   Velvet is a 'cut warp-pile fabric, originally of silk, in which the cut ends of the fibres form the surface of the fabric'. See Beech, S.R., C.A. Farnfield, P. Wharton and J.A.Wilkins, eds., *Textile Terms and Definitions*, 8th Edition, Manchester: The Textile Institute, p. 271.

   Mashru is a silk-cotton sateen; it is a weft-faced fabric and has a silk warp and a cotton weft.

4   Sanskriti Kendra, *Sanskriti Museum of Indian Textiles*, New Delhi: Sanskriti Kendra, p. 4.

5   Burnard, J., *Chintz and Cotton. India's Textile Gift to the World*, Kenthurst NSW: Kangaroo Press Ltd, p. 11.

6   Sharma, D.P. and Madhuri Sharma, *Panorama of Harappan Civilization*, New Delhi: Kaveri Books, pp. 60–61.

7   Macauley, G.C.,trans., *Herodotus. The History*, 2 vols., London: Macmillan, p. 765.

8   Casson, L., *The Periplus Maris Erythraei*, Princeton: Princeton University Press, p. 81.

9   Temple, R., *The Itinerary of Ludovico di Varthema of Bologna, 1502–1508*, London: Hakluyt Society, p. 29.

10 Forbes Watson, J., *Textile Manufactures and Costumes of the People of India*, 18 vols., London: Wm. H. Allen and Co., p. 2.

11 Agrawal, Y., *Silk Brocades*, New Delhi: Roli Books, p. 13.

12 Agrawal, p. 13.

13 Varadarajan, L. and Krishna Amin-Patel, *Of Fibre and Loom. The Indian Tradition*, Ahmedabad and New Delhi: National Institute of Design and Manohar Publishers, p. 264.

14 Cultivated silk is reeled from the cocoon of the silk moth (*Bombyx mori*) which is fed on mulberry leaves.

15 Casson, p. 16.

16 Agrawal, p. 16.

17 Kapur Chishti, R. and Rahul Jain, *Handcrafted Indian Textiles*, New Delhi: Roli Books Pvt Ltd, p. 103.

18 Gibb, H.A.R., trans., *Ibn Battuta. Travels in Asia and Africa, 1325–1354*, New Delhi: Asian Educational Services.

19 Bayly, C.A., 'The Origins of *Swadeshi* (Home Industry): Cloth and Indian Society, 1700–1930', in Arjun Appadurai, ed., *The Social Life of Things. Commodities in Cultural Perspective*, Cambridge: Cambridge University Press, p. 290.

20 Singh, C., *Textiles and Costumes from the Maharaja Sawai Man Singh II Museum*, Jaipur: Maharaja Sawai Man Singh II Museum Trust, p. xvii.

21 Dhamija, J., *Woven Magic. The Affinity Between Indian and Indonesian Textiles*, Jakarta: Dian Rakyat, p. 82.

22 Steven Cohen offers the following identification of *lampas*: 'These are the complex, loom-woven silk cloths generally known in Western Europe as *lampas* and *samite*, in the Ottoman Empire as *kemha* and *serenk*, and most probably known in Iran and India as particular varieties of *kimkhab* or *kamkhab* and *zarbaft*'. See Cohen, S., 'A Group of Early Silks. The Tree Motif', in Dhamija, J., ed., *Woven Silks of India*, Bombay: Marg Publications, p. 19.

23 Abu'l-Fazl Allami, *Ain-i-Akbari*, vol. 1 (trans. H. Blochmann), Delhi: Low Price Publications, p. 93.

24 Dhamija, J., ed., 'Introduction. Woven Silks of India', in *The Woven Silks of India*, Bombay: Marg Publications, p. 6.

25 Smart, E.S. and Dale C. Gluckman, 'Cloth of Luxury: Velvet in Mughal India', in Krishna Riboud, ed., *In Quest of Themes*

and Skills—Asian Textiles, Bombay: Marg Publications, p. 39.

26 Foster, W., ed., *Early Travels in India, 1583–1619*, London: Oxford University Press, pp. 117–118.

27 Sen, S.N., ed., *Indian Travels of Thevenot and Careri*, New Delhi: National Archives of India, pp. 163–164.

28 Sardar, pp. 328–329.

29 Cohen, p. 19.

30 Crill, R. and Steven Cohen, 'Courtly and Urban Textiles', in Barnes, R., Steven Cohen and Rosemary Crill, *Trade Temple and Court. Indian Textiles from the Tapi Collection*, Mumbai: India Book House Pvt Ltd in association with Garden Silk Mills Ltd, p. 188.

31 Lalbhai, R., 'Ashavali Saris of Ahmedabad. Revival of a Technique', in Dhamija, J., ed., *The Woven Silks of India*, Bombay: Marg Publications, p. 126.

32 Chakraverty, A., *The Master Naqshaband of Banaras Brocades*, Chennai: Crafts Council of India, p. 35

33 Cohen (1995), p. 19.

34 Varadarajan and Amin-Patel, p. 103.

35 Cohen (2002), p. 188.

36 Watt, G., *Indian Art at Delhi*, Delhi: Motilal Banarsidass, p. 255.

37 Postans, M., *Cutch or Random Sketches of Western India*, New Delhi: Asian Educational Services, p. 16.

38 Personal communication, Vishram Valji Vankar, September 1997.

39 For the definitive book on the technique of ply-split braiding, see Collingwood, P., *The Techniques of Ply-Split Braiding*, London: Bellew Publishing. For a text that focuses specifically on the technique in western India, see Quick, B. D. and Judith A. Stein, *Ply-Split Camel Girths of West India*, Los Angeles: Museum of Cultural History, University of California.

40 Personal communication, Soma Sava Rabari and Kana Bhima Rabari, March 1997.

4 Dyed, Printed and Painted Textiles

Gujarat has an extensive history of producing dyed, colourfast textiles, and diverse methods of patterning cloth with dyes and pigments have evolved for which the state is renowned. In this chapter, these are organised into two main categories: dyed textiles which involve immersion of the cloth in dye and the use of mordants; and painted textiles where pigment or dye is applied directly to the surface of the textile with a brush or a *kalam* (pen). Dyed textiles have been sub-divided into resist-dyeing which includes tie-dye and ikat, and block-printing.[1] Some textiles defy easy classification as they combine a number of techniques. In the production of *Mata-ni-pachedi* (cloth of the Mother Goddess), for example, various areas are drawn, painted, block-printed and dyed. Similarly, *ajrakh* which is block-printed features the use of a resist paste and is thus also an example of resist-dyeing.

HISTORY OF TEXTILE DYEING, PRINTING AND PAINTING

The exact evolution of printing and dyeing is not clear, but archaeological finds suggest that the production of colourfast cotton textiles in this part of India dates back to the period of the Indus Valley Civilisation.[2] The discovery of a dyer's workshop and cotton fibres reportedly dyed with madder (radio-carbon dated to 1760 ± 115 years) at the Harappan site of Mohenjodaro (in present-day Pakistan) indicates that the Harappans were cultivating and processing cotton and had a complex dyeing technology in place by the second millennium BCE that included knowledge of mordants.[3]. Further evidence of the longevity of the Indian dyer's craft is to be found in references to the trade in coloured cotton textiles from the subcontinent in the Greek period *Periplus* and the Roman period Pliny, and much later in travellers' accounts and the trade records of the East India Companies.[4]

The dyers' palette relied on the local availability of colour-producing plants, minerals and insects. Red dyes came from many sources, including sappan wood (*Caesalpina sappan*), chay (*Oldenlandia umbellata*) and the

FIG 4.1

Harvesting indigo, Tamil Nadu

Indigo production is now centred on Tamil Nadu and Andhra Pradesh in south India. Sarkhej in Gujarat and Bayana near Agra were the main sites for indigo cultivation and processing in the 17th and 18th centuries. The Gujarati industry has long since disappeared.

lac-producing insect (*Coccus lacca*), although madder root (*Rubia tinctorum*) and *al* root (*Morinda citrifolia*) were the most common. Black dye was made by fermenting rusting horseshoes, scrap iron and jaggery (boiled cane syrup); yellow came from safflower (*Carthamus tinctorius*), marigolds (*Tagetes patula*), catechu (*Acacia catechu*), pomegranate skins (*Punica granatum*), onion skins (*Allium cepa*) and turmeric root (*Curcuma domestica*); and blue came from indigo leaves (*Indigofera tinctoria*). Indigo, which still grows wild in parts of the subcontinent, was a significant commodity in its own right. It is listed in *The Periplus* with cotton cloth and garments, and silk cloth and yarn as one of the goods exported from the port of Bharuch. By the early seventeenth century, Sarkhej in Ahmedabad, and Bayana near Agra were the two principal centres in India for the manufacture of indigo, and the product from these two sources was identifiable by shape: the square tablets of Sarkhej were known as 'flat indigo' and the indigo balls of Bayana as 'round indigo'.

In western India, the East India Companies established their 'factories' at Surat from where they exported all manner of goods, notably textiles, but also indigo which was used in Europe to dye wool.[5] The competition for indigo was intense—the English and Dutch factors vied with merchants from Mongolia, Armenia and Persia to secure the limited supply. The manufacturers, taking advantage of their monopoly, became notorious for bulking up the weight of indigo with sand and oil. English East India Company records of 1638 note the adulteration: 'Two bales of flat indigo were found to contain nothing but black earth'.[6] Evidently the manufacturers' sharp practice continued and in 1640 disgruntled English merchants brought it to the attention of the Viceroy of Ahmedabad, Azam Khan. His unequivocal response was recorded by the German traveller, Mandelslo: 'He threatened no less than death to him that should hereafter mix sand or oyle, or any other substance than what nature gives to indico.'[7] By the eighteenth century the East India Company had developed other sources of indigo both in India—notably in Bengal—and outside the subcontinent, and production at Sarkhej gradually declined.[8]

At the end of the nineteenth century synthetic indigo, which had been developed in Germany by Badische Anilin und Soda Fabrik (BASF) in 1897, was introduced into India. Cost effective and easy to use, "German indigo"—as it is still known in the subcontinent—rapidly replaced natural indigo; today nothing remains of the Gujarati indigo industry and commercial production is now centred on Tamil Nadu and Andhra Pradesh.

FIG 4.2

Indigo cakes, Tamil Nadu

This producer cuts the indigo into square tablets that are sold by weight. In the 17th century, this format was referred to as 'flat indigo' in East India Company records.

Most natural dyes require a mordant or metallic salt to permanently bond the colour to fabric. Treated with different mordants but dyed in the same dye bath, fabrics will produce a range of colours and shades. It was the manipulation of mordants that was the basis of the Indian dyer's technical pre-eminence which reached its zenith in the seventeenth and eighteenth centuries when their multi-hued, colourfast cotton textiles were all the rage with European consumers. Iron (ferrous sulphate) and alum (potassium aluminium sulphate or soda ash) were the most important mordants, although copper, tin and chrome were also used. Their efficacy was assisted by the use of tannins mostly commonly derived from myrobalan (*Terminalia chebula*), known locally as *harde*, although pomegranate rinds were another source used particularly for yellow dyes. However, natural dyes fell into gradual decline after synthetic dyes became commercially available in India in the late nineteenth century and by the early 1950s few Gujarati dyers were using them. They were won over by the cost effectiveness and ease of use of synthetic dyes. There has been a concerted effort to revive the use of natural dyes initiated in the 1970s by the Gujarat State Handicrafts Development Corporation and the National Institute of Design (NID) in collaboration with a few dyers who still sustained the practice. Since the mid-1970s, the number of craftspeople using natural dyes has steadily increased as their renewed commercial viability has been established.

Dyed Textiles

Gujarat has long been famous for fine cottons dyed in plain colours, especially red and blue that were produced at several centres and exported from Surat. Tavernier, a French jeweller who visited Gujarat during the reign of the Mughal emperor Aurangzeb, noted their production in Ahmedabad: 'The *baftas*, or cotton cloths required to be dyed red, blue, or black are taken uncoloured to Agra and Ahmedabad because these two towns are near places where indigo is made'.[9] But the state's enduring reputation rests on the variety and quality of its decorated textiles which rely on the manipulation of dyes and mordants to produce a pattern; various forms of resist-dyeing are used and also block-printing.

Resist-dyeing

Resist-dyeing relies on creating a barrier between the cloth and the dye either through a tied resist or by applying a resist medium—in Gujarat wax or a paste of lime and gum arabic are in common use and, more rarely now,

FOLLOWING PAGES

FIG 4.3

Khatri tying a silk textile, Bhuj, Kachchh

Tie-dye (*bandhani*) is a resist-dyeing technique of great antiquity for which Kachchh is famous, notably the towns of Bhuj, Mandvi, Mundra and Anjar. Khatris, who dominate the craft, are known especially for exquisite silk textiles that are used for weddings and other important ceremonies.

FIG 4.4

Laheriya ('waves') textiles, cotton, from Jaipur, Rajasthan

This form of tie-dye creates stripes, zig-zags and checks. The cloth is rolled diagonally and then bound at intervals to create stripes. It takes several stages of binding and dyeing to produce the more complex patterns such as zig-zags and checks.

mud (*dabu*). Application of the resist medium is mostly by use of printing blocks; textiles produced by this method are discussed in a later section on block-printing. But the state is perhaps best known for the use of a tied resist, a category of textiles that includes *bandhani* (Gujarati for tie-dye) and ikat.[10]

Bandhani

Bandhani patterns are created by binding tiny areas of the cloth with thread which blocks the absorption of dye when the fabric is immersed in the dye bath. The pattern is typically composed of small dots or *bindi*. Variations of the technique include a stitched resist, or *tritik* (a Malay term), and *laheriya* (Sanskrit/Hindi for 'waves') for which Jaipur and its environs in Rajasthan are noted. Cloth is rolled diagonally and bound at intervals to create stripes, and in more complex pieces, zigzags and checks. Based on evidence of mordant dyeing technology from Mohenjodaro it seems probable that resist-dyeing techniques such as *bandhani* were known during the period of the Indus Valley Civilisation. However, the earliest visual evidence of tie-dyed fabrics in use in western India is in Buddhist murals at the Ajanta Caves in Maharashtra. In Cave 1 (460–478 CE) female figures are depicted wearing bodices with a spotted pattern and ikat skirts. In the *Harshacharita*, or the Life of King Harsha of Kanauj (606–648 CE), written approximately a century and a half later, the court poet Bana refers to 'old matrons [who] were skilled in many sorts of [textile] patterning, some of which were in the process of being tied'.[11]

In terms of actual cloth, the oldest examples with a tie-dyed design are medieval, consisting of fragments of cotton block-printed in western India in imitation of tie-dye, retrieved from Fustat and other sites in Egypt (see Chapter 1). The medieval period provides further visual and

textual evidence of tie-dye in use: women are depicted wearing tie-dyed dress in Jain manuscripts painted in Gujarat in the fourteenth century;[12] and the first specific mention of Gujarati *bandhani* is to be found in inventories known as *varnaka*, compiled between the fourteenth and sixteenth centuries, which refer to *bandhalaya*, or tie-dye. A fifteenth century text notes the importance of Mandvi in Kachchh as a centre for tie-dyed *odhani* (veilcloths), which is still the case today.[13] In the modern period, other centres noted for *bandhani* are Jamnagar in Saurashtra, and the towns of Bhuj and Mundra in Kachchh district.

The craft is dominated by the Khatris, a hereditary caste of dyers and fabric printers in Gujarat, composed of both Hindus and Muslims; Muslim Khatris are the majority in Kachchh, and Hindus in Saurashtra.[14] The work, from production to sales, is generally organised by men through family networks. Although men are active throughout the process, much of the routine labour of tying is done as piece work by women at home. Prior to being distributed, the cloth is prepared in workshops where designs are stencilled onto fine cotton (*mulmul*) or silk using a fugitive dye mixed with kerosene. Designs on wool are marked using a thread dipped in soot and kerosene. Guided by these outlines, the women pinch the fabric into tiny peaks, with the aid of a finger nail or a small metal point worn on a finger, and then bind the fabric tightly with thread, looping a knot around it and moving swiftly to the

FIG 4.5

Bandhani workshop, Jamnagar, Saurashtra

The pattern to be tied is hand-printed onto silk with a fugitive dye. The cloth is distributed to female outworkers for tying, who return the tied textiles to the workshop. Dyeing and finishing is done by male dyers, most of whom belong to the Khatri caste.

FIG 4.6 | LEFT

Khatri marking out *bandhani* designs, east Kachchh

Using a length of string dipped in a mixture of soot and kerosene this craftsman maps out the patterns to be tied on a woollen veilcloth. Known as *sat batili* ('seven designs'—see fig. 4.14), the veilcloth is worn by Vagadia Rabari women.

FIG 4.7 | RIGHT

Khatri woman tying a woollen veilcloth, east Kachchh

After the design has been marked out, the textile goes to outworkers for tying. This woman is using her teeth to compress the coarse *desi* (local) wool in order to achieve a tight tie.

next *bindi* (dot) without breaking the thread. For bulkier fabrics like wool, some compress the cloth using their teeth. The cloth is customarily folded in half or even quarters for tying, with *bindis* applied through multiple layers of the cloth which reduces the labour and results in a mirrored design. The tied fabric then goes to the dyers for colouration. Complex designs require several stages of tying and dyeing. In some cases, once the dyeing process has been completed women re-wind the thread with admirable economy on to a matchbox to be used again. The work provides Khatri women with a valuable source of income; it does not bring them into conflict with social conventions such as *purdah,* and it accommodates their domestic duties.[15] In contrast, dyeing is almost exclusively a male preserve with knowledge and skills passed on through the generations. Synthetic dyes are widely used, although in the past decade, a few of the craftsmen in Bhuj, Kachchh, have revived the use of natural dyes and now produce a limited amount of work using this older technology.

Jamnagar: *Gharcholu and Panetar*

Bandhani has enduring presence in the domestic market and there is a growing export trade to Europe, North America and Japan. In particular, Japan has become a strong market thanks in part to its own highly regarded tradition of resist-dyeing known as *shibori*.[16] *Bandhani* has been an important

component in caste dress; it is a marking of identity both in general use and at the times of important rites of passage such as marriage when garments made of tie-dyed fabrics are worn by women . A range of fabrics was used for tie-dye, including wool, cotton and silk, but silk *bandhani* was the most prestigious; it was labour-intensive to produce and used expensive materials like *gajji*, a satin made of imported Chinese silk. Cost tended to restrict its use on a large scale to wealthy merchant castes although smaller pieces of tie-dyed silk and *mashru* were used by other castes for bridal and festival blouses.

The Khatris' repertoire has been shaped by the specific needs of their local clients and regional specialities have developed that endure, especially in rural areas of the state. The *bandhani* of Jamnagar, a former princely state in Saurashtra, developed under the patronage of the ruling Jams who sponsored diverse crafts, including weaving, printing and furniture making. Many Khatri dyers have migrated to Jamnagar from Kachchh over the past fifty years and the Census of India confirms that this pattern of migration goes back at least four hundred years.[17]

The Khatris of Jamnagar are famous for the production of fine tie-dyed saris especially wedding saris known as *panetar* and *gharcholu* (lit. 'house dress') worn by brides from the Jain and Hindu merchant castes of Gujarat.[18] These two garments mark a woman's transformation into a bride and future mother and symbolise her transfer from her natal home to that of her in-laws, attendant upon which is the transfer of responsibility for her welfare from her father to her husband. Thus a white silk *panetar* is the last gift a bride receives from her parents. During the wedding ceremony she is given a red cotton *gharcholu* by her mother-in-law that she will wear thereafter. A *gharcholu is* replete with motifs of flowers, vines, lotuses and other auspicious emblems which symbolise fertility; implicit in its designs is the duty incumbent on a wife to bear children. Although cheaper block-printed copies and synthetic versions of both *gharchola* and *panetar* are popular, the significance of these garments persists as symbols of marital union, family alliances and expressions of social hierarchies.[19] Jamnagar is also the site of large scale production of tie-dyed cotton *dupatta* and "suits", co-ordinating three-piece sets for *dupatta*, *salwar* and *kamiz* that are worn by women throughout India. Much of the tying is outsourced to women in Kachchh where local agents, who are often members of the same extended family, organise distribution, collection, quality control and payment.[20]

FIG 4.8 | FACING PAGE

Detail of sari, *gajji* silk, tie-dyed, L 414 x W 104 cm, Saurashtra, late 19th or early 20th century

The complex design of this sari shows figures, birds and animals among trees, possibly mango trees (*ambo*). The field is framed by borders of birds, animals and flowers and a flowing creeper design (*pan vel*).

V&A: IS 200-1960

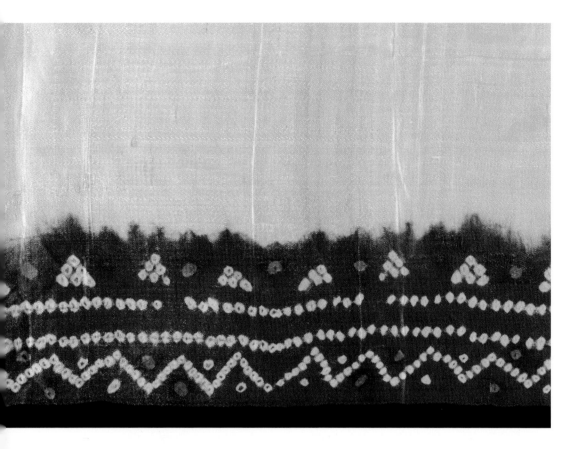

Kachchh: *Chandrokhani* and Other Textiles

Kachchh has a reputation for the finest tie-dyed textiles. Of particular note are tie-dyed saris made of *gajji* which were worn by 'the higher Hindu castes of Gujarat and Rajasthan' and remain perennial favourites with urban castes throughout India.[21] For their own community the Khatris make exquisite *rumal*, or head scarves and veilcloths known as *chandrokhani* (lit. 'moonlit textile') that are worn by brides. Older examples of *chandrokhani* are made of two lengths of tie-dyed silk that feature the mirrored halves of the circular 'moon' design. The centre seam of the textile is sumptuously decorated with gold or silver *jari* braid which is known locally as 'lace'; symbolically this is auspicious, deflecting malign influences and creating a large enough textile for deep veiling. The use of costly silk, gold and complex *bandhani* displays the wealth of the bride's family and represents an investment in the future of the bride and groom. This 'conspicuous consumption' also used to be evident among Muslim clients for whom Khatris made lengths of silk *bandhani* for the wedding dress; for the *maldharis* (herders) of Banni in north Kachchh they made black, dark green, or navy blue silk *bandhani* for the *aba*, or tunic

FIG 4.9 | LEFT

Part of a sari, *gajji* silk, tie-dyed, W 65 cm, Ahmedabad, c. 1867

This appears to be a fragment of a white silk sari known as *panetar*, traditionally part of the dowry for brides from the Jain and Hindu merchant communities of Gujarat.

V&A: 4939 IS

FIG 4.10 | ABOVE

Dyer removing tied cotton cloth from a dye vat, Jamnagar, Saurashtra

This workshop is one of many in Jamnagar that produces tie-dyed textiles for everyday wear for the domestic market. Lengths of tie-dyed cotton and synthetics for "suits" (*salwar kamiz* and *dupatta*), saris and *dupattas* are hand-made in large numbers.

FIG 4.11 | ABOVE

Khatri woman wearing a tie-dyed silk veilcloth decorated with gold braid

This type of bridal veilcloth (*chandrokhani*) is made and worn by Muslim Khatris. In the traditional red and black of Khatri wedding dress, it is decorated with a large central medallion and the non-figurative designs preferred by Muslims.

Photograph courtesy of Abduljabbar Khatri

FIG 4.12 | ABOVE RIGHT

Rumal, silk, tie-dyed, L 64 x W 69 cm, Kachchh, early 20th century

This head scarf or coverlet was made for use by women of their own caste by Muslim Khatris. It is in the red and black associated with Khatri bridal dress.

V&A: IS 157-1984

worn as wedding dress by women of clans such as Jat, Mutwa, Sameja, Node, Hingorja, Haliputra and Raisiputra. These garments, now no longer in vogue, were embellished with minute mirrorwork embroidery for which the women of Banni were renowned.

The Muslim Khatris also made key items of dress, such as turbans, skirt lengths, blouse pieces and veilcloths for the Hindu population of Kachchh, including Patel and Banushali farmers, and Ahir and Rabari herders. *Bandhani* has been integral to the sartorial identity of many of these groups and persists particularly among Rabaris whose modesty code dictates the use of a tie-dyed woollen veilcloth by a woman after marriage. A Rabari woman's dowry used to include a series of five different tie-dyed veilcloths that featured particular patterns, colour combinations and embroidery that were considered to be auspicious. Although the rules governing marriage have been revised, reducing the number of veilcloths to not more than three, tie-dyed veilcloths are still required wear and mark the property transfers of marriage.[22]

Bandhani is widely perceived as auspicious in Gujarat and continues to be a feature of wedding dress for women of many different communities. In the recent past, silk and *mashru bandhani* were particularly prized for dowry items, especially blouses. Although the use of *bandhani* is gendered to a degree—it is associated with women and it is far more apparent in women's dress—it has been worn traditionally by men of the Kachchhi Rabari subgroup who wear a cotton *rumal* or turban in dark brown, maroon or black decorated with red *bandhani*. For many years, however, Kachchhi Rabari men have worn a block-printed copy and the original is no longer produced.

Since polyester became widely available, synthetic *bandhani* mass-produced by industrial giants such as Reliance Industries has been the fabric of choice for many throughout the state. The vivid colours are popular, the fabric is cheap and easy to maintain, and the variety of designs for saris, veilcloths, blouses and skirt lengths caters to every taste. This development and changing fashions have eroded the local market for handmade *bandhani* and many Khatri *bandhani* producers have taken up other trades. But a few persist with fine *bandhani* and have found a niche in the Indian fashion world making sophisticated tie-dyed scarves, stoles and fabrics for urban fashionistas. There is also a developing export market; *bandhani* is popular with the South Asian diaspora, and increasingly with foreign clients for fashion and furnishings.

FACING PAGE

FIG 4.13 | ABOVE

Muslim woman's dress (*aba*), silk, tie-dyed, embroidered and decorated with mirrors, L 124 x W (across hem) 96 cm, Kachchh, early 20th century

Style worn by the cattle herders of Banni, Kachchh. The front panel was embroidered on a separate piece of *bandhani* and attached to the dress, which suggests it may have been reused *See appendix ill. 4 for garment analysis.*

V&A: Circ. 817–1912

FIG 4.14 | BELOW

Woollen veilcloth (*sat batili*), in two pieces, drying after dyeing and washing

Rabari veilcloths like this are typically woven in two pieces which the women join together with a decorated seam. Veilcloths are part of a Rabari woman's dowry and use auspicious colours and patterns (see also figs 4.6 and 4.7).

FIG 4.15 | RIGHT

Detail of blouse (*kanchali*), silk, tie-dyed, embroidered and decorated with mirrors, east Kachchh, mid-20th century

Tie-dyed silk in red or green was the fabric of choice for blouses worn by Dhebaria Rabari women for weddings and festivals. Heavily embroidered, they were an important component in a woman's dowry.

Private collection

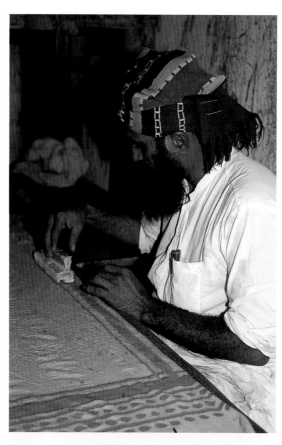

FIG 4.16 | ABOVE LEFT

Kachchhi Rabari shepherd, west Kachchh

This man's cotton turban cloth (*rumal*) has been block-printed to look like a tie-dyed design. The precedent for printing imitation tie-dye is to be found in the medieval cotton fragments found at Fustat, Egypt. (see fig. 1.10).

FIG 4.17 | ABOVE RIGHT

Khatri printing a Rabari *rumal*, Dhamadka, east Kachchh

A *rumal* requires several stages of printing and dyeing; here the printer is printing a resist of lime and gum.

FIG 4.18 | BELOW LEFT

Meghwal women, Khavda, north Kachchh

These women are in their best dresses for a profit-sharing event organised by the NGO they belong to. Their polyester veilcloths are industrially printed with tie-dyed designs.

FIG 4.19 | BELOW RIGHT

Lakme Fashion Week, Mumbai, 2006

The model is wearing a dress designed by Rahul and Firdous. It is fashioned from silk specially designed and tie-dyed by Abduljabbar Khatri of Bhuj, Kachchh.

FIG 4.20

Sari, cotton, with silk warp in the borders and silk wefts in the end stripes, warp ikat, supplementary warp patterning, L 410 x W 122 cm, Gujarat, probably Ahmedabad, c. 1872–1873

This type of sari was made for everyday use.

V&A: 0831 IS

Ikat

Although related to *bandhani*, ikat is distinct because the tied resist is applied to yarn rather than woven fabric. The warp or weft threads are bound with impermeable yarn that resists dye prior to dyeing and then weaving the fabric; in the case of double ikat, both warp and weft are tied. Even the most simple ikat fabrics require meticulous preparation at the tying and dyeing stage followed by careful warping up and weaving in order that the desired pattern appears in the finished cloth. In this category are coarse cotton saris, waist cloths, head covers and carrying cloths featuring weft ikat that were woven by the Khatri weavers in Mandvi for Chodhri tribal women.[23] Slightly more upmarket were cotton saris, *dhotis* and turban cloths that used to be made in Ahmedabad and Surat for everyday use and featured narrow warp ikat borders worked in silk. Stylistically these are closely related to the ikat saris of Madhya Pradesh. No longer produced, some striped *mashru* satins were woven with narrow stripes of ikat chevrons, a style that was probably derived from Turkish *mashru* introduced to Gujarat during the sixteenth century.[24]

FIG 4.21 | LEFT

Salvi woman binding *patolu* warp, Patan, north Gujarat

Salvi weavers, who are Jains, spend weeks tying and dyeing the warp and weft threads of a *patolu*, part of the painstaking preparation required for weaving these extraordinary double ikat textiles.

Patola

Supreme among Indian ikats is the *patolu*, a double ikat silk textile traditionally dyed with natural dyes. Made by Jain weavers of the Salvi caste, production is now confined to a single extended family in Patan. The painstaking process of drafting, tying, dyeing and weaving restricts production to a handful of pieces each year and the waiting time for orders runs to several years.[25] *Patola* were part of the textiles trade with Southeast Asia for over five hundred years. Although some designs were used both in India and Indonesia, others were developed specifically for the export market; export *patola* were of a looser weave than those used domestically and were further differentiated by longitudinal borders of cotton. Such was their prestige in Indonesia that they were worn as court dress and preserved as ceremonial cloths known as *maa'* believed to possess magical power.[26] In India *patola* were used as ceremonial saris chiefly by Nagar Brahmins, Hindu or Jain Mahajan (merchants) and Bohra Muslims, notably in Gujarat and Maharashtra; particular designs were favoured by each community. Traditionally associated with weddings—*patola* were often worn by the

FIG 4.22

Salvis weaving a *patolu*, Patan

The warp beam on the looms used for *patola* is asymmetrical. The weavers often work in pairs, carefully realigning warp and weft threads with each pass of the shuttle in order to keep the ikat design sharp.

FIG 4.23

Ceremonial cloth, silk, double ikat, cotton warps in outer borders, L 480 x W 100 cm, Gujarat probably Patan, c. mid-19th century, possibly earlier

Patola of this type were made for export to Indonesia where their function was ceremonial; known as *maa'* they were preserved as sacred objects.

V&A: IS 74-1993

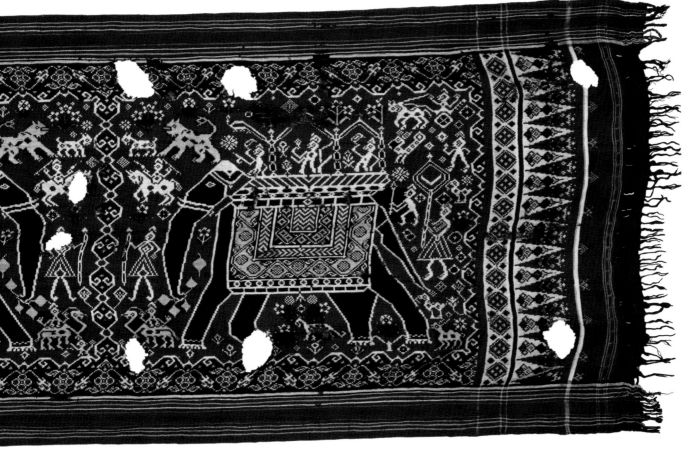

mother of the groom and given as wedding presents—they were rarely worn as bridal saris. A song passed down through generations of Nagars in Ahmedabad in which a girl beseeches her fiancé to buy her a *patolu*, conveys the desirability of these auspicious textiles:

'Chelaji bring me a costly *patolu* from Patan
Drawn with beautiful peacocks of bright hue
A *kesuda* [golden yellow] border and a *pallav* brimming with life...'[27]

Belief in the protective potency of *patola* meant that they were also worn by expectant mothers for the *simant* ritual that takes place in the seventh month of pregnancy.

Nowadays the use of *patola* in such customs has declined and they are chiefly bought by wealthy Patel diamond merchants in Surat and Kachchhi Bhatias (merchants) settled in Mumbai.[28] Cheaper imitations have evolved, notably the so-called 'patola' of Rajkot in Saurashtra which are not true double ikat but single (weft) ikat silk saris. An ikat workshop established in Rajkot in the 1950s as part of a government training scheme has spawned a host of popular designs drawn from the original *patola* which are now done in single ikat, making them much more affordable for a mass audience. Like many other prestigious handmade textiles in India there are now industrially-printed synthetic versions of *patola*; although lacking the cachet of the original textile they are an example of the constant re-invention that has marked the textile culture of Gujarat.

Block-printing

As with tie-dyeing, it is tantalising to review the finds from ancient India and surmise that block-printing was practised in the Indus Valley region over four thousand years ago. However the evidence is inconclusive; it shows that the people of the time were decorating cloth but it is unclear what methods they used. Nonetheless, the similarity between the trefoil design on the mantle of the male figurine found at Mohenjodaro (fig. 1.2) and the cloud pattern (*kakkar*) that features in the repertoire of contemporary *ajrakh* printers of Kachchh and Sindh has been noted, suggesting some degree of continuity from India's ancient past.[29] The oldest surviving block-prints from Gujarat are the fragments of medieval trade cottons retrieved from sites in Egypt. These and similar textiles of comparable age discovered in Southeast Asia in Toraja, Central Sulawesi, share

FIG 4.24

Trousers made from *patolu* fabric tailored in Central Java, Indonesia, silk, double ikat, L 106 x W (across waist) 54 cm, probably Patan, c. 1900

These were worn at court in Yogyakarta, Java. The *patolu* design, *Vohra gajji bhat*, was worn by Ismaili Vohras in Gujarat and is non-figurative, composed of heart-shaped leaves and geometric motifs.

V&A: IS 74-1993

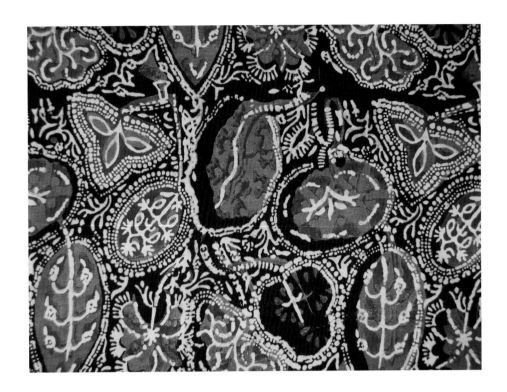

FIG 4.25

Detail of silk fabric, resist- and mordant-dyed, block-printed, Ajrakhpur, Kachchh

This contemporary textile made by Ismail Mohammad Khatri is based on a ceremonial banner found in Toraja, central Sulawesi. The original is held at the V&A and has been radiocarbon-dated to 1340 ± 40 years (see fig. 1.12).

Private collection

common techniques and designs and are technically related to the contemporary block-prints of Gujarat, especially those of Kachchh. Growing awareness of these historical links among some of the printers has led them to exploit their design heritage and produce 'antique' fabrics for fashion and furnishings based on Gujarati textiles retrieved from sites in Egypt and tombs in Southeast Asia.

Block-printing is practised throughout the state with significant centres at Ahmedabad which produces floral spray patterns and imitation *bandhani* (these are also screen printed); Kachchh district where Dhamadka, Ajrakhpur and Khavda villages are famous for complex geometric prints known as *ajrakh* that are printed on both sides of the cloth; and to a lesser extent at Deesa in northern Gujarat, which is known for a variety of striped designs. Like tie-dyeing, the craft is dominated by Khatris, but in Ahmedabad there are significant enclaves of Chhipa printers who are heavily involved in all aspects of textile production, and also a sub-group of Vagharis who produce votive cloths used in *Mata* (Mother Goddess) worship. Ahmedabad, which became known as 'the Manchester of the East' in the nineteenth century because of its modern cotton mill industry and commercial pre-eminence, is also an historic block-printing centre. This is attested to by Georges Roques, an agent of the French Compagnie des Indes, who provided the earliest description of cotton printing in India, written

FIG 4.26 | ABOVE

Sari, resist- and mordant-dyed, block-printed, cotton, L 343 x W 45 cm Ahmedabad, c. 1880

This type of sari printed with a centrefield design of red spots enclosing stars and end borders of a large floral motif, was worn by Bhils.

V&A: IS 114-1883

FIG 4.27

Detail of length of fabric, resist- and mordant-dyed, block-printed, cotton, Deesa, north Gujarat, 2002

Narrow stripes alternating with a creeper design (*pan vel*) and small buds (*butis*) are typical of the block-prints associated with this area although the patterns are now produced throughout western India.

Private collection

between 1678 and 1680. His detailed account makes particular mention of the properties of the River Sabarmati and its part in successful dyeing: 'The water has this faculty of contributing much to it, and it was known from experience that the river at Ahmedabad had that virtue above other waters'.[30] The Sabarmati has continued to play a central role in textile production in Ahmedabad until the present decade; in addition to the cotton mills, many of the small screen-printing and block-printing workshops run by Chhipas—there is a notable cluster in Jamalpur—have used the river for washing cloths and its banks for drying, bleaching (in the sun) and finishing. These activities are now being phased out as the area is being re-developed by the Ahmedabad Municipal Corporation as part of the Sabarmati River Front Project.[31]

FIG 4.28–4.31

Chhipa printers, Sabarmati River, Ahmedabad, 1995

Generations of printers and dyers have used the Sabarmati for washing textiles and its banks have provided an area for sun-bleaching and drying cloth. These activities are now being phased out as the area is being redeveloped by the municipal corporation.

Chhipas of Ahmedabad and *Saudagiri*

Older Chhipas recall the final years of the trade with Southeast Asia. Many families in Ahmedabad had been involved in the production of block-printed cottons known as *saudagiri* (from the Persian *sauda* or 'trade goods') that were exported to Thailand between the mid-nineteenth and mid-twentieth century.[32] The trade ended with the Second World War, concluding five hundred years of commerce between India and Thailand.[33] *Saudagiri* were intended for the mass market to be worn as *pha nung chong krabeng* (a unisex kind of sarong) or used as a women's shawl known as *pha sabai*. Scant attention was paid to production standards; *saudagiri* were typically made of coarse cotton much of which was imported from England in the nineteenth century, printed with a mud resist (*dabu*) which is now chiefly used in Bagru, Rajasthan, and featured small repeated geometric and floral motifs with an end border panel known as *tumpal*.

FIG 4.32

Competitors in the Miss Thailand 1938 pageant

The three finalists are dressed in sarongs made of *saudagiri* fabric. The trade in these textiles ceased with the advent of the Second World War.

Photograph courtesy of Yasin Savaijiwala/ Maskati and Co.

บ้าพเจ้า(พิศมัยโชติวุฒิ)นุ่งผ้าลาย   เข้าประกวดและได้รับตำแหน่งนางสาวไทยพ.ศ.๒๔๘๑

ตลอดจนสตรีไทยทุกชั้นนิยมใช้กันแพร่หลายมาหลายสิบปีแล้วเพราะใช้ผ้าเนื้อดี ดอกเด่น สีสด จากนายช่างผู้ปราณีตอย่างดีเลิศ

FIG 4.33 | ABOVE

Woman applying mud to cotton textiles, Bagru, Rajasthan

Mud has been used as a resist throughout western India where the practice is known as *dabu* printing.

FIG 4.34 | RIGHT

Samples of *saudagiri*, cotton, for the Thai market, acquired between 1855 and 1879

Saudagiri textiles were made chiefly in Ahmedabad and Pethapur for export to Thailand. Often crudely printed and dyed, they were utilitarian textiles for the mass market.

V&A: IS 1707

Exported from Gujarat's chief port, Surat, their origin was indicated by their Thai names of *pha surat*, and *pha gujarat*.[34] The blocks or stamps with which they were printed were engraved by the Gajjar carpenters' community and surviving pattern books at Pethapur near Gandhinagar are annotated with the names of popular designs and the merchants involved in the trade, most of whom were Bohra Muslims.[35] Although *saudagiri* disappeared in the 1940s, a revival is currently underway in Ahmedabad launched by a Chhipa family formerly involved in the trade. The new work is printed on high quality cotton, using natural dyes and the products are aimed at the international fashion and soft furnishings market.[36] Chhipas based in Ahmedabad also supplied the highly segmented domestic market. Until thirty or forty years ago they printed

designs to suit the specific requirements of each client's caste, typically producing turban cloths, saris, half-saris (*sadla*), veilcloths and skirt lengths (*ghaghra*). There was also a minor trade in printing outlines for embroidery designs for skirt and sari borders, a service that is still available on the steps of Rani-no-Hajiro in Ahmedabad.

Vagharis of Ahmedabad: *Mata-ni-pachedi* and *Mata-no-chandarvo*

Distinct in style and usage from other dyed and printed textiles in Ahmedabad are votive cloths known as *Mata-ni-pachedi*, 'the cloth of the Mother Goddess' and *Mata-no-chandarvo*, 'the canopy of the Mother Goddess'. Formerly produced at several places in Gujarat (as well as Agar, Madhya Pradesh) they are now made only in Kheda district and Ahmedabad by Vagharis using a combination of drawn, painted, printed and dyed elements.[37] The cloths feature representations of the *Mata*, or Mother Goddess, who is worshipped by many marginalised communities throughout western India, including the Vagharis themselves. Their imagery draws on folk narratives derived from the Puranas and they are used to enclose outdoor shrines during rituals involving animal sacrifice which are led by a *bhuvo*, or shaman, to request relief from illness or misfortune for devotees.[38] In Gujarat, seven forms of the *Mata* are worshipped, each of which has a different *vahana* or vehicle. Devotees worship a particular form depending on their caste and clan affiliations and artisans are commissioned accordingly. The artisan uses a *babul* twig (*Acacia arabica*) as a *kalam* or pen to paint the cloth with a mordant, for which reason these cloths are also known as *kalamkari*, although the term is more commonly associated with the temple cloths of Srikalahasti and Masulipatnam in Andhra Pradesh. *Pachedi* and *chandarvo* are predominantly blood red and were formerly dyed with madder; synthetic alizarin is now more common.[39] The black outlines are drawn with an iron sulphate paste, and the white areas are bleached by drying in the sun. The centre panel of *pachedi* and *chandarvo*—dominated by the goddess—is customarily drawn and painted by hand using mordants; the surrounding panels featuring sequences of more minor figures, animals and birds are mordant-printed with stamps.

FIG 4.37 | ABOVE

Printing workshop at the Calico Dyeing and Printing Works, Ahmedabad

This company, owned by a Chhipa family that used to be involved in the *saudagiri* trade, has revived production of a number of *saudagiri* patterns.

FACING PAGE

FIG 4.38 | BELOW

Printer, Rani-no-Hajiro, Ahmedabad

This printing service is run on the steps of an imperial mausoleum. Women bring skirt lengths and sari borders to the printer who stamps them with outlines for embroidery. Each block has a single motif and the range includes parrots, peacocks, flowers, dancing girls and elephants.

FIG 4.39

Ceremonial cloth, resist- and
mordant-dyed, block-printed and
painted, cotton, W 272 x H 137 cm,
Ahmedabad, c. mid-20th century

Mata-ni-pachedi ('cloth of the mother
goddess') is used in worship by several
marginalised communities in western
India. Produced by Vagharis, chiefly in
Vasna and near the General Post Office
in Ahmedabad.

Given by Margaret Hall.
V&A: IS 6-1967

Once all stages of drawing and printing have been completed, the cloths are washed in flowing water, then laid flat to bleach in the sun. Dyeing follows which is carried out by Muslim Chhipas.[40] Although *pachedi* and *chandarvo* are still used for *Mata* worship, attempts to expand commercial opportunities for the Vagharis have seen the development of small panels for use as cushion covers and wall hangings; these are also applied to T-shirts and used for decorating shirts and tunics.

Khatris of Kachchh: *Ajrakh* and Batik

Four hundred kilometres to the west of Ahmedabad lies the desert district of Kachchh—one of India's leading areas for block-printing and dyeing. It is renowned for the variety of its block-prints and several villages have established reputations for a particular style or technique. Changing patterns of consumption in Kachchh over the past fifty years have put many Khatri printers out of business. Those Khatris who continue with the craft have been compelled to make the transition from supplying the local market to producing year-round for internal and overseas export. Prior to that production and sales were seasonal; the former

FIG 4.40 | LEFT

Vaghari drawing the outline of a *mata-ni-pachedi*, Vasna, Ahmedabad

The black outlines are drawn in iron sulphate paste using a *kalam* (pen) fashioned from a *babul* twig. Important parts of the cloth like the central figure of the mother goddess are hand-drawn but border designs and minor characters are block-printed.

FIG 4.41 | RIGHT

Vaghari family painting a mordant onto a *mata-ni-pachedi*, Vasna, Ahmedabad

The cloths are predominantly red and a mordant is required to permanently fix the colour to the cloth.

was governed by the climate, the latter by the cycle of religious festivals. Much of the work was done in the open air so there would be a lull in production during the monsoon rains when printers repaired their equipment in readiness for the next two seasons. Peak sales coincided with the Muslim festival of Eid, the Hindu festivals of Mahashivaratri ('the night of Shiva') and Janmashtami (Krishna's birthday) and the marriage season from November to January—all of which required new clothes. Some sales were made directly from the Khatris' workshops as their customers often lived nearby; cloth was also available from merchants in the local bazaar. Pockets of local trade remain but are diminishing; Khatri merchants in Bhachau still sell block-printed *sadla* (half-saris) to Patel (farmers caste) women of north-east Kachchh.

For many Khatris seasonal sales were made by hawking goods from village to village, an experience that is within living memory for the Khatris of Dhamadka and Nakhatrana.[41] Few families could afford to hold stock (this is still the case) so knowledge of the social and religious life of their customers and their dress codes was crucial in order to have the appropriate goods ready for marriages and festivals. Dhamadka's strategic position on a migration route used by nomadic Rabaris meant that the Khatris were able to capitalise on sales of veilcloths, skirt lengths and turbans when the *dhangs* (migratory groups) returned to Kachchh to celebrate Janmashtami. They also made a variety of textiles for the cattle herders (*maldharis*) of Banni in north Kachchh. These included: *sirakh* which were quilt covers for newly-weds; *malir* which is still worn as a shoulder cloth by Jat and Meghwal men; a variety of patterned skirt lengths such as *haidharo, jimardhi* and *limai;* and *ajrakh*, a prestigious textile worn by cattle herders in Banni. Among these rustic block-prints it is *ajrakh* that has been transformed from an item of local dress to a textile of international acclaim.

Ajrakh

The name *ajrakh* is probably derived from *azrak*, the Arabic for blue—the textile is predominantly blue with accents of red and white and was originally dyed with indigo and madder.[42] It is stylistically and technically linked to the medieval cotton fragments found at Fustat and other sites in Egypt although modern *ajrakh* displays greater refinement and is typically printed on both sides of the cloth, with the alignment of the designs demonstrating the mastery of the printer. There are between fourteen and sixteen different stages of resist-printing and mordant-dyeing—the resist areas are printed with a paste of lime and gum arabic but oral history suggests that wax may also have been used in

FIG 4.42 | FOLLOWING PAGE

Resist- and mordant-dyed, block-printed cotton, printed on both sides of the cloth, dyed with indigo and madder, L 252 x W 189.5 cm, Ajrakhpur, Kachchh

Known as *ajrakh*, this double-sided textile is made by Khatri block-printers in only a few places and probably takes its name from Arabic for blue (*azrak*).

V&A: IS 5-2007

FIG 4.43 | ABOVE

Abduljabbar Khatri printing
the outline of an *ajrakh* border,
Dhamadka, Kachchh

A resist of lime and gum is printed to
reserve white areas. The cloth has been
prepared by calendering and soaking
in a pre-mordant. This is the first of 14
stages of printing and dyeing required
to produce *ajrakh*.

FIG 4.44 | ABOVE RIGHT

Khatri printing *ajrakh* border design,
Dhamadka, Kachchh

A thick paste of gum, clay, millet flour
and alum (a mordant) is printed on the
border areas that will be red when the
textile has been dyed in madder
or alizarin.

the past. The process takes up to three weeks to complete and uses twenty or
more engraved printing blocks.[43] *Ajrakh* conforms to Islamic principles of non-
figurative design and features complex geometric patterns that are influenced by
architecture and regional floral styles, as well as designs based on coins such as
kori (Kachchhi currency before 1947), *mohur* (a Mughal coin) and *riyal* (currency
in Saudi Arabia) which reflects Gujarat's earlier trade with the Middle East.

Previously made in several parts of western India, *ajrakh* is now produced only
in Barmer, Rajasthan, and three villages in Kachchh: Dhamadka, Ajrakhpur
and Khavda. It also survives in the neighbouring province of Sindh which was
ceded to Pakistan in 1947. *Ajrakh* was worn exclusively by Muslims; in Sindh
it has become emblematic of Sindhi identity while in Kachchh it is associated
particularly with the Muslim cattle herders of Banni in the north of the district
although it has been adopted by neighbouring communities of Meghwals,
who are Dalits, in all likelihood to escape the stigma of untouchability.[44] In
Kachchh, it is male attire worn as a turban, *dhoti, lungi* and multi-purpose
shoulder cloth but in Sindh women wear it as a *chaddar* (veilcloth) and *dupatta*,
and it is also used as a bed sheet.[45] Attributed with protective properties

FIG 4.45 | ABOVE LEFT

Khatri dyeing block-printed cotton in indigo, Dhamadka, Kachchh

The fabric is dipped in the indigo vat and then laid to dry in the sun. To achieve a deep shade of blue, cloth has to be dipped repeatedly for the colour to build up.

FIG 4.46 | ABOVE CENTRE

Washing and calendering block-printed cloth, Dhamadka, Kachchh

After each stage of printing and dyeing, *ajrakh* and other block-prints are washed to remove any excess dye and beaten to smooth the cotton fibres.

FIG 4.47 | ABOVE RIGHT

Block-printed bedspreads laid to dry in the sun, Dhamadka, Kachchh

Sunlight plays a vital role in the production process; heat helps the colours to develop and light bleaches white areas of the printed designs.

FACING PAGE

FIG 4.48 | BELOW

Detail of *ajrakh* centrefield design known as *kori*

The pattern is based on a coin from Kachchh. The district had its own mint and the *kori* was the main unit of currency until 1947 when Kachchh became part of the Indian union.

Private collection

FIG 4.49 | RIGHT

Detail of *ajrakh* centrefield design known as *riyal*

The pattern is based on a coin from Saudi Arabia and reflects the influence of centuries of trade between Gujarat and the Arab world.

Private collection

against the harsh environment of Banni, it is believed to be auspicious and is given as a gift to bridegrooms who wear it on their wedding day. Nowadays, the local use of handmade *ajrakh* dyed with natural colours has all but disappeared as the herders favour polyester *ajrakh* which costs a fraction of the price. A few Khatris—notably those of Dhamadka and Ajrakhpur—continue to print *ajrakh* using natural dyes. But this is *ajrakh* adapted for urban tastes in furnishings and fashion; now printed on wool and silk as well as cotton, it features new colourways and new products such as bedsheets, duvet covers, cushions, *dupatta*, saris, dress material and silk scarves. Few of these goods find their way on to the local market; they sell in India's metropolitan centres and overseas.[46]

Batik

Like *ajrakh*, batik is made by Muslim Khatris in Kachchh and features the use of a resist medium, wax, which is printed rather than drawn as in other parts of India and Southeast Asia.[47] A number of older Khatris recall the use of a form of wax known as *kanka* in the Kachchhi dialect, notably in Chobari village in north-east Kachchh which was an important centre for all aspects of printing and dyeing until the mid-twentieth century. A distinction is made between *kanka* which was a forest product derived from the seeds of the *pilu* (jojoba) tree and *min*, the Kachchhi term for beeswax or paraffin wax. Paraffin wax is used in contemporary batik production.[48] The wax is printed using engraved wooden blocks for the larger designs; the stamps for finer areas are made of strips of copper plate that have been twisted to the shape of the pattern and set in a wooden base. The fabric, chiefly cotton, is dyed in synthetic dyes which are purchased in Anjar and Ahmedabad. Manufacture of modern batik is centred on the port towns of Mandvi and Mundra and the nearby village of Bhujpur which produce saris and "suits" (co-ordinating *salwar, kamiz* and *dupatta*), bed covers and yardage; the designs are often supplied by clients or their agents. Much of the batik produced is dispatched to Ahmedabad and Mumbai and local sales are made chiefly through merchants based in the district capital, Bhuj.

FIG 4.50 | ABOVE

Meghwal cattle herder in *ajrakh lungi* and shoulder cloth, Banni, north Kachchh

Ajrakh, which is worn by Banni Muslims as caste dress, has also been adopted by some Hindu Meghwals. This man uses *ajrakh* in part to escape the stigma of his caste and like his hero, the Dalit leader Dr Ambedkar, is a Buddhist.

FIG 4.51 | BELOW

Wax printing on cotton, Mundra, south Kachchh

The Khatri printer works at a low print table, the surface of which is packed with sand. Batik designs are printed with carved wooden blocks and small stamps made of strips of copper plate, using commercial paraffin wax as the resist medium.

FIG 4.52 | RIGHT

Jain cosmological *mandala*: plan of Jambudvipa, W 55 x H 54.5 cm, pigment painting on cloth, Gujarat, 19th century

Textiles have been a feature of the religious culture of western India and were widely produced in Gujarat. This is an example of a *pata*, a sacred hanging used in Jain temples.

V&A: Circ. 91-1970

Painted Textiles: Pigment Painting on Cloth

Although a number of types of Indian textiles have been described as 'painted'—chintz for example which was painted with dyes and mordants—this section confines itself to textiles painted with pigments.[49] Pigment painted textiles tend to be confined to ceremonial use because the medium is not robust enough to withstand regular wear but fabrics decorated with *roghan* painting which was used to embellish dress and textiles until the mid-twentieth century is a notable exception.

Ceremonial Cloths: *Patas*, *Gyana baji*, *Panchanga* and *Pichhwais*

Textiles have been a feature of the religious culture of western India and votive cloths made of cotton and painted with pigments were widely produced in Gujarat and Rajasthan. Their use in Jain and Hindu worship produced a number of distinct forms. *Patas* are sacred hangings used in

FIG 4.53

Pichhwai, cotton, painted, L 199 x W 227 cm, Gujarat, late 19th or early 20th century; *Gopashtami Utsava*

*Pichhwai*s are temple hangings of the Vallabhacharya sect who worship Krishna. This example celebrates the festival of *Gopashtami* which marks Krishna's promotion from herder of calves to full cowherd.

Calico Museum of Textiles (Acc. No. 1646)

Jain temples that feature diagrams alluding to tantric texts, drawings of pilgrimage sites such as Shatrunjaya in Saurashtra, and cosmic diagrams. Related to *patas* are *gyana baji,* game boards painted on cloth which were a forerunner of the modern game of snakes and ladders; although not used in worship, they reflect Jain beliefs about good and evil.[50] Executed in the same medium but for quite a different purpose, *panchangas* (lit. 'five limbs') are calendars used by Hindu astrologers to determine auspicious timings for events and the dates of festivals; they are usually in the form of a long, cotton scroll, the main body of which is painted with numerical diagrams and a list of instructions for each day, bordered by folk imagery. But perhaps the best known examples of pigment paintings on cloth are *pichhwais,* the temple hangings of the Vallabhacharya sect, depicting Krishna as Shrinathji; their production is particularly associated with Nathadwara in Rajasthan, the site of the Shrinathji shrine since the mid-seventeenth century.[51] The cult of Shrinathji spread throughout western India, making Nathadwara a major pilgrimage site, especially for Gujaratis. Reflecting that popularity, *pichhwais* were produced in nearby Gujarat: mostly embroidered, block-printed and brocade versions, although a number of painted *pichhwais* held at the Calico Museum, Ahmedabad, have also been attributed to Gujarat.

Roghan

Distinct in use and style from the religious traditions of cloth painting, *roghan* textiles are made by drawing a design on to cloth with an iron pen known as a *kalam* using a medium made from boiled castor oil to which pigments have been added. This paste is known as *roghan* which means

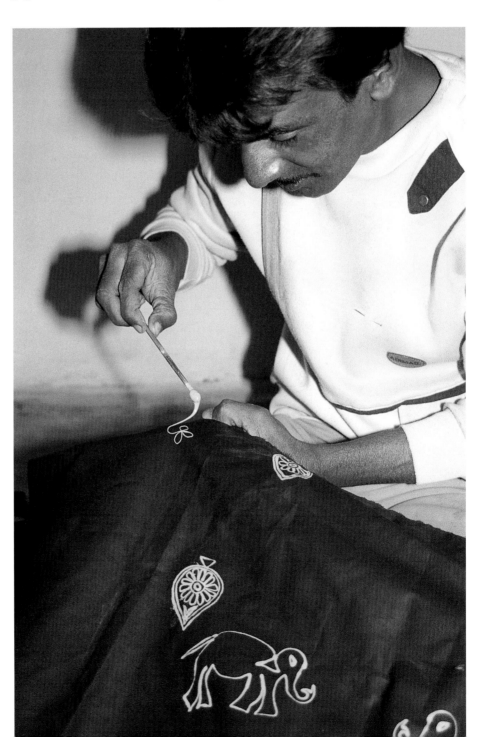

FIG 4.54

Abdul Gafur Khatri, Nirona, Kachchh, drawing a design on cotton with *roghan* paste

Roghan was previously used as an inexpensive substitute for embroidery on clothes and domestic textiles.

'resin' in Gujarati. When the design has been completed, it is pressed against another piece of fabric or the other half of the same piece to create a mirror image of the original design. In Kachchh, *roghan* was used as an inexpensive substitute for embroidery on skirts, veilcloths, *toran* (hanging over threshold) and a textile known as *dharaniyo* which was used to cover stacked quilts; the custom of using *roghan*, however, died out forty or fifty years ago. Now practised by a single family of Muslim Khatris in the village of Nirona in Kachchh district, *roghan* was formerly produced at Chobari in Kachchh, Ahmedabad, Vadodara and Patan. In Ahmedabad a type of *roghan* known as 'tinsel work' was used to decorate saris worn by wealthy women; in this context *roghan* was block-printed rather than painted and the designs were sprinkled with mica or crushed gold leaf. Tinsel work is still produced near Manek Chowk in Ahmedabad but the block-printers simply print commercial adhesive onto cloth and sprinkle it with glitter for saris worn only by the poor.[52] There have been interventions by agencies working in the craft sector to revive *roghan* but the painstaking process and limited market appeal have thus far prevented success.[53]

CONCLUSION

As demand for painted and dyed textiles has declined due to social changes wrought by independence, the availability of cheap synthetic alternatives and the influence of the media and fashion, many craftspeople have struggled to make a living. Now a majority of people in Gujarat wear synthetic fabrics and use them for domestic and votive textiles as well. In order to survive, craftspeople have been forced to look for new markets outside their local territory. In Kachchh many Khatris have sustained their businesses by adapting traditional block-prints and *bandhani* to suit the taste of the urban elite whose style alludes to Indian and western cultures. In this respect, Ahmedabad has been an important design and trade hub which in the 1970s saw the foundation of the Gujarat State Handicrafts Development Corporation (GSHDC) and its retail outlet, Gurjari. The task of the GSHDC was to bridge the gap between traditional craft and urban consumers, providing an interface between craftspeople and new clients.

FIG 4.55

Veilcloth, cotton, *roghan* decoration,
L 243 x W 121 cm

Made in Nirona, Kachchh for use as a
wedding veilcloth for a Rajput bride in
Thar Parkar, Sindh; pre-Partition.

Private collection

Notes

1 For a useful classification system of resist-dyeing techniques, illustrated with line drawings, see Bühler, A., Eberhard Fischer and Marie-Louise Nabholz, *Indian Tie-Dyed Fabrics*, Ahmedabad: Calico Museum of Textiles, pp. 1–5.

2 Marshall, J. H., *Mohenjo-Daro and the Indus Civilization*, Delhi: Indological Book House, pp. 32–33.

3 Barnes, R., *Indian Block-Printed Textiles in Egypt*, 2 vols, Oxford: Clarendon Press, vol. 1, pp. 70–71.

4 For Pliny, see Bostock, John and H.T. Riley, trans., *The Natural History of Pliny*. VI, London: Henry G. Bohn. *The Periplus* is discussed in Chapter 1 (note 5).

5 The East India Companies' (British, Dutch, etc) foreign trading stations were known as 'factories' and their agents as 'factors'.

6 Foster, W., *The English Factories in India, 1637–1641*, Oxford: Clarendon Press, p. 58.

7 Mandelslo cit. Commissariat, M. S., *A History of Gujarat with a Survey of its Monuments and Inscriptions. Volume 2. The Mughal Period from 1573 to 1758*, Bombay, Calcutta, Madras, New Delhi and Hyderabad: Orient Longmans, pp. 303–304.

8 The exploitation of indigo farmers in Bengal by the British eventually provoked the 'Blue Mutiny' which saw demonstrations and rioting among the peasant workers in Lower Bengal in 1859. See Balfour-Paul, J.,1998, *Indigo*, London: British Museum Press, pp. 70–76.

9 Crooke, W., ed., *Tavernier's Travels in India (1676)*, vol. 2, trans., Valentine Ball, Oxford: Oxford University Press, p. 5.

10 The Hindi term *bandhej* is also used in Gujarat, especially in urban centres such as Ahmedabad. The root of both the Gujarati and the Hindi terms is Sanskrit, from the verb *bandhna*, 'to tie'. Other terms are also used to refer to specific tie-dyed cloths or patterns such as *chundadi* and sat *bhatilo*.

11 Bühler et al, p. 108.

12 Murphy, V. and Rosemary Crill, *Tie-dyed Textiles of India*, London and Ahmedabad: V&A Publications in association with Mapin Publishing, p. 12.

13 Chandra, M., 'Costumes and Textiles in the Sultanate Period', in *Journal of Indian Textile History*, VI, pp. 5–61.

14 Hindu Khatris prefer to be known as Brahmakshatriya, indicating their status as Kshatriyas (warrior caste). In other parts of northern India, the Khatris are known as entrepreneurs, traders and merchants. See Trivedi, R.K., ed., *Census of India, vol VI. Selected Crafts of Gujarat. Bandhani*

or Tie and Dye Sari of Jamnagar, Delhi: Government of India, pp. 7–11; Edwards, E.M., 'Contemporary Production and Transmission of Resist-Dyed and Block-Printed Textiles in Kachchh District, Gujarat' in *Textile: The Journal of Cloth and Culture*, 3, 2, pp. 186–187. Oral history suggests that the Khatris either migrated via Champaner to Gujarat, or from the Punjab to Sindh (now in Pakistan) and settled in Kachchh during the medieval period with further migrations to Saurashtra. Although there were conversions in Sindh, many Khatris converted to Islam in Gujarat under the influence of Muslim missionaries from the Fatimid dynasty in Cairo (969–1171 CE); members of the Sufi orders from West Asia also spread the faith. See Varadarajan, L., *Ajrakh*, Ahmedabad: New Order Book Co., p. 13. A more prosaic account of the conversions gives their cause as the onerous costs of marriage and other ritual services provided by Brahmin priests (Personal communication, Ismail Mohammad Khatri, 5 January 2001).

15 *Purdah* literally means 'curtain' or 'veil' (Urdu/Persian *pardah*). The term refers to the custom of screening women from men and strangers prevalent in Muslim and Hindu societies.

16 The Japanese term *shibori* (meaning to 'wring, squeeze or press') is now in common use around the world to cover a range of resist-dyeing techniques in which cloth is tied, clamped, folded, or held back during dyeing, to prevent some areas from taking up dye colour. See the World Shibori Network: http://www.shibori.org.

17 Trivedi, p. 5.

18 Murphy and Crill, pp. 23–24.

19 Johnson, Donald C., 'Pragmatism and Enigmas: The "Panetar" and "Gharcholu" Saris in Gujarati Weddings', in Foster, H.B. and Donald C. Johnson, eds., *Wedding Dress Across Cultures*, Oxford and New York: Berg, pp. 85–92.

20 Personal communication, Umar M. Khatri, Jamnagar, December 2008.

21 Bühler et al, p. 105.

22 Edwards, E.M. 'The Role of Veilcloths Among the Rabaris of Kutch, Gujarat, Western India', in Costume, vol. 43, pp. 19–37.

23 Fischer, E. and Haku Shah, *Simple Weft Ikat from South Gujarat, India*, Ahmedabad: Calico Museum of Textiles, pp. 2–17.

24 Crill, R., *Indian Ikat Textiles*, London: V&A Publications, p. 139.

25 Personal communication, Bharat K. Salvi, December 2008.

26 Bühler, A. and Eberhard Fischer, The *Patola of Gujarat*, vol. 1, Basle: Museum of Ethnography and the Rock Foundation, New York, pp. 280–281.

27 Personal communication, Padmaja Dhruv and Manjari Divangi, December 2008.

28 Personal communication, Rohit Salvi and Bharat K. Salvi, December 2008.

29 Bilgrami, N., *Sindh jo Ajrak, Karachi*: Department of Culture and Tourism, Government of Sindh, p. 18.

30 Schwartz, P.R., *Printing on Cotton at Ahmedabad, India, in 1678*, Ahmedabad: Calico Museum of Textiles, p. 8.

31 http://www.sabarmatiriverfront.com

32 Personal communication, Yasin Savaijiwala, November 2006.

33 Guy, p. 151.

34 Archambault, Michèle, 'Blockprinted Fabrics of Gujarat for Export to Siam: An Encounter with Mr Maneklal T. Gajjar', no publication details.

35 Personal communication, Maneklal Gajjar, November 1994. See also Jain, Jyotindra, 'Saudagiri Prints. Textiles for Far Off Siam', *India Magazine*, October 1985, pp. 54–63.

36 Savaijiwala, Yasin, *Revival of Saudagiri*, Ahmedabad: Yasin Savaijiwala, pp. 1–6.

37 The Vagharis describe their original occupation as hunting but in Gujarat they pursue many occupations including work as itinerant vegetable sellers, traders in second hand clothes and embroideries, and tattooists. In the case of those at Mirzapur and Vasna, Ahmedabad, they are known for making *Mata-ni-pachedi* and *Mata-no-chandarvo*.

38 The Puranas are Sanskrit sacred writings on Hindu mythology and religious instruction.

39 For a technical description of *Mata-ni-pachedi* and discussion of their usage, see Erikson, J., *Mata Ni Pachedi. A Book on the Temple Cloth of the Mother Goddess*, Ahmedabad: National Institute of Design.

40 Muslim Chhipas are also known as *rangrez*. There is a further subdivision of the group into *neelgar* who specialise in indigo dyeing. See Varadarajan, L., *Ajrakh*, Ahmedabad: New Order Book Company, p. 41.

41 Personal communication, Khatri Mohammad Siddik, September 1997.

42 Varadarajan, p. 20.

43 Personal communication, Ismail Mohammad Khatri, September 1997.

44 Meghwals are leatherworkers who also keep cattle. Formerly known as 'Untouchables'—their occupation is ritually impure according to the orthodoxies of the caste system—they use either the name Harijan ('children of god') given them by Mahatma Gandhi, or the more political term Dalit ('oppressed'). Personal communication, Basser Bhura, Meghwal, December 1994.

45 Bilgrami, N., *Sindh jo Ajrak*, Karachi: Department of Culture and Tourism, Government of Sindh, p. 11.

46 Edwards, E.M., 'Cloth and Community: The Local Trade in Resist-Dyed and Block-Printed Textiles in Kachchh District, Gujarat', in *Textile History*, 38, 2 (2007), pp. 190–193.

47 Kerlogue, F., *Batik. Design, Style and History*, London: Thames and Hudson, pp. 18–21.

48 Personal communication, Ismail Mohammmad Khatri and Hajji Haroun Khatri, November 2006.

49 Crill offers a useful definition of the technique of chintz. See Crill, R. (2008), *Chintz. Indian Textiles for the West*, London: V&A Publishing, p. 7.

50 Talwar, K. and Kalyan Krishna, *Indian Pigment Paintings on Cloth*, Ahmedabad: Calico Museum of Textiles, pp. 75–76.

51 Ambalal, A., *Krishna as Shrinathji. Rajasthani Paintings from Nathdvara*, Ahmedabad: Mapin Publishing.

52 Lynton, L., *The Sari*, London: Thames and Hudson, pp. 32–35.

53 Personal communication, Khatri Abdul Gafur Daud and Arab Hasan Khatri, Nirona, December 1994.

5   Embroidery

Western India is the richest area of the subcontinent for embroidery, a category of textiles that also embraces appliqué, quilting and beadwork. The strong cultural ties between Gujarat, Rajasthan and Sindh in Pakistan are evident in common styles of embroidery. This is particularly evident in embroideries made for dowry. Unlike most of the textiles discussed in this book which are made by professional craftspeople whose hereditary caste occupation is printing, or dyeing, or weaving, a good deal of Gujarati embroidery has been made by women and has tended to be viewed as a leisure activity. The circulation of dowry embroidery, originally in the domestic realm, meant that it did not have the same status as other types of textiles. Made for private use rather than for sale, it was culture not commerce. However, that distinction has become blurred in the past fifty years with the development of the international trade in dowry embroideries which has added another facet to Gujarat's long history of commercial textiles.

Written records have focused on professional craft work which in terms of the history and development of embroidery has rendered women's contribution largely invisible. Thus far more is known about the history of trade embroidery—much of which was made by men—than that produced by women for domestic use. Information on commercial embroidery has been gleaned from various sources, including the accounts of travellers in western India. Imperial chronicles, notably the *Ain-i-Akbari*, Abu'l-Fazl's vivid record of the reign of Emperor Akbar; the trade records of the British East India Company; and John Forbes Watson's epic survey of Indian textile manufactures. Forbes Watson described Indian embroideries (and brocades) as 'exquisite productions' and concluded that British textile manufacturers simply could not compete with Indian artisans, observing that, 'There may be little hope of Europe ever being able to make these cheaper than India herself can; but, as a mere lesson in taste, the study of them may prove useful to the Home manufacturer.'[1]

Information on embroidery in everyday use in Gujarat is scanty prior to the twentieth century, although there are a number of studies that deal with the post-colonial era, during which period the tradition of dowry embroidery started to decline.[2] One of the few early commentators was Marianna Postans; her published recollections of a five-year residence (1834–1839) in the then princely state of Kachchh include descriptions of local women's embroidered dress, as well as details of the commercial embroidery at Bhuj made by men belonging to the Mochi (leatherworkers) caste who played a prominent role in the history of Gujarati embroidery.[3] The silk embroidered cotton hangings, bedspreads and fashion fabrics made by Mochi embroiderers for export to Europe brought Gujarat international acclaim in the seventeenth and eighteenth centuries. During the same period, Mochis also worked in Mughal ateliers making embroideries for use at court. These two distinct markets provided ample work for Mochi embroiderers and allowed the craft to flourish. However, as the Mughal Empire fell into decline after Aurangzeb's death in 1707, the Mochis lost their imperial patronage and were compelled to seek work elsewhere.

In the nineteenth and twentieth centuries other types of commercial work developed in Gujarat such as the *chinai* (Chinese) embroidery made by Chinese immigrants in Surat; and in the past forty years, embroidery made by women based on dowry pieces has been developed for sale by non-governmental organisations (NGOs).

HISTORY OF EMBROIDERY

At present the oldest known Gujarati embroideries are two votive textiles used by Jains that have been dated to the fifteenth or sixteenth century.[4] They depict female deities, characterised among other things by the protruding eye, and were influenced by western Indian figurative painting of the twelfth to sixteenth centuries. Although few examples of embroidery survive from before the sixteenth century, the discovery of bronze needles at the Harappan site of Mohenjodaro indicates knowledge of sewing. Patterned drapery represented on a steatite figurine excavated at the same site suggests that embroidery, as well as other forms of decoration such as printing and weaving, was part of a sophisticated material culture that developed in the Indus Valley. Early literature and painting provide only speculative evidence of the craft. The Greek geographer Strabo, drawing on the writings of Megasthenes, now

lost, Greek ambassador to the Mauryan court in the late fourth century, reported the Indian love of finery, describing court dress as 'worked in gold and ornamented with precious stones', noting 'flowered garments of the finest muslin'.[5] Exactly how these textiles were made is unclear but they are redolent of the later use of *jari* and *badla* (flat metallic thread) embroidery on sheer cottons during the Mughal period and thereafter. Similarly, it is impossible to determine whether textile designs depicted in the Buddhist wall paintings at Ajanta are brocaded or embroidered but as John Irwin observed, they 'are relevant to the study of embroidery'.[6] He drew a parallel between the designs of chevrons, circles, stripes and checks on the textiles depicted in the paintings

FIG 5.3 | LEFT

Detail of piece of *gajji* silk, silk embroidery, Thar Parkar, Sindh or Kachchh, mid-20th century

Suf ('triangle') embroidery made by Sodhas, Hindus from Sindh who sought refuge in Kachchh after the conflicts with Pakistan in 1965 and 1971. *Suf* designs are composed of triangles, worked mainly in satin stitch using silk floss.

Private collection

FIG 5.4 | ABOVE

Mochi (leatherworkers/cobbler's caste) woman at work, Ahmedabad

This woman is embroidering a shoe upper using a hook known as an *ari* which is a refined version of a cobbler's awl. *Ari* embroidery is typically worked in a chain stitch and metallic thread is often used, especially for shoes.

FIG 5.5

Equipment used by Mochis for making shoes

The awl (centre) is the same design as the *ari* used for embroidery but it is far larger, appropriate for stitching through the tough leather used for shoes and sandals.

and the *phulkari* ('flower work') embroidery tradition of the Punjab in which similar motifs are worked in a darning stitch—a style that is in turn closely related to the *suf* embroidery of western India which features patterns built up of small triangles embroidered chiefly in satin stitch.

The Venetian adventurer Marco Polo provides the earliest substantive evidence of embroidery in his account of the tanning industry in Gujarat in the late thirteenth century. He praised the leather mats and cushions made there as 'skilfully embroidered with gold and silver wire', a craft still practised by Mochis today.[7] But he makes no mention of the silk chain-stitch embroidery on cotton for which Gujarat was acclaimed in the sixteenth and seventeenth centuries—either he had not seen it or that type of work did not develop until somewhat later. It is referred to in the early sixteenth century by the Portuguese trader, Duarte Barbosa, who remarked on the 'very beautiful quilts and testers of bed finely worked' produced in Cambay by 'Moorish washer-women', the production of which was also noted by the Dutch traveller, Linschoten in 1585.[8] The earliest surviving examples of what were referred to at the time as 'Cambay quilts', are probably a set of hangings from Ashburnham House in Sussex and a bedspread preserved at Hardwick Hall in Derbyshire which have been dated to the seventeenth century.[9] When the East India Company started trading in India in the early seventeenth century, local factors were urged to send these acclaimed Gujarati embroideries to England.[10]

Cultural Ties

The popular embroidery of western India reveals the close cultural ties between Gujarat, Rajasthan and Sindh in Pakistan where rural communities share common styles of decoration. But the dowry embroideries made by Gujarati women were barely known outside the state until fifty years ago when the craft traditions of India started to be brought to public attention around the world. This was due to several factors including the arrival of foreign tourists in India, many on the so-called 'hippy trail' and the foundation of the All India Handicrafts Board (AIHB) in 1952 which started to showcase crafts, including regional styles of embroidery, at cultural festivals and exhibitions in India and overseas.[11]

Tourists, scholars, collectors, entrepreneurs, designers and curators have been drawn to Gujarat by the wealth of its embroidery; since the 1970s this has engendered the development of specialised tourism focused on embroidery and craft, and has also seen a steady outflow of old embroidery from the state, sold to visiting enthusiasts by entrepreneurs based in Bhuj and Ahmedabad, and the tourist centres of Udaipur, Jaipur, Mumbai and New Delhi.[12] The exodus of these unique cultural artefacts and the dwindling production of dowry embroidery due to changing fashions and the entry of women into the wage labour market has prompted Gujarat State Handicrafts Development Corporation (GSHDC) and NGOs to establish projects to both preserve examples of old embroidery and sustain the production of new work. These endeavours have transferred women's embroidery skills from dowry production to commercial work, generating livelihoods for the rural poor, and resulting in the professionalization of thousands of embroiderers.

TRADE EMBROIDERIES FOR EUROPE

The popularity of the commercial embroideries made by the Mochi community for use as soft furnishings, including hangings, valances, and canopies for beds, and dress fabrics in Britain lasted for nearly two hundred years. From the early seventeenth century until the nineteenth century they were among the most lucrative commodities handled by the East India Company. The embroideries were particularly associated with Cambay although the town's importance as a port and a centre of textile production had declined by the late sixteenth century due to the silting up of the Gulf of Cambay. Surat had subsequently become the chief port of western India as well as

FIG 5.6 | FACING PAGE

Hanging, cotton, silk embroidery, L 190 x W 164 cm, Gujarat, c. 1700

This type of chain stitch embroidery was exported from Cambay by the East India Company. It was made by professional male embroiderers of the Mochi community using an *ari* and a needle.

This piece was used at Ashburnham House, Sussex.
V&A IS: 155-1953

a significant production centre where the British and Dutch East India Companies established their headquarters in the early seventeenth century. Nonetheless, in the early eighteenth century, Alexander Hamilton, a trader and sometime employee of the East India Company, still wrote of the people of Cambay that they 'embroider the best of any people in India, and perhaps in the world'.[13] But embroideries—by then exported from Surat—were actually made at several sites in Gujarat. Patan in northern Gujarat, which was better known for *patola* weaving, was a centre of note, confirmed by reference to the town in a Royal Proclamation issued in 1631 by Charles I of England which listed 'quilts of Pitania [Patan] embroydered with silk' among the articles of private trade that employees of the East India Company were allowed to bring home with them.[14]

The trade embroideries were typically worked in chain stitch using coloured silk floss on a white cotton ground. In the late eighteenth century satin stitch worked on a silk ground was introduced which was popular as dress material

FIG 5.7–5.9 | BELOW AND FACING PAGE

The late Adam Sanghar and family, professional embroiderers using *ari* hooks, Bhuj, Kachchh

Ari embroideries of this size are worked by stretching the ground fabric onto a wooden frame which creates a taut surface for the embroidery. The design is either traced onto the cloth (cotton in this example) or drawn freehand. The *ari*, which the embroiderer works from the top of the cloth, penetrates the fabric and the thread, held beneath it, is looped on to the hook.

The textile illustrated is on display in the Embroidery Gallery at the Calico Museum of Textiles, Ahmedabad.

into the nineteenth century.[15] Earlier 'Ashburnham type' embroideries featured a very dense chain-stitch and the use of deep shades of blue, green, red and pink thread, with meandering florals, leaves and trees in which are nestled birds and small animals of unknown genus. The Mochi craftsmen used a hook known as an *ari* for chain-stitch embroidery, an implement adapted from a cobbler's awl which harked back to their caste origins as leatherworkers and shoe makers, and *ari bharat,* or hook embroidery, is also known as *Mochi bharat* (Mochi embroidery).

By the end of the seventeenth century embroidery designs bore a marked European stamp, which suggests that European prototypes were sent to India to be copied. Rosemary Crill has drawn attention to the similarity between Gujarati trade textiles and, variously, English crewel work, Jacobean embroidery, French *bizarre* silks and Dutch engravings which resulted in the emergence of a 'hybrid chinoiserie style' by the late seventeenth century.[16] A cross-over between the designs of chintz produced in South India and those of

Gujarati trade embroidery is also apparent which suggests that the East India Company was exporting co-ordinating sets of chintz and embroidered hangings to Europe. Mochi embroidery illustrates the overlapping histories of the East India Company's European trade and imperial production under the Mughals; chain-stitched embroideries graced the domestic interiors of wealthy Europeans as well as adorning the sumptuous surroundings of the Mughal courts. The ability of the Mochi embroiderers, like other Gujarati artisans, to respond to the needs of diverse consumers by producing highly differentiated products, enabled them to sustain the craft well into the twentieth century.

Court Embroidery

The Mughals

Some of the most exquisite examples of Mochi embroidery were made for the Mughals. Embroidered floorspreads, bolsters, hangings and canopies were a feature of court decor and were also used in the luxurious tents inhabited by royalty and their entourages during frequent tours to maintain the cohesion of the empire. Court dress made from the finest fabrics was also extensively embroidered with silk and *jari*. In an account of Emperor Aurangzeb's court in the mid-seventeenth century, the Frenchman François Bernier, conveyed the sheer luxury of the bodices worn by women at court: 'They are often worth ten and twelve crowns, and sometimes more when they are of the workmanship which I have seen, enriched with these fine needle-embroideries'.[17] His observation also reveals that embroidery worked with a needle as well as that made with a hook was part of imperial production. Under Mughal administration embroiderers among other artisans served in the imperial workshops which had been established at leading centres of Mughal power such as Ahmedabad. The output of these workshops would, according to Abu'l-Fazl who chronicled Akbar's reign, 'astonish experienced travellers'.[18] Bernier's account offers a glimpse of how the workshops operated: 'In one of these halls you see the embroiderers occupied in their work with the master who supervises them.' Bernier also reveals the hereditary nature of craft as an occupation, an aspect of the caste system that persists in contemporary India: 'All the artisans come in the morning to the *karkhanas*, work there the whole day long, and return in the evening to their own houses, each one slipping his life away patiently without aspiring any higher than his station. The embroiderer makes his son an embroiderer...'[19]

The embroideries made in the imperial workshops were for the most part quite different from those produced for Europe. The designs were a synthesis of Persian aesthetics and Indian traditions; recurring use of the *mihrab* (niche in a mosque) arch above a blossoming plant on hangings and a repeated *buti* (small floral motif) as well as other florals on fine cotton turban cloths and men's sashes known as *patka* were typical of Mughal style. The Mughal fashion for elaborate sashes as part of male finery drew on the customs of Safavid Persia. The original Persian accessory was decorated with heavy silk, gold and silver fringing; in India this became the *patka* which was generally made of fine muslin and embroidered with a variety of patterns including chevrons and stripes, and end borders featuring flowers or plants. Many were worked in a satin stitch using silk floss and metallic thread.

Broadly described as *zardozi* or 'gold embroidery', metal embroidery was popular with royalty and the nobility and was used extensively during the Mughal era. A plethora of types evolved: in *kamdani*, *jari* was embroidered directly onto fabric; *badla* work featured flattened metal strips that were laid on fabric; in a technique known as *mukesh*, metal strips were stitched through the fabric using the point of the strip instead of a needle to form

FIG 5.10
Man's sash (*patka*), cotton embroidered
with silk floss and gold-wrapped
thread, satin stitch, W 52.5 cm, Mughal,
early 18th century

V&A: IM 29-1936

FIG 5.11 AND 5.12

Muslim women making braid with metallic thread, Surat

These women are employed as outworkers by local *jari* manufacturers. They produce a variety of handmade braids which are edged and finished using a crocheting hook.

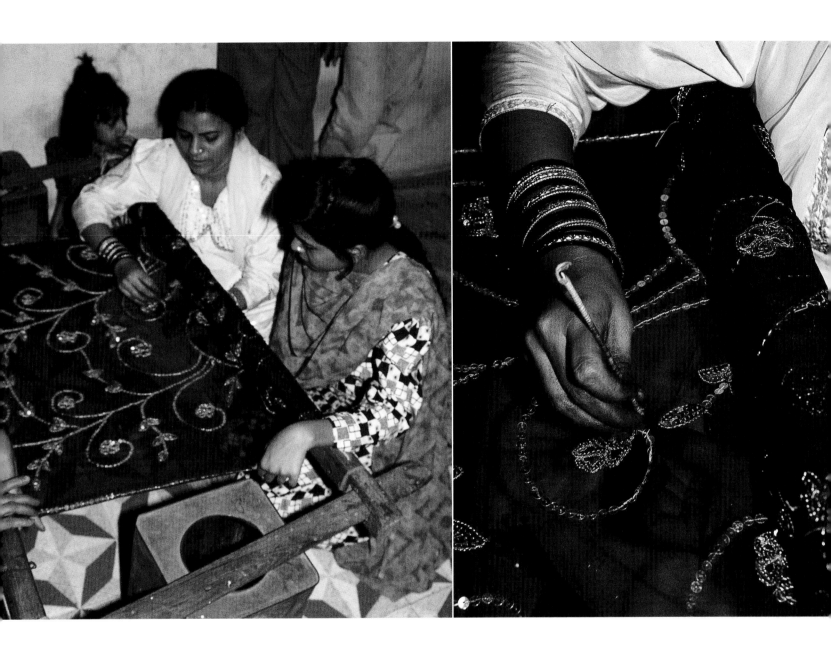

FIG 5.13 AND 5.14

Professional embroiderers working
with metal threads and sequins, Surat

These women do outwork for local *jari*
manufacturers and specialise in metal
work embroidery. Using an *ari*, they
produce lengths of fabrics, shawls and
other items embellished with chain
stitch in gold and silver and metallic
sequins.

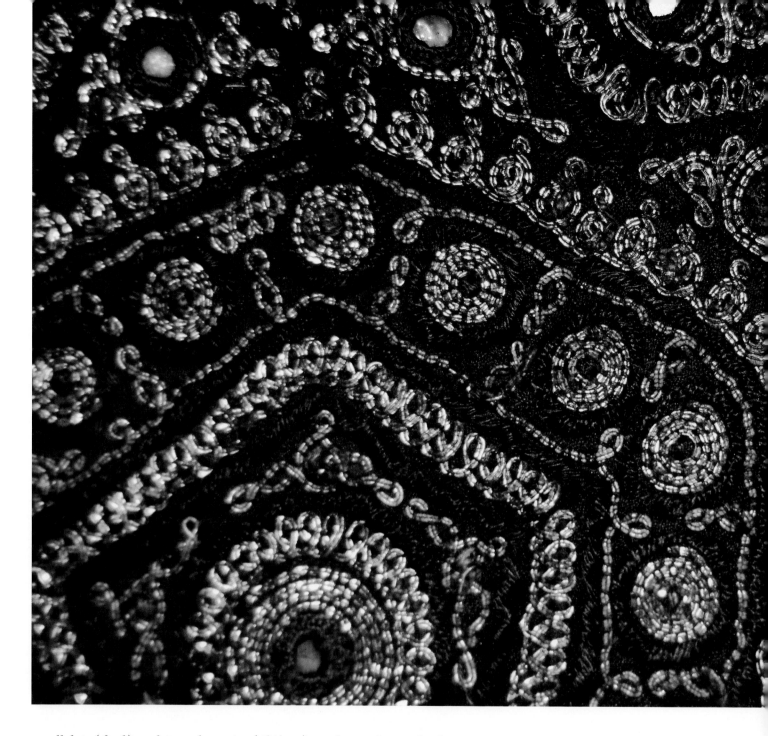

small dots (*fardi*), eyelets and sequins (*tiki/tara*); an alternative method was to draw the strip through the fabric with a needle and thread.[20] Metallic thread was produced in a variety of forms. Apart from flattened strips, embroiderers had a choice of tiny spirals (purls) called *salmo* or *sadi*, concertina-like forms known as *nakshi*, sequins, and ribbon known as *gota* which was woven from metal strips and silk, often used to edge garments or for appliqué work.[21] Both Mughal interiors and court dress scintillated with precious metals on lustrous fabrics. The legacy of these shining cloths is to be found today in contemporary embroideries and passementerie made by female embroiderers

FIG 5.15

Detail of embroidered blouse from Banni, Kachchh, cotton, mirrors, gold and silver metallic thread, mid-20th century

In this style of embroidery which is known locally as *muko*, metallic thread is couched on to the ground fabric of blouses made for a woman's dowry.

Private collection

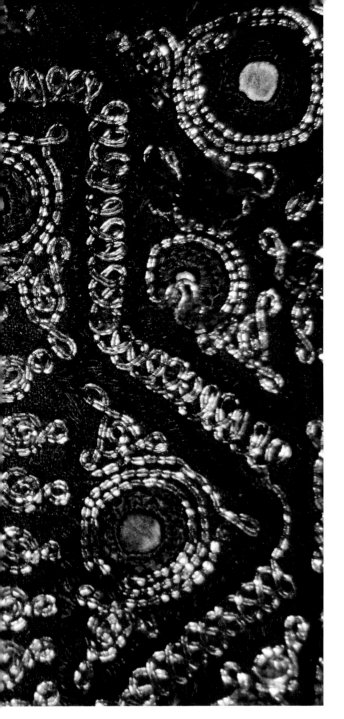

in Surat for mostly Muslim clients in Mumbai, Delhi and Kolkata, whose products are also exported to Bangladesh and the Gulf countries. It is also evident in the dowry embroidery of the herders of Banni in northern Kachchh where *muko* (laid work with *jari*) has been a feature of bags and bodices.

Regional Courts

After the death of Emperor Aurangzeb in 1707 the 'golden age' of the Mughals began to wane; the imperial coffers had been drained by constant warfare and the court was forced to retrench. Patronage of the arts and crafts diminished and the imperial workshops at Ahmedabad, Delhi and Lahore gradually dispersed; embroiderers like other artisans were laid off. This coincided with the gradual decline of the European market for Indian embroidery; thus in the eighteenth century the two main sources of patronage for embroiderers started to disappear. In Gujarat the embroiderers found work at the regional courts, notably in Kachchh and in Kathiawar (now Saurashtra) where their main activity was embroidering dowry items for Kathi (nobility/landowners) brides.[22] They also embroidered for local royalty and the nobility, producing ceremonial dress which was lavishly decorated, notably with heavy gold *zardozi* on silk and velvet.

By the nineteenth century, Bhuj, the Kachchhi capital, had become the leading centre for Mochi embroidery. The Maharaos of Kachchh kept many Mochis in almost continuous work. Nanavati, Vora and Dhaky noted the Mochis' 'prodigious output... during royal marriages, the occasions of [that] kind being quite frequent in former times in Kutch. The richly embroidered silks were needed as gifts for a British Political Agent, Governor, or Viceroy during his visit to the State'.[23] Their output included fans, *chakla* (square embroidered wall hangings, usually in pairs), *toran* (pennanted door hanging), purses and items of dress including chain-stitched hats, bodices, sari borders and *ghaghra* (drawstring skirts) worn at court by royalty and the nobility which were often included in a bride's dowry. Royal *ghaghra*, in particular, were extravagant in their dimensions and decoration. In an interview with fashion designer Ritu Kumar published in 1999, Kunverba, the Rajmata of Bhuj, recalled

FIG 5.16 | FACING PAGE

Sher Muhammad Khan Bahadur, Nawab of Palanpur, early 20th century

This formal portrait shows the Nawab of Palanpur (north Gujarat) in a tunic encrusted with heavy metalwork embroidery. Gold thread, sequins and other spangles have been couched on to the ground fabric (velvet).

Photograph courtesy of Abhishek and Radhika Poddar Collection

FIG 5.17 | RIGHT

The Rana Sahib of Porbandar, early 20th century

A formal portrait of the ruler of the princely state of Porbandar (Saurashtra) which shows him in a tunic heavy with *zardozi* (metalwork) embroidery. Indian royal dress was a marker of status and featured sumptuous textiles embellished with gold, silver and gems.

Photograph courtesy of Abhishek and Radhika Poddar Collection

FIG 5.18 | FACING PAGE

Detail of embroidered skirt, ivory satin, coloured silk, Kachchh, early 20th century

The embroidery is entirely in chain stitch and was made by the Mochi community.

See page 8 for full garment.

V&A: IM 246-1920

discovering a skirt made from a piece of gold embroidered fabric seventy-seven yards long as well as several other exquisite skirts in the clothing store of her ancestor, Naniba Jhali, the wife of Maharao Pragmalji II (r. 1860–1876).[24] A number of fine examples of Mochi embroidered skirts and bodices have survived from the nineteenth and early twentieth century preserved in royal clothing stores or treasured as heirlooms by the families of the nobility and court officials.[25]

A witness to the industry of the Mochis at Bhuj in the mid-nineteenth century, Marianna Postans observed that, 'The embroiderers display much taste in their native designs; but the most remarkable characteristic of their talent is the surprising correctness they display in the art of imitation [copying].'[26] The Mochi work of Bhuj was typically embroidered with a hook in silk floss on silk satins known as *gajji* and *atlas* in a tonal scale of particular colours; in other parts of Gujarat, Mochis used a greater range of stitches. The imitative ability of the Mochi remarked on by Mrs Postans led to a consistent style throughout the state that featured Mughal-influenced *butis* (floral motifs) interspersed with peacocks, female figures known as *putali* or *dingali* (doll), florals, foliage and more rarely caparisoned horses or elephants; borders were often composed of alternating parrots and floral motifs.

The embroiderers kept pattern books that included their own or commissioned sketches of designs from which clients would make a selection. One such volume is preserved at the Kachchh Museum, Bhuj, which includes sketches, handwritten notes and details of royal commissions compiled by Karsandas Gopalji Jhansari Bharatwala (1843–1937/38). Donated to the museum by the Karsandas family, it represents a record of one of the last Mochis in royal service whose work for Maharao Khengarji III (r. 1876–1942) is within living memory. As his grandson, Jethalal Jhansari recalls: 'He [Karsandas] did a lot of work for the royal family of Kachchh and Gondal. If any new orders came from the royal family, that work took priority... It took a lot of time to complete and my grandfather would stay at different palaces for months at a time.'[27] In his retirement, Karsandas was given the honorific duty of tying the Maharao's turban on ceremonial occasions; turbans were part of the insignia of royalty and covering the head symbolised respect for god.[28] The honour was subsequently conferred on his heirs and Jethalal Jhansari ties the turbans of the current incumbent of the Kachchhi *gaddi* (throne), Pragmalji Madansinhji III.

19

20

21

22

23   24

FIG 5.19–5.24

Pages from a hand-drawn and painted pattern book used by Mochi embroiderers, Bhuj, Kachchh, mid-19th to early 20th century

Kachchh Museum Collection

19. & 20. The book served as a design catalogue for patrons and this page shows variations of the paisley or mango design (keri)—see detail (20). Many of the pages have been annotated by the embroiderers in Gujarati.

21. This page shows designs of peacocks and girls dancing and a floral border, similar in style to that of the skirt in fig. 5.18.

22. This page shows three designs for embroidered hats. The florals, leafy stems and peacocks are recurrent motifs in Mochi embroidery.

23. This page shows designs for embroidered shoes, with patterns for uppers and side panels.

24. This page shows a design for the still popular board game chaupad.

Urban Embroidery in the Nineteenth and Twentieth Centuries

Royal commissions undoubtedly burnished an artisan's status and thus took priority over other work, but Mochi embroiderers also attracted patrons from the mercantile and wealthy land-owning castes of Gujarat, including Banias (merchants) and Kanbi Patels (farmers). Some of the finest examples of Mochi embroidery from the nineteenth and twentieth centuries are temple hangings known as *pichhwais* that were commissioned by the Bhatias of Kachchh, wealthy merchants who belonged to the Vallabhacharya sect who worshipped Krishna in the form of Shrinathji.[29] Such high status work was the exclusive domain of skilled male artisans; Mochi women were active as embroiderers but they were confined to journeyman work, as Jethalal Jhansari notes: 'The men's work was very intricate and the women's work was more rough [made] for people in Vagad [east Kachchh]—Banias and Kanbi Patels.'[30]

FIG 5.25 | LEFT

Portrait of Maharao Khengarji III of Kachchh, satin, silk embroidery, Bhuj, Kachchh, early 20th century

The work of a Mochi embroiderer from Bhuj, this portrait was made with an *ari* in chain stitch. It is based on a formal photograph of the Maharao taken at the Delhi Darbar in 1911.

Private collection

FIG 5.26 | RIGHT

Portrait of Maharao Khengarji III of Kachchh, early 20th century

Photograph courtesy of Abhishek and Radhika Poddar Collection

Although Bhuj was the acknowledged centre of Mochi embroidery, there were also active Mochi communities in Anjar and Mandvi. Jethalal recalled his grandfather telling him that the port of Mundra had formerly been a production centre as well: 'But by [1910] it had finished due to people migrating from the town to other areas. For example the Patels all left [emigrating to east Africa].'[31] However, it was not only in Mundra that demand had declined; the wider market for Mochi embroidery had largely petered out by the beginning of the twentieth century and royal commissions ceased altogether when the Republic of India was established in 1950.[32] Nonetheless the influence of Mochi embroidery persists in the popular embroidery of Gujarat made by women for domestic consumption.

The broad appeal and use of Mochi embroidery contrasted with another style of commercial embroidery that developed in Surat in the nineteenth century. *Chinai* (Chinese) embroidery was made by Chinese immigrants specifically for the Parsi community, chiefly for items of dress, including saris and sari borders, girls' blouses, caps and children's dresses. Most *chinai* work was embroidered on a silk ground, occasionally on velvet, with either silk floss or a tightly plied silk thread that was used for finer details. The design repertoire reflected

FIG 5.27

Sari border (*kors*), satin, silk embroidery, early 20th century

This style of embroidery, known as *chinai* (lit. 'Chinese') was made for Parsis by Chinese embroiderers based in Surat. It was worked in satin stitch, usually in pale colours on a dark background; Parsi women favoured purple and black for saris.

Private collection

the Chinese origins of the embroiderers: fauna, including deer, cranes and cockerels nestled in flora, typically drooping willows and clusters of blossoms. Linda Lynton has also suggested that they were influenced by the designs of eighteenth century Chinese export embroideries and Indian chintz.[33] Much of the embroidery was white satin stitch, with details in colour; changes in the direction of the satin stitch introduced subtle tonal variations. Knot stitch and occasionally chain stitch were also used. The pale lustre of the embroidery contrasted with the dark coloured grounds favoured by the Parsis; the women wore saris of black and deep purple, some entirely covered with *chinai* work, others were limited to an embroidered border. A Parsi bride's trousseau used to include one fully embroidered sari known as *gara* with white embroidery and one sari with an embroidered border known as *kor-ni-sari*. *Gara* were worn during the wedding celebrations but not for the formal ceremony. Some of the most elaborate pieces of *chinai* work were girls' sleeveless tunics known as *jubla* which was worn with loose trousers and an embroidered cap. As the nineteenth century drew to a close, the market for *chinai* embroidery had dwindled due to a combination of changing fashions among the Parsis and from the 1880s onward the availability of cheaper imported silk and velvet borders (*kors*) made using a mechanised jacquard loom.[34] Thus by the mid-twentieth century the commercial production of *chinai* embroidery like that of Mochi embroidery had disappeared.

POPULAR EMBROIDERY

The custom of dowry has generated much of the popular embroidery made in Gujarat. Although dowry has been illegal in India since the introduction of the Dowry Prohibition Act of 1961, it persists across all sectors of Indian society and among the farmers and herders of rural Gujarat women are still required to make an embroidered trousseau in preparation for marriage. They continue to embroider after marriage for their husbands, children, homes and religious shrines. The embroideries produced conform to caste styles and have been significant markers of caste identity that reveal details of religious affiliation, age, marital status and economic standing. They have also provided an opportunity for artistic expression and have been a source of pride. As one woman put it, 'When you make your own *kanchali* (bodice) it is attached to your desire to wear it and there is always some emotional attachment to your own embroidery anyway. You put lots of colour, a lot of effort, many different motifs—flowers, *abhla* (mirrors)—it looks so beautiful'.[35]

FIG 5.28 | FACING PAGE

Parsi girl's tunic (*jubla*), *gajji* silk, silk embroidery, L 56 x W 53.5 cm, Surat, c. 1870

Jubla provide some of the finest examples of chinai embroidery; they were worn by girls with loose trousers and a round embroidered hat.

V&A: 1426a-1874

FIG 5.29 | ABOVE LEFT

Instalment of Vagadia Rabari woman's dowry, east Kachchh

Vagadia Rabari women still make an embroidered trousseau in preparation for marriage. In recent years dowry inflation has become a problem across all the Rabari subgroups in Kachchh which led the Dhebaria council to ban embroidery in 1995.

FIG 5.30 | BELOW LEFT

Fakirani Jat woman embroidering a dress (*churi*) for her daughter in preparation for her marriage, Kachchh

Jats, who are Muslims, create densely embroidered non-figurative designs stippled with tiny mirrors. They use a restricted palette of black, white, orange, green, blue and two shades of red.

FACING PAGE

FIG 5.31 | ABOVE RIGHT

Gracia Jat girl in an embroidered *churi*, west Kachchh

*Churi*s are worn by females of all three subgroups of Jats in Kachchh (Fakirani, Gracia and Dhanetah). Most are black although red, as in this case, is sometimes used, especially by young girls.

FIG 5.32 | RIGHT

Node women, Pachcham, north Kachchh

Node are Muslim cattle-herders who decorate their blouses (*kanchali*) with embroidery. These and other embroidered textiles are important components of a dowry.

FIG 5.33 | LEFT

Suthar women, Banni, north Kachchh

Hindu Suthars are woodworkers who also herd a few cattle. The women wear a long embroidered *kanchali* similar in style to that worn by neighbouring Muslim clans.

FIG 5.34 | RIGHT

Meghwal women, Khavda, Kachchh

Like other Hindu groups living in the Banni area, the style of dress and embroidery of Meghwals is influenced somewhat by that of the Muslim cattle herding clans.

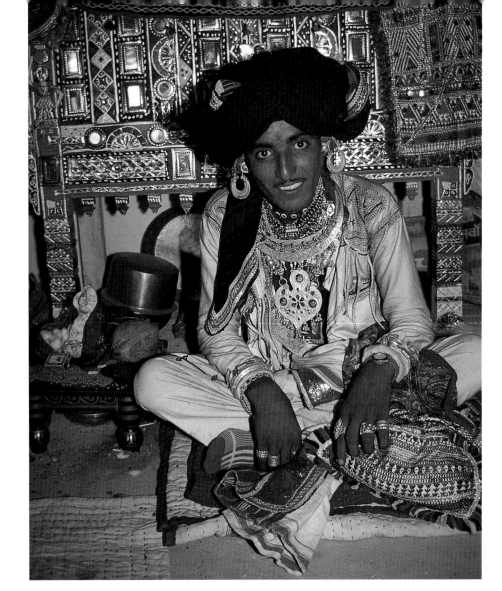

FIG 5.35

Vagadia Rabari groom on the eve of his wedding, east Kachchh

His smock, his bag filled with *prasad* for wedding guests, and the domestic textiles that surround him, were embroidered by his mother and sisters. They are laden with auspicious symbols which Rabaris believe ward off malign influences and express their distinctive aesthetic style.

FIG 5.36 | BELOW LEFT

Vagadia Rabari woman and her sister, east Kachchh

This young bride has recently moved to her husband's village to live in the marital home. She is resplendent in embroidered dress made for her dowry which marks her transition from daughter to wife. The dress is rich with fertility symbols, anticipating her future role as a mother.

FIG 5.37 | BELOW RIGHT

Vagadia Rabari woman making embroidery for her dowry, east Kachchh

Many Rabaris arrange partners for their children when they are still young. This young woman, engaged from the age of two, and now in her early twenties, embroiders in earnest as the day of her wedding approaches.

Since 1947 there has been widespread dowry inflation, partly due to the entry of women into the wage labour market. This has been problematic particularly in the rural areas of the state, notably Kachchh, Saurashtra and northern Gujarat which have been the principal areas for embroidery. In some communities the amount of embroidery had escalated to such a level that it was taking years to complete and was impeding the process of marriage. Among the Dhebaria Rabaris of Kachchh the burden of dowry became so onerous that in 1995 the caste council imposed a total ban on embroidery and fined anyone who did not comply. Arjanbhai Rabari, the architect of the ban, explained it thus: 'According to my calculation [we] used to spend seventy thousand rupees for embroidery; this is not a small amount... so if a father has four daughters, think what money he is spending... Five or six of us decided that like Gandhi [who] starved, was beaten and went to jail for the independence of the country... to abolish this sin from our society, we would go through the same process.'[36] The ruling was enforced with conviction and the making and use of embroidery by Dhebaria Rabaris effectively ceased in 1995.

The volume of embroidery required for a woman's trousseau has affected most communities, whatever their faith. In Banni, northern Kachchh, among Meghwal leatherworkers and Muslim clans of cattle-herders such as Jat, Mutwa, Node, Hingorja, Haliputra, Raisiputra, Sameja, Samma and Brahui, women have traditionally made twenty-one quilts, or *dadki*, for dowry. These are displayed on a stand facing the entrance to the home, covered by an appliqué hanging as a symbol of prosperity and hospitality. They are offered to guests to sit on and serve as bedding for the family. In 2003, a newly-married bride from the Mutwa community displayed a stack of over fifty quilts which her mother-in-law said was the norm; closer scrutiny revealed that many were machine-stitched, decorated with metallic braids and the amount of hand embroidery and appliqué, or *kutab,* was minimal. The matriarch, an accomplished embroiderer in her

FIG 5.38 | FACING PAGE

Ahir woman, central Kachchh

Newly married, this young woman is wearing the embroidered dress typical of her community. Glittering with mirror decoration, it is rich with floral designs and parrots worked in chain stitch which reveals the enduring influence of Mochi embroidery (fig. 5.18).

fifties, voiced her concerns about this development: 'We are worried about our traditional style; all the young girls have stopped doing embroidery and we are afraid it will die out'.[37]

This change reflects a general trend in Gujarat—embroidery is widely seen as old-fashioned and the younger generation is abandoning it in favour of machine-made decoration such as sequins and braids applied to glossy synthetics. This marks a significant shift from earlier times. In 1966, Saurashtra like Kachchh had been identified in a study published by the Government of Gujarat as a significant area where embroidery and beadwork of many 'schools' were flourishing.[38] By the 1980s, fashions had changed, as Emma Tarlo observed during fieldwork in Saurashtra. Her study of 'clothing matters' among Kharaks (farmers), Bharwads (shepherds) and Kanbis (farmers) and others revealed numerous changes: although embroidery still featured in a Kharak dowry, few young women relished wearing it; Kanbi women no longer made or used embroidery and were wearing synthetic saris; among the more conservative Bharwads, men's dress and the women's *ghaghra* and *kapadu* (bodices) were decorated with machine embroidery done by local tailors.[39] Thus between the 1960s and 1980s, the popular embroidery of Saurashtra went into steep decline. Kachchh remains the last bastion of hand-embroidered dress in Gujarat, its customs preserved by the remoteness of the district. Fashions are gradually changing there, too, but it is still possible to see a range of embroidery techniques largely because of the work of non-governmental organisations (NGOs) in Kachchh. While providing sustainable employment for local women as embroiderers, three NGOs—the Shrujan Trust, KMVS (Kutch Mahila Vikas Sangathan) and Kala Raksha—have also aided the preservation of cultural heritage by incorporating the use of the full variety of local stitches into the embroidered products they sell.[40]

Techniques of Popular Embroidery

Mirrorwork and Embroidery Stitches

One of the most striking features of popular Gujarati embroidery has been the use of mirrored glass known as *abhla*—a custom thought to have originated with the use of mica, a naturally-occurring shiny silicate found in the desert area of western India. Sheila Paine has suggested that mirrors are used to deflect the evil eye which can be 'overpowered by anything that dazzles and makes it blink'; shells, beads, tassels and buttons affixed to the

FIG 5.39

Mutwa home, Dhordo, Kachchh

Mutwa women traditionally make
21 quilts for their trousseaux; the
number is now far higher because
of dowry inflation. Decorated with
embroidery, patchwork and appliqué,
they are displayed on a stand facing the
threshold of the home. They symbolise
fecundity, literally filling up the home,
and hospitality.

edges of garments, bags and hangings serve the same purpose.[41] It seems
probable that mirrorwork is part of India's Islamic inheritance. The use of
reflective surfaces was a feature of Islamic architecture which was introduced
to India during the Sultanate period and later consolidated by the Mughals.
According to Indo-Persian philosophy, light was a manifestation of the divine
at work in the world, which Christopher Bayly has suggested, 'gave rise to the
enormous taste for mirrors and shiny fabrics'.[42] Whatever its origins, now the
use of mirrors is dictated by custom; girls learn mirrorwork from older female
relatives along with other aspects of embroidery. Large fragments of mirror
glass hand-blown at Kapadvanj near Ahmedabad are bought by weight; those
fragments are then cut to approximately the desired shape with scissors
adapted for the purpose, and the rough edges are smoothed on a roof tile.[43]
The mirrors are secured onto fabric, usually with some form of herringbone
stitch.[44] Industrialisation has brought other options for embroiderers; factory-
made glass pre-cut into small squares, diamonds, circles and triangles is
available as are mirror pieces set into a machine-embroidered frame; sequins
and sequin-covered fabrics are also popular.

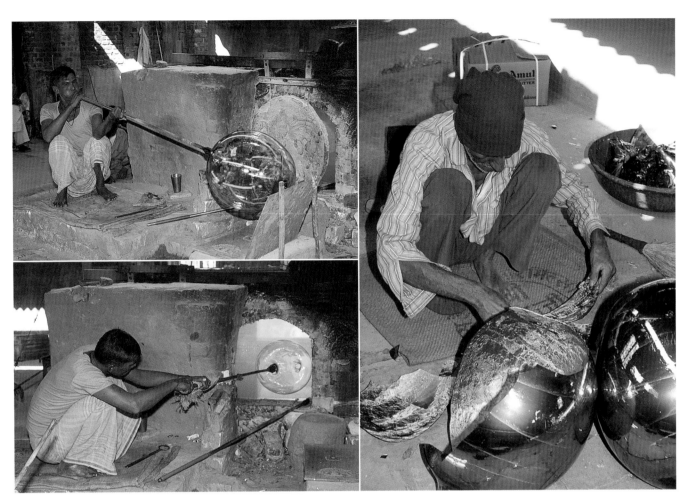

FIG 5.40–5.42 | ABOVE AND RIGHT

Glass-blowing at Kapadvanj, Gujarat

Globes of mirrored glass are handmade by Muslim craftsmen at this small workshop, the last of its kind in Gujarat. The globes are broken up and the fragments are graded by hand; thicker pieces are used for architectural decoration and thinner pieces for mirrorwork embroidery. Much of the glass is dispatched directly to merchants and the shards are sold by weight in bazaars throughout western India. But some of it goes to Limbdi in Saurashtra for further processing. It is cut into small geometric shapes in workshops run by Jain merchants and then sold by weight to haberdashers.

FIG 5.43 | BELOW RIGHT

Kachchhi Rabari girl, Bhujodi, Kachchh

This girl is cutting fragments of handmade mirror glass, bought in nearby Bhuj, into small geometric shapes using scissors specially adapted for the purpose. The mirrors will be stitched onto a shawl by her mother who works part-time for a local weaver.

Apart from mirrorwork, women use a range of stitches: chain stitch, running stitch, backstitch, herringbone, fishbone stitch and satin stitch are used to build up a dense bas-relief of embroidery that often obscures the ground fabric. They stitch forwards from the body rather than across it as is the Western custom. Australian writer Jim Masselos attributes the prevalence of chain stitch which is used throughout Gujarat to the influence of the Mochi embroidery of Bhuj: 'While male embroiderers were becoming successful professional specialists their technique was spreading out into the villages where women adopted it for their own purposes. Later the technique would spread across and over into Kathiawar where it became one of a number of stitches used by village women.'[45] In Kachchh, Rabaris, Kanbis and Ahirs use both simple chain stitch and square chain stitch worked in yellow or white cotton thread (with a needle rather than a hook) to define shapes and establish boundaries between pattern areas; these stitches were formerly used by Kanbis, Kharaks and Bharwads in Saurashtra.

An interlacing stitch worked on a frame of Cretan stitch known as *bavaliyo*—a reference to the thorny acacia (*baval*) that grows in the desert—is widely used throughout Gujarat and may have been introduced from the Near East.[46] Many of the Kachchhi embroiderers use areas of *bavaliyo* interspersed with mirrors: known as *tek bavaliyo* by Rabaris and Ahirs, it is used for borders on dowry

FIG 5.44 | ABOVE

Dhebaria Rabari *kanchali*, tie-dyed silk, coloured cotton thread, mirrors, plastic buttons; made for a woman's dowry, east Kachchh, c. 1970-80

Mirrorwork is a characteristic of embroidery made throughout northwest India, and that of Kachchh is especially acclaimed. Dhebarias have produced some of the most vibrant examples of the craft.

See appendix ill. 7 for garment analysis.

Private collection

FIG 5.45 | FACING PAGE

Detail of fig. 5.44

The designs are embroidered mainly in open chain stitch. Mirrors of various shapes are secured in a frame of herringbone stitch that has been worked into using buttonhole stitch. The palette is typical of Dhebarias; orange and white predominate with accents of other colours.

bags and skirts; among the Muslim groups of Banni, Mutwas are famous for their minuscule stitches, fine *bavaliyo* and use of tiny mirrors. In Saurashtra, Kharak women used to cover their skirts in dense *bavaliyo* until seventy years ago. Patanwadi Rabaris of northern Gujarat still embroider deep borders of *bavaliyo* in deep pink cotton or silk floss on their *sadla* (half-saris).

The use of monochrome silk floss, usually maroon or deep pink, was prevalent in Saurashtra in Mahajan embroideries and those commissioned by Kathis (landowners) until the twentieth century; *chakla* and *toran* featuring geometric designs were worked in herringbone stitch, darning stitch and satin stitch

FIG 5.46 | LEFT

Detail of Dhebaria Rabari dowry sack, cotton, cotton thread, mirrors, tassels, quilted, embroidered, east Kachchh

Stitches include: chain, herringbone, Cretan, buttonhole and an interlacing stitch. The large floral motifs alternating with stylised parrots are also evident in embroidery by other communities and show the influence of Mochi designs (figs 5.18, 5.38 and 5.53).

Private collection

FIG 5.47 | BELOW

Detail of cuff of Dhebaria Rabari smock, satin, cotton, cotton thread, silk floss, mirrors, buttons, east Kachchh

Mirrors alternate with blocks of herringbone and interlacing stitches in the band of *tek bavaliyo. Tek* is a Rabari term for 'mirror' and *bavaliyo* refers to *baval*, the thorny acacia tree that grows in the desert.

Private collection

FIG 5.48 | FACING PAGE

Detail of trouser cuff, Mutwa, cotton, cotton thread, mirrors, Dhordo, Banni, Kachchh

The Muslim cattle herders of Banni are renowned for their minute *bavaliyo*. Many of the girls no longer want to do these complex interlacing stitches and describe them as '*dukhi kam*' or painful work.

Private collection

using silk floss. *Suf* (also known as *kachho*, meaning 'raw' or 'weak') embroidery in which patterns are built up of triangles worked in satin stitch using silk floss was introduced into the repertoire of Kachchh by Hindu Sodhas from Thar Parkar in Sindh, Pakistan, who sought refuge in the district after the Indo-Pakistani War of 1971. The designs created by embroiderers reflect their membership of a particular community and their religious beliefs; those of Muslim women in Banni, Kachchh, comply with the Quranic proscription against figurative representation and rely on the interplay of geometric and floral motifs and bold use of colour. The embroidery made by the Hindu Meghwals of Banni who are Dalit leatherworkers has absorbed many of

FIG 5.49

Detail of Mahajan hanging, cotton cloth, silk floss, mirrors, embroidery and appliqué, Saurashtra

This is one of a pair of *chakla* (s. *chaklo*), textiles that are hung either side of a doorway. Satin stitch and herringbone worked in deep pink silk floss is particularly associated with Saurashtran embroidery.

Private collection

FIG 5.50

Detail of Node blouse piece, *gajji* silk, silk floss, cotton thread, mirrors, east Banni, Kachchh

Node like other Muslim groups in Banni use non-figurative designs like this large medallion on their textiles. Most of the black silk floss has perished with use.

Private collection

FIG 5.51 | FACING PAGE

Detail of panel for Gracia Jat dress, cotton cloth, cotton thread, mirrors, west Kachchh

This panel (*angoti*) combines abstract florals and geometric designs worked in a variety of stitches including; satin, open chain and buttonhole. Typical of Jat work, the dense embroidery completely covers the background fabric.

FIG 5.52 | RIGHT

Hindu Suthar woman in embroidered *kanchali*, Banni, Kachchh

The vocabulary of stitches, organisation of patterns and absence of figurative imagery on this woman's blouse has much in common with nearby Mutwas who are Muslims. Stylistic exchange has been a feature of the embroidery of Kachchh.

FIG 5.53 | FACING PAGE

Detail of Kanbi child's hat (*toplo*), *gajji* silk, cotton cloth, silk floss, cotton thread, west Kachchh

As with other groups of Hindus in the district, Kanbi embroidery reveals the influence of Mochi work in its use of floral motifs, stylised parrots and chain stitch.

Private collection

FIG 5.54 | RIGHT

Wall hanging with image of the deity Ganesh (*Ganesh sthapana*), cotton embroidered with silk, mirrors, herringbone stitch and chain stitch, L 66 x W 52 cm, Kanbi community, Saurashtra

Used in worship by a bride and groom as part of the marriage ceremony.

V&A: IS 18-1967

the motifs and patterns of their Muslim neighbours. This imitation may originally have developed as a strategy to avoid the stigma of 'untouchability' but it has prompted Mutwas, and other communities, to change their style of embroidery in order not to be taken for Dalits.[47] Nonetheless, Meghwal women have earned a reputation as some of the most skilful embroiderers in Kachchh whose rich *pakko* (strong, enduring) embroidery is vibrant with florals, repeated geometrics and mirrors.

A strong narrative element is evident in the embroidery of the Ahirs, Kanbis, Rajputs and the three subgroups of Rabaris in Kachchh—Kachchhis, Dhebarias and Vagadias. The embroidery of these communities combines motifs of rural life with symbols of Hindu mythology. Garments, dowry bags and quilts used for weddings and festivals are replete with shrines, mango trees, thorn bushes, flowers, parrots, peacocks and elephants, girls fetching water and churning butter. In Saurashtra, Kanbis and Charans used to embroider *Ganesh sthapana*, a distinctive five-sided hanging for household shrines that featured the elephant-headed god Ganesh, with his attendants Siddhi and Buddhi on either side. The hanging, made for dowry, was used in worship by the bride and groom as part of the marriage ceremony.[48]

Quilting, Patchwork and Appliqué

Quilted textiles, patchworks and appliqués are widely made throughout Gujarat. Among the Meghwals and Muslims of Banni in Kachchh, quilts are an intrinsic part of a dowry, which also includes quilted bags for storing clothes and jewellery, and the Quran (an envelope bag known as *jild*). At a utilitarian level they are patchworks of recycled clothes quilted with a simple running stitch, used on a daily basis as sleeping mats and seating for guests.[49]

FIG 5.55 | LEFT

Quilts airing in the sun, Dhamadka, east Kachchh

The quilts in daily use are patchworks of recycled clothes, quilted with a simple running stitch in a coarse cotton thread.

FIG 5.56 | RIGHT

Kachchhi Rabari woman making a quilt from woollen veilcloths, Bhujodi, Kachchh

Among Rabaris quilts are gendered according to the clothes from which they are made. As this one is being made from old veilcloths, it is female and its use will be restricted to females in compliance with the community's modesty code.

FIG 5.57

Quilt, cotton cloth, cotton thread, patchwork and quilting, Banni, Kachchh

Made for dowry by a woman from a Muslim herding clan, this quilt has a centre panel of *ajrakh*, a prestigious block-printed textile worn by men in Banni.

Private collection

FIG 5.58

Quilt, cotton cloth, cotton thread, patchwork, appliqué, reverse appliqué and embroidery, Banni, Kachchh

Made by Hindu Meghwals, the centrefield of this quilt is composed of squares of reverse appliqué (*kutab*) while the surrounding borders combine strip patchwork and appliqué.

Private collection

Among the Rabaris of Kachchh, men's and women's clothing is recycled separately and quilts are gendered. According to a Rabari *barot* (caste genealogist), they retain the essence of the wearer and use is bound by the community's modesty code: 'A quilt is made out of the clothes that the women have worn so if a man covers himself with those clothes, that is a kind of dishonour to him. That's why they don't do it; it's a question of *sharam* (modesty).'[50] Although patchworks are functional objects, in India, and other parts of Asia, they also have a religious resonance—Sufi renouncers wore patched clothes as a sign of poverty and humility. However, as Steven Cohen has observed, drawing on Mughal albums of paintings and calligraphy known

FIG 5.59

Detail of Dhebaria Rabari dowry sack (*kothali*), cotton cloth, silk floss, cotton thread, plastic buttons; quilting, appliqué and embroidery; chain stitch, open chain, running stitch, interlacing; east Kachchh, c.1980

Dhebarias were known for their fine appliqué, evident in the floral (*buti*) and stylised parrot motifs (*sudo*) that decorate this sack.

Private collection

FIG 5.60

Dhebaria Rabari woman with a beadwork head ring for a sacred coconut or water pot known as *indhoni-ni-choti*, east Kachchh

This object is used for ceremonial purposes. It is fashioned from cotton cloth, cotton thread, metallic foil, plastic beads and is decorated with beadwork and passementerie.

as *muraqqá* (Persian for 'patched' or 'patched garment'), there are instances where the patched clothing of the religious figure depicted is anything but humble, 'rather it consists entirely of valuable loom-woven silk.'[51] This 'conspicuous consumption' derails any notion of poverty and is comparable to some of the dowry quilts from Banni which are made in profusion from purpose-bought fabrics. They feature dazzling geometric patchwork and appliquéd *kutab* (lit. 'cut up') and are often backed with fragments of *ajrakh*, the prestigious block-printed textile worn by men of the area. Appliqué is also a feature of Rabari work and tends to be reserved for textiles that have a ceremonial purpose. The quilts provided for a groom to sit on as he awaits the *phera*, votive hangings and a bride's dowry bags are decorated with appliqué and embroidery laden with auspicious symbols. Some of the finest Rabari appliqué is also evident on the trappings adorning their camels, indicative of the high status of these animals for Rabaris. In Saurashtra, Mahajans and Kathis used to make large festival hangings, canopies (*chandarvo*) and animal trappings featuring a white ground with stylised animals and flowers, and geometric shapes in red and blue appliqué.[52]

Beadwork

Beadwork is made throughout Kachchh and Saurashtra. Early examples such as the bullock cloths in the collection at the Junagadh Museum in Saurashtra were made by professional Mochi embroiderers and date back to the late nineteenth century.[53] The seed beads used were Venetian glass from Murano which reached India via East Africa and the Arabian peninsula but these are no longer manufactured.[54] Although glass beads made in Varanasi have been available since 1981, most embroiderers now use plastic beads.[55] By the twentieth century, the craft had been taken up by Kathi women who made *toran*, *chakla* and *dandia* (sticks used in dance) and more recently, it has been adopted by the Rabaris, Ahirs and other groups in Kachchh. Rabaris make beaded *dhabak* (large protective discs worn over their temples by little girls), necklaces, pot stands known as *indhoni*, children's toys, and ceremonial objects such as bead-covered coconuts used in worship and the sword sheaths worn by bridegrooms.

Notes

1   Forbes Watson, J., *The Textile Manufactures and Costumes of the People of India*, London: Wm. Allen and Co, p. 6.

2   See Nanavati, J.M., M.P. Vora and M.A. Dhaky, *The Embroidery and Bead Work of Kutch and Saurashtra*, Baroda: Government of Gujarat; Elson, V.C., *Dowries from Kutch*, Los Angeles: University of California; Fisher, N., ed., *Mud, Mirror and Thread*, Ahmedabad: Mapin Publishing Pvt Ltd.

3   Postans, M., *Cutch or Random Sketches Taken During a Residence in One of the Northern Provinces of Western India*, New Delhi: Asian Educational Services, p. 175.

4   The embroidery of both pieces is worked in coloured silks and *kusha* grass—sacred to the Jains—on a cotton ground and both include representations of sixteen female deities known as *Vidyadevis*. One piece is held at the Calico Museum of Textiles, Ahmedabad, for details see Irwin and Hall, p. xiv; the other piece was part of the A.E.D.T.A. (Association for the Study and Documentation of Asian Textiles) Collection, which is now known as the Riboud Collection and held at Musée Guimet in Paris. For discussion of this piece, see Berinstein, V. 'An Early Jain Embroidery', in Riboud, K., ed., *In Quest of Themes and Skills —Asian Textiles*, Bombay: Marg Publications, pp. 2–3.

5   Quoted in Irwin, J. (1951), *Indian Embroidery*, London: HMSO, p. 3.

6   Irwin, J. and Margaret Hall (1973), *Indian Embroideries*, Ahmedabad: Calico Museum, p. 1.

7   Yule, H. and Henri Cordier, trans., *The Book of Ser Marco Polo*, vol.2, Delhi: Munshiram Manoharlal Publishers Pvt Ltd, p. 394.

8   Duarte Barbosa and Linschoten quoted in Irwin and Hall, pp. 2–3.

9   Levey, S. (1998), *Elizabethan Treasures. The Hardwick Hall Textiles*, London: National Trust, pp. 28–29. The Ashburnham hangings were divided between the V&A, the Calico Museum at Ahmedabad and the Museum of Fine Arts, Boston.

10 Irwin and Hall, p. 29.

11 See Nanda, R., *Kamaladevi Chattopahdyaya. A Biography*, New Delhi: Oxford University Press, pp. 123–158.

12 For discussion of the development of the trade in dowry embroideries, see Tarlo, E., 'The Genesis and Growth of Business Community: A Case Study of the Vaghri Street Traders in Ahmedabad', in Cadène, P. and Denis Vidal, eds., *Webs of Trade. Dynamics of Business Communities in Western India*, New Delhi: Manohar Publishers, pp. 53–84.

13 Hamilton, A., *New Account of the East Indies*, vol. 1, London: Argonaut Press, p. 86.

14 Irwin and Hall, p. 29.

15 Crill, R. (1999), *Indian Embroidery*, London: V&A Publications, p. 8.

16 Crill, p. 8.

17 Bernier quoted in Irwin and Hall, pp. 5–6.

18 Blochmann, H., trans., *The Ain-i-Akbari*, vol. 1, Delhi: Low Price Publications, p. 94.

19 Bernier quoted in Irwin and Hall, p. 6.

20 For an outline of contemporary metal work techniques including *badla* and *muko* (*mukesh*), see Morrell, A., *Badla, Kamdani or Mukesh—A Metal Work Embroidery Technique in India*, Monograph Folder Series No. 1, Ahmedabad: Calico Museum of Textiles.

21 Personal communication, Kaushikbhai Patel, *jariwala*, 29.4.97.

22 Nanavati et al, pp. 11–12.

23 Nanavati et al, p. 19.

24 Kumar, R., *Costumes and Textiles of Royal India*, London: Christie's Books Ltd, p. 67.

25 See Dhruv, J., 'Untouched: Textile Heirlooms of the Family of the Diwan of Kachchh', *Embroidery*, vol. 53 (May 2002), pp. 25–27.

26 Postans, p. 175.

27 Personal communication, Jethalal and Pushpaben Jhansari Chauhan, Mochi, 11.8.03.

28 For a discussion of the significance of the turban, see Cohn, B.S., 'Cloth, Clothes and Colonialism. India in the Nineteenth Century' in Annette B. Weiner and Jane Schneider, eds., *Cloth and Human Experience*, Washington and London: Smithsonian Institution Press, pp. 303–353.

29 The painted form of *pichhwai* is better known, for which the town of Nathadwara in southern Rajasthan, also the site of the Shrinathji shrine, is the principal centre of production.

30 and 31 Personal communication, Jethalal Jhansari Chauhan, 11.8.03.

32 See Masselos, J. (n.d.), 'The Artist as Patron: Women's Embroidery in Gujarat', *Popular Art in Asia: The People as Patrons*. Working Papers No. 1, Sydney: The University of Sydney Centre for Asian Studies, p. 47 #1; Irwin, J. and Babette Hanish, 'Notes on the Use of the Hook in Indian Embroidery', *The Bulletin of the Needle and Bobbin Club*, vol. 53, nos. 1 and 2, p. 5.

33 Lynton, L., *The Sari*, London: Thames and Hudson, p. 151.

34 The Crafts and Commerce in pre-Independence India exhibition held at the Crafts Museum, New Delhi in 2007, displayed examples of sari borders for the Parsi market manufactured in Krefeld, Germany, using a mechanised jacquard loom; the embroidered effect was achieved by use of supplementary warps. These were exported to India and to the UK where there was also a Parsi community.

35 Personal communication, Poopliben, Mutwa embroiderer, 21.8.03.

36 Personal communication, Arjanbhai Rabari, Dhebaria council member, 21.6.97. For further discussion of the Dhebaria embroidery ban, see Edwards, E., 'Marriage and Dowry Customs of the Rabari of Kutch: Evolving Traditions', in Foster, H.B. and Donald C. Johnson, eds., *Wedding Dress Across Cultures*, Oxford and New York: Berg, pp. 67–84.

37 Personal communication, Poopliben, Mutwa embroiderer, 21.8.03.

38 Nanavati et al, p. 19.

39 Tarlo, E., *Clothing Matters. Dress and Identity in India*, London: Hurst and Co Ltd, pp. 202–283.

40 For details of these non-governmental organisations, see: http://shrujan.org; KMVS (Kutch Mahila Vikas Sangathan) via http://craftrevivalimpact.com; http://www.kala-raksha.org.

41 Paine, S., *Embroidered Textiles. Traditional Patterns from Five Continents*, London: Thames and Hudson, p. 132.

42 Bayly, C.A., 'The Origins of *Swadeshi* (Home Industry): Cloth and Indian Society, 1700–1930', in Appadurai, A., ed., *The Social Life of Things. Commodities in Cultural Perspective*, Cambridge: Cambridge University Press, p. 291.

43 For a description of glass-blowing at Kapadvanj, see Rivers, V.Z., 'Kaleidoscopic Images', *The India Magazine*, vol. 13 (May 1993), no. 6, pp. 6–15.

44 There are various ways of stitching mirrors to fabric, see Morrell, A., *The Techniques of Indian Embroidery*, London: B.T. Batsford Ltd, pp. 75–95.

45 Masselos, p. 35.

46 Crill, p. 12.

47 Personal communication, Poopliben, Mutwa embroiderer, 21.8.03.

48 Hitkari, S.S., *Ganesha-Sthapana. The Folk Art of Gujarat*, New Delhi: Phulkari Publications, pp. 23–32.

49 Ormsby Stoddard, P., *Ralli Quilts. Traditional Textiles from Pakistan and India*, Atglen, Pennsylvania: Schiffer Publishing Ltd, p. 33.

50 Personal communication, Gelamir, *barot*, 16.1.98.

51 Cohen, S., 'Textiles, Dress, and Attire as Depicted in the Albums', in Wright, E., ed., *Muraqqá. Imperial Mughal Albums*, Alexandria, Virginia: Art Services International, p. 181.

52 Irwin and Hall, p. 118.

53 Irwin and Hall, pp. 124–125.

54 For a discussion of the manufacture and trade in beads, see Sciama, L.D., 'Gender in the Making, Trading and Uses of Beads: An Introductory Essay', in Sciama, L.D. and Joanne Eicher, eds., *Beads and Bead Makers. Gender, Material Culture and Meaning*, Oxford and New York: Berg, pp. 1–45.

55 Crabtree, C. and Pam Stallebrass, *Beadwork. A World Guide*, London: Thames and Hudson, p. 111.

6   Craft Development and Entrepreneurship

This chapter identifies several initiatives taken by state agencies, NGOs, entrepreneurs and artisans that address the problem of how to make the production of handcrafted textiles relevant and viable in the modern, industrialised state of Gujarat. As the preceding chapters reveal, in contemporary Gujarat the local market for block-prints, tie-dyes, woven silk, woollen and cotton textiles and the home production of embroidery has greatly diminished since synthetic alternatives have become available in the past forty years. Many people now prefer synthetic fabrics because they are brightly coloured, easy to maintain and cheap. Similarly braids, sequins and other manufactured embellishments have numerous points of appeal: they are far less labour-intensive than embroidery which as women enter the wage labour market they no longer have time for, and they are more modern compared to embroidery which is increasingly seen as old-fashioned. These shifts in taste were made possible by advancements in textile technology, most notably the polyester boom of the 1950s, which occurred as part of the rapid industrialisation of Gujarat after independence in 1947. If industrialisation has widened the range of fabrics available in the state, then urbanisation and modernisation have impacted on the popular styles of dress by bringing disparate communities into closer contact and introducing diverse influences such as television, soap operas, popular Hindi films and the internet into previously remote areas. In rural districts such as Kachchh, for instance, although women's dress is still predominantly a three-part ensemble of drawstring skirt, bodice and veilcloth there is now widespread use of Western dress by men, and pan-Indian garments such as the *salwar kamiz* have been adopted by some women, despite the problems these garments present in conservative communities, an issue discussed earlier.

Thanks to early attention by Gandhi and others at the beginning of the twentieth century, the precarious state of handcrafted textiles was a charged political issue by the time of Indian independence. Indeed, Jawaharlal Nehru the first prime minister of independent India (in office from 1947–1964) remarked that 'the history of India may well be written with textiles as its leading motif.'[1] Crafts thus became an area of focus in the development of modern India. Crafts represented something intrinsically Indian; revitalised they would create employment compatible with a society that was still largely agrarian, generating increased exports and stimulating economic growth.[2] Thus, after independence, Nehru introduced a series of five-year plans both to effect the rapid industrialisation of all sectors of production and to preserve crafts and revive artisanal production. As part of this new attention to crafts development, a slew of institutions emerged after 1947. At the national level these included: the All India Handicrafts Board (AIHB) which was founded in 1952 to co-ordinate craft development across the subcontinent, preserving traditional artisanry and creating new markets for craft products. The same decade saw the founding of the National Handicrafts and Handlooms Museum (better known as the Crafts Museum) at New Delhi, likewise dedicated to preserving the country's craft traditions.[3]

A plethora of organisations was also established at state level that directly affected the craft sector; in Gujarat these included private cultural institutions, educational institutions, state agencies and non-governmental organisations (NGOs). Among the private cultural foundations of note are the Calico Museum of Textiles, Ahmedabad, which opened in 1949 and which houses a world-renowned collection of historic Indian textiles; the Shreyas Folk Museum, established in Ahmedabad in 1977, which displays the popular arts and crafts of Gujarat; and the TAPI (Textiles and Art of the People of India) Collection of Textiles at Surat which is supported by Garden Silk Mills Limited.[4]

In the education sector, the National Institute of Design (NID) was inaugurated in 1961 at Paldi in Ahmedabad to provide design education, producing professional designers who would shape the material and visual culture of independent India and take Indian products to the world. In 1986, the National Institute of Fashion Technology (NIFT) was founded at Gandhinagar to train designers for the nation's burgeoning fashion industry.[5] The state crafts agency— the Gujarat State Handicrafts and Handlooms Development Corporation (GSHDC) and its retail outlet, Gurjari—were founded at Ahmedabad in 1973, entrusted with 'making handicrafts marketable and preserving the traditionality of these crafts.'[6]

Among the non-governmental organisations (NGOs) working in the craft sector in Gujarat are: the Shrujan Trust which was set up in 1968–69 and works with women in Kachchh and north Gujarat; the trade union SEWA (Self Employed

Women's Association) which is based in Ahmedabad (registered in 1972) and organises poor, self-employed women throughout Gujarat; Kutch Mahila Vikas Sangathan (KMVS) which works to uplift rural women— including twelve hundred craftswomen—and was established in Kachchh in 1989;[7] Kala Raksha, a trust 'dedicated to the preservation of traditional arts' which was set up in Kachchh in 1993 and which founded the Kala Raksha Vidhyalaya in 2005 to provide design education for traditional artisans.[8]

Apart from interventions in the craft sector by state agencies and others, entrepreneurs have also created new opportunities for craftspeople. Gujaratis— not least the craftspeople themselves—are known for their mercantile flair, and entrepreneurship has also contributed to the regeneration of handicrafts and handlooms in the post-colonial era. A number of local companies have set out to adapt traditional handmade textiles for contemporary applications in furnishings, fashion and accessories aimed at urban clients in India and overseas, providing sustainable markets for the craftspeople with whom they collaborate. Notable among these are: Bandhej, Rajka Designs and Honeycomb International, all based in Ahmedabad.[9]

It is apparent that there are many different kinds of organisations currently working in craft development in Gujarat and the variety of initiatives launched in the period since independence is considerable. Therefore the organisations and individuals highlighted in this chapter have been chosen to represent three distinct categories: a state organisation, an NGO, and an entrepreneur. They have also been selected because they pioneered new ways of working in textiles and crafts which have proven to be successful over several decades, resulting in sustainable livelihoods for the craftspeople involved and contributing to the preservation of traditional crafts. But the role of the artisans in these successful ventures should not be underestimated. They are equal partners in each collaboration, contributing unique skills and expertise, besides which they are powerful advocates for the relevance of craft in modern India as an aspect of cultural heritage as well as a source of income.

GSHDC, NID AND THE BLOCK-PRINTERS OF DHAMADKA

In the mid-1970s, GSHDC initiated a state-wide scheme to regenerate the state's moribund crafts working in conjunction with NID to develop new products that would be marketed and sold in the commercial centre of Ahmedabad at the

FIG 6.1 | FACING PAGE
Khatri Mohammad Siddik carving a printing block, Dhamadka, Kachchh

Gurjari shop. NID faculty and other professional designers spent time in the workshops of village weavers, dyers, printers, leatherworkers, wood carvers and embroiderers to understand the nature of production, assess how particular crafts might be adapted for contemporary applications and collaborate with individual artisans to develop new products aimed at urban consumers. One of the communities targeted was the Khatris who were known for their work as dyers and block-printers. In the village of Dhamadka in east Kachchh, the GSHDC found a willing participant in the late Khatri Mohammad Siddik.

From the 1950s onward, like most Khatri dyers, Mohammad Siddik had used chemical dyes; unlike many of his peers, however, he also retained a passion for the older practice of natural dyeing. Already aware that the only way to sustain his craft was to find a new clientele, he had determined to specialise in block-prints dyed with colours derived from plants and minerals and to revive production of handmade *ajrakh* which his forebears had supplied to the cattle-herders of Banni for several generations. Knowledge of dyeing was central to his identity as a Khatri, a legacy to be nurtured and passed on to his three young sons, Razzak, Ismail and Jabbar, then barely teenagers. In an interview with Professor Jyotindra Jain, former director of the National Crafts Museum, he described this essential link: 'As I savour the alum on my tongue, my eyes visualize the corresponding shade of red. The son of a Khatri can never get a girl in marriage until he passes this test of being able to judge the right proportions of ingredients by using his senses and not gadgets'.[10] The collaboration with GSHDC and NID was to be transformative; it provided him with the opportunity to develop his business, to revive the use of natural dyes and to restore the status of *ajrakh*. As he summed it up, 'Allah smiled at me and changed things.'[11]

With the help of professional designers, Mohammad Siddik and his family adapted the designs of *ajrakh* and other block-prints for bedspreads, table cloths and cushion covers, suitable for a modernising society. As the second son, Ismail Khatri recalled: 'When I was about 14 or 15 we did some Gurjari work... some NID students and their teachers came here to use our cloth for fashion design and soft furnishings. Those people would live in our home for a few days and they enjoyed our hospitality... I was interested in looking at the new [modern] world'.[12] The products sold well at Gurjari and at the exhibition-cum-sales organised in New Delhi and other metropolitan centres. These events connected artisans directly with potential customers and thus stimulated further business opportunities. As a result of this exposure, Mohammad Siddik attracted international attention and his small workshop at Dhamadka drew design historians, dyers, designers, textile collectors and entrepreneurs alike—the business flourished and the village became a tourist destination for anyone interested in handicrafts. Mohammad Siddik was in demand to give demonstrations of his craft in India and around the globe and to contribute his wisdom to ongoing debates about craft development in India, serving on the advisory panels of several organisations. His own skill in printing earned him the honour of a National Craft Award in 1981.

As his business expanded, Mohammad Siddik hired local workers to help his sons with dyeing and printing, creating jobs in an area of Gujarat with limited employment opportunities. At the time of his death in 1999, his sons inherited the largest block-printing concern in Kachchh which employed fourteen workers in addition to members of the extended family. Moreover the company's success had demonstrated the commercial viability of natural dyes, with the result that an increasing number of dyers and printers in Kachchh have since started using vegetable dyes for at least a part of their production. Acknowledging Mohammad Siddik's influence, M.B. Khatri, whose family produces tie-dyed textiles in Bhuj, also identified the rise of 'green consumption' among foreign customers as crucial to sustaining the craft: 'Our cultural demand was satisfied with the chemical dyes. But gradually, environmentally, people from Western countries started clamouring for vegetable dyes... Mohammadbhai Siddik—he, I think, revived these vegetable dyes... And then his sons also started doing [the] same thing. But the main hurdle was demand. Demand was not so much in our local market because people were not aware of this danger [of chemical dyes].'[13]

Mohammad Siddik's sons, Razzak, Ismail and Jabbar, have continued to develop the company, diversifying from their staple fabric, cotton, to include wool and silk, and developing a range of scarves and shawls. While a greater

FIG 6.2 | RIGHT

Interior of Gamthiwala Cloth Centre at Manek Chowk, Ahmedabad

This family business specialises in block-printed fabrics dyed with natural colours. Their collaborations with the block-printers and dyers of western India have proved fruitful, commercially and in terms of promoting the region's rich culture of cloth.

FIG 6.3 | ABOVE

Cloth merchant Ahmedbhai Shaikh of Gamthiwala with a sample book developed in conjunction with the Khatris of Dhamadka

This is one of a series of sample books assembled to illustrate the range of designs and colourways available as block-printed yardage.

proportion of their goods are exported to foreign clients—Maiwa Handprints based in Vancouver, Canada, is their largest client—one of their most fruitful collaborations has been with the Gamthiwala Cloth Centre at Manek Chowk in Ahmedabad, a retailer and wholesaler that specialises in block-printed textiles dyed with natural colours. Working with Ahmedbhai Shaikh they have developed *ajrakh* yardage, expanding the traditional palette from blue/red/black to include all permutations offered by the natural dyes available to them.[14] Expanding the business brought new challenges. Foreign clients expected year-round production which was difficult as much of the work was carried out in the open and production necessarily ceased during the monsoon season. Many customers also wanted a range of plain fabrics to co-ordinate with the patterned prints and demanded a high level of quality control; some dyes, such as black and yellow, which were daubed onto cloth with a rag produced uneven results which had previously been concealed in the highly-patterned prints but were unacceptably blotchy as a plain colour. The demands of the export market especially prompted the Khatris to expand their range of products and to devise new techniques; moreover the environmental concerns of their clients prompted them to embrace eco-friendly production. In this regard, following the disaster of the Gujarat earthquake in 2001 which devastated Dhamadka, much of the Khatris' production has moved to a new village, Ajrakhpur, where the village planning includes a common water treatment plant that when installed will re-use water five times before finally releasing it for use in agricultural irrigation. In addition, Razzak, Ismail and Jabbar are gradually increasing their use of organic cotton and silk.[15] In many respects, the evolution of Mohammad Siddik and Co. has embodied much that the GSHDC aimed to achieve: it combines an historic craft with a sustainable business that is internationally renowned both as an expression of Indian culture and as a producer and exporter of contemporary commodities.

'THREADS OF LIFE': THE SHRUJAN TRUST AND EMBROIDERY

The Shrujan Trust has been in the vanguard of NGO activity in the craft sector in Gujarat for over forty years. Originally set up by Chandaben Shroff in 1968–69 as part of a drought relief programme in Kachchh run by the Ram Krishna Mission, Shrujan is a grassroots organisation that has tackled rural poverty by channelling local women's embroidery skills—honed by making dowry items—into the production of commercial embroidery. It has offered a viable alternative to women whose choices were limited to either the hard labour of road-digging under government drought relief schemes known as 'scarcity work', or selling dowry embroidery. Local women often preferred the latter, as one local embroiderer explained: 'Selling embroidery was like winning the lottery; we got lots of money for it without doing hard labour. We used it for our homes and our cattle'.[16] These sales—typified as 'distress sales' or 'hardship sales' by NGOs—left the material culture of Kachchh depleted. As Shrujan has developed, its work has expanded from providing income generation to preserving cultural heritage and conserving local embroidery. An archive of regional styles of embroidery has been established at the Shrujan Design Centre at Bhujodi village (eight kilometres from Bhuj, the district capital) and a travelling archive known as the 'Design Centre on Wheels' goes out to villages as a source of reference and inspiration for the embroiderers. Women have been encouraged to revive stitches that had fallen into disuse, although not always with total conviction as indicated in the use of the term *dukhi kam* (lit. 'painful work') applied to some of the minute interlacing stitches for which the Banni area of northern Kachchh was noted.

Over the past forty years, Shrujan has generated sustainable employment for thousands of local women and has engaged them in an active programme of capacity building; as a result the women have developed into accomplished professional artisans. The work is organised to accommodate social conventions such as *purdah* and the women's domestic responsibilities, notably child care and fetching water which can take several hours a day, thus most embroiderers work at home. At the outset, the women embroidered borders for saris which sold by word-of-mouth and at private sales held in the homes of Shrujan trustees, chiefly in Mumbai. Shrujan now produces a varied range of fashion items, including saris, skirts, shirts, *kurtas*, *salwar kamiz* and shawls; soft furnishings such as throws, cushion covers and bedspreads; and accessories including purses, bags, binders, mobile phone covers; and most recently—art panels. Chandaben Shroff has been active as a designer since Shrujan's inception, working closely with gifted local artisan-designers and aided by Shrujan trustee, Kirit Dave, a professional architect and designer. Product development, distribution of embroidery materials, tailoring, finishing, quality control and marketing are handled through the Design Centre which also has an exhibition space and retail outlet. The goods are promoted on-line as well as being marketed through exhibitions and sales throughout India.

For the women, their professional status brings them respect, not least because of their earning capacity. For the craft, local perceptions have changed from seeing embroidery as a domestic 'time-pass' (hobby) to appreciating its considerable commercial potential. The income from embroidery has enabled the women to build *pukka* (strong) homes, educate their children and buy health care when they need it. In the challenging environment of Kachchh, Shrujan's motto, 'threads of life', is apt.[17]

BANDHEJ AND CONTEMPORARY DESIGN

The design company Bandhej (Hindi for 'tie-dye') was started in the early 1980s by Archana Shah, a graduate of NID who had specialised in textiles. The first Bandhej shop opened in Ahmedabad in 1985 and there is now a chain of eight shops across India. The company retails stylish contemporary fashions—

FOLLOWING PAGES

FIG 6.4 | LEFT

Workshop run by the Shrujan Trust with embroiderers in Kachchh

Shrujan has an ongoing programme of workshops to train local women as commercial embroiderers and to upgrade the skills of those who already work for the trust.

FIG 6.5 | RIGHT

Ahir women at a training workshop for embroiderers run by the Shrujan Trust, Kachchh

including accessories and jewellery, soft furnishings, ceramics and some furniture. It works with hundreds of artisans in Gujarat and other parts of India, harnessing traditional crafts such as tie-dyeing, block-printing and embroidery to a contemporary design sensibility to produce goods that are relevant and appealing to urban consumers. At the time of its inception, Bandhej was unique. As Archana Shah puts it, 'People were still trying to find out what direction design should take and what design was all about and in what context one would use it in India. So of course there was no concept of fashion—there was no such thing in India.' Studying at NID was a formative experience for Shah:

> '…Just before Gurjari was set up, the director there decided to give NID this project in terms of how you deal with various crafts of Kachchh; how do you produce products that would then be sold in urban areas? …I spent fifteen days with Mohammad Siddik doing prints… It was all terribly new. Although one lived in India, one didn't realise the richness there was in our traditional textiles. We'd been to the Calico Museum but [did] not really see people using these things in daily life. The Calico Museum had just one kind of textiles which is more the classical style—the textiles of the rich. … It was a very exciting journey for me and I decided that this was what interested me and I would like to continue.'[18]

From the outset the challenge for Bandhej has been to reconcile fashion's demand for innovation each season with the artisan's need for sustainable work. Over the past twenty-five years, the company has established enduring relationships with particular artisans based on an understanding of the possibilities and limitations of the craft and the craftsperson. As Archana Shah recounts:

> 'I firmly believe that by observing it [the craft process] one comes to understand… you start thinking and imagining that just by twisting here, changing it a little there, adding a little, the [new] product emerges… They [traditional artisans] have to start to understand the very basic difference between craft for the [general urban] market and craft which has always been done for a particular market. For example, Mohammadbhai's family [Mohammad Siddik, block-printer] always did [work] for *somebody*. He knew it was for Rabaris, or Jats, or whomever.'[19]

The company has been committed to improving the quality of craft techniques and to providing continuous work for the craftspeople with whom it has

FIG 6.6

Detail of tie-dyed woollen coat made by Bandhej, Ahmedabad

This company harnesses the region's craft skills and gives it a contemporary design sensibility to produce a fashion range and products for interiors.

Private collection

worked; it has seen the rise of a new generation of craftspeople *au fait* with contemporary design. In its endeavour to marry craft and contemporary fashion with an Indian sensibility, Bandhej has been a catalyst in securing a viable future for several hundred Indian artisans.

CONCLUSION

In the examples illustrated above, the overlapping histories of different types of initiatives in the handicrafts and handlooms sector are apparent. The narrative of a single textile craft, indeed of a single craftsman—that of block-printing and Khatri Mohammad Siddik—reveals some of the ramifications of the GSHDC's craft development policy; it also shows how these aligned with the educational and developmental imperatives of NID, and the entrepreneurial aims of Bandhej and the Gamthiwala Cloth Centre. The examples chosen illuminate remarkable and enduring achievements by committed people. Inevitably, there are also many examples of crafts that have not flourished despite similar interventions. For example, the craft of *roghan* painting in Kachchh has failed to find a sustainable market niche, in spite of input from the GSHDC and the expertise, energy and advocacy of master craftsman, Abdul Gafur Daud. Similarly, the *patola* weavers of Patan struggle against the odds to sustain their exquisite craft despite global recognition for this unique textile. Their market has shrunk to a handful of clients and since the 1950s, popular understanding of what constitutes a *patolu* has been formed by cheaper imitations such as the so-called "*patola*" developed in Rajkot, originally as part of a government training scheme. The backing of government agencies and others, with professional design input allied to the expertise of the craftspeople, then, is no simple guarantee of success. Therefore, successes should be celebrated where they occur. The handmade textiles discussed in this book lie at the intersection of culture and commerce, embodying something distinctively Indian yet with global appeal. But their relevance to the modern material world and their survival rests on the ability—demonstrated through successive epochs—of Gujarati artisans to adapt to changing circumstances and new markets.

Notes

1 Quoted in Kumar, R., *Costumes and Textiles of Royal India*, London: Christie's Books, p. 81.

2 McGowan, A., *Crafting the Nation in Colonial India*, New York: Palgrave Macmillan, p. 189.

3 For a discussion of the Crafts Museum, see Greenough, P., 'Nation, Economy and Tradition Displayed. The Indian Crafts Museum, New Delhi', in Carol A. Breckenridge, ed., *Consuming Modernity: Public Culture in a South Asian World*, Minneapolis and London: University of Minnesota, pp. 216–248.

4 The Calico Museum is supported by the Sarabhai Foundation and was named after the Calico Mill, one of the earliest textile mills to be established in Ahmedabad (1880). See http://www.calicomuseum.com. For further information on the Shreyas Folk Museum, see Jain, J., *Folk Art and Culture of Gujarat. Guide to the Collection of the Shreyas Folk Museum of Gujarat*, Ahmedabad: Bodhi Press. For information on the TAPI Collection, see http://www.tapicollection.com.

5 NID's marketing slogan is 'Designed in India, Made for the World'. For further information, see: http://www.nid/edu.

6 GSHDC (n.d.), *A Note on the Working of the Gujarat State Handicrafts Development Corporation Limited*, Gandhinagar: GSHDC, p. 2.

7 See: http://www.craftrevivalimpact.com.

8 See: http://www.kala-raksha.org.

9 For information on Bandhej, see: http://www.bandhej.com; Rajka: http://www.rajka.com.

10 Jain, J., 'The Implicit and the Manifest in Indian Folk Art and Mythology', in Nora Fisher, ed., *Mud, Mirror and Thread. Folk Traditions of Rural India*, Ahmedabad: Mapin Publishing Pvt Ltd, p. 47.

11 Personal communication, Khatri Mohammad Siddik, 14.9.97.

12 Personal communication, Ismail Khatri, 10.1.01.

13 Personal communication, M.B. Khatri, 7.12.06.

14 For a discussion of the development of Mohammad Siddik and Co., see Edwards, E.M., 'Contemporary Production and Transmission of Resist-Dyed and Block-Printed Textiles in Kachchh District, Gujarat', *Textile: The Journal of Cloth and Culture*, vol. 3, no. 2, pp. 168–189. For information on Maiwa Handprints, see: http://www.maiwa.com.

15 Personal communication, Ismail Khatri, 30.11.06.

16 Personal communication, Sariyaben, embroiderer, 23.8.03.

17 Personal communication, Chandaben Shroff and Kirit Dave, 12.7.02. For information on the Shrujan Trust, see: http://shrujan.org.

18 Personal communication, Archana Shah, 22.11.03.

19 Personal communication, Archana Shah, 22.11.03.

Appendix
Garment Analysis

In this appendix the construction of a selection of garments illustrated in use and discussed in the main text is analysed. The drawings are based on garments held in the collection at the Victoria and Albert Museum, London. Although the drawings are intended to show representative styles of dress in Gujarat, the Museum number is indicated to enable interested readers to access these garments at the V&A or through the V&A website.

ILLUSTRATION 1.

Man's robe (*angarkha*) of Ahmedabadi brocade, lined with silk and decorated with zardozi embroidery at neck.

See pp. 2–3.

V&A: 05648 IS

Front View

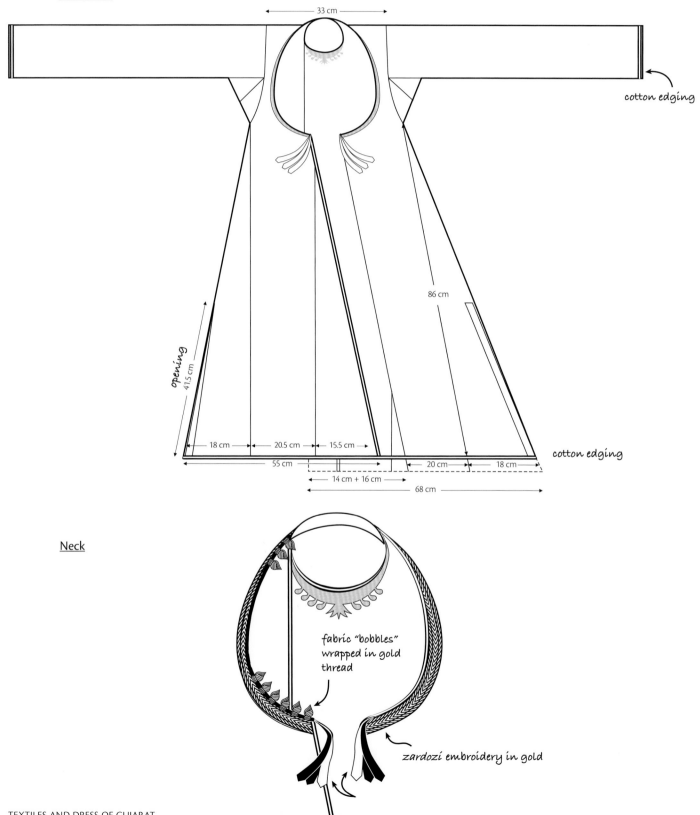

33 cm

cotton edging

opening
41.5 cm

86 cm

18 cm

20.5 cm

15.5 cm

55 cm

20 cm

18 cm

cotton edging

14 cm + 16 cm

68 cm

Neck

fabric "bobbles"
wrapped in gold
thread

zardozi embroidery in gold

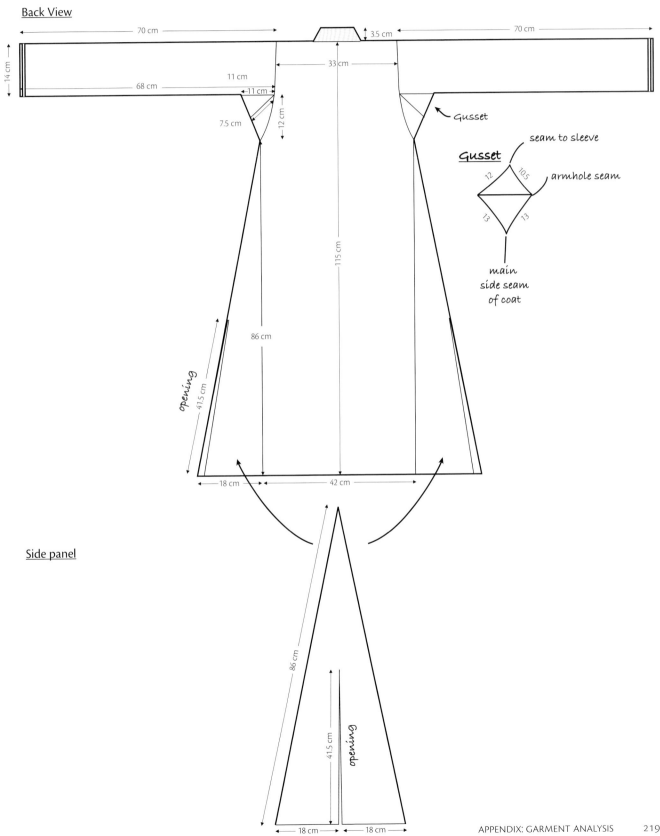

70 cm

3.5 cm

70 cm

14 cm

33 cm

11 cm

68 cm

11 cm

7.5 cm

12 cm

Gusset

seam to sleeve

Gusset

12

10.5

armhole seam

13

13

main
side seam
of coat

115 cm

86 cm

opening

41.5 cm

18 cm

42 cm

Side panel

86 cm

41.5 cm

opening

18 cm

18 cm

ILLUSTRATION 2. Dhebaria Rabari man's smock (*kediyun*) of heavy white cotton with hand embroidery on yoke.

See fig. 2.48.

V&A: IS 145-2007

Front View

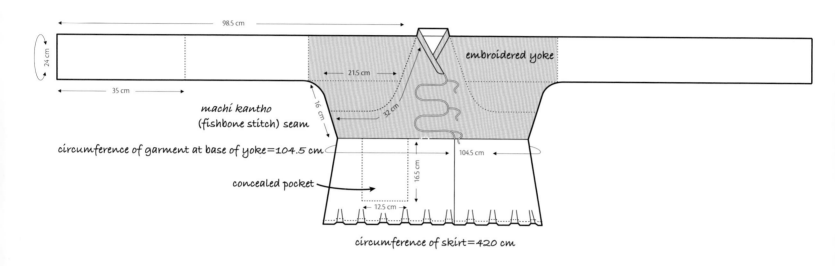

98.5 cm

24 cm

35 cm

21.5 cm

embroidered yoke

16 cm

machi kantho (fishbone stitch) seam

32 cm

circumference of garment at base of yoke=104.5 cm

104.5 cm

concealed pocket

16.5 cm

12.5 cm

circumference of skirt=420 cm

Back View

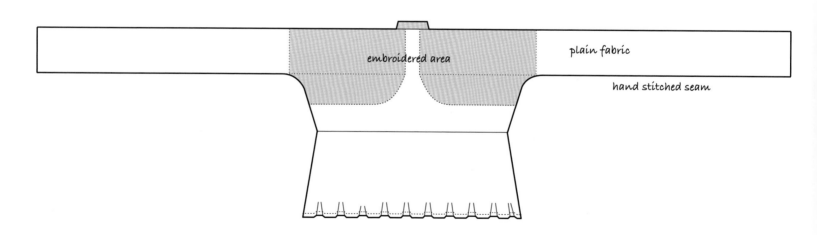

embroidered area

plain fabric

hand stitched seam

ILLUSTRATION 3.

Vagadia Rabari child's smock
(*jhuli/jhurdi*) of white cotton with hand
embroidery on yoke.

A comparable example is illustrated in fig. 2.49.

V&A: IS 7-2008

<u>Front View</u>

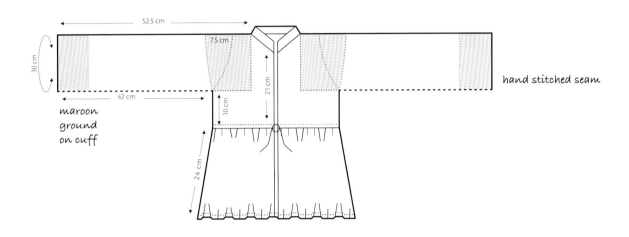

hand stitched seam

maroon
ground
on cuff

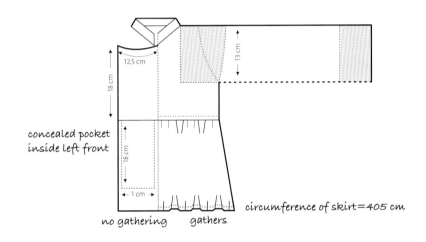

concealed pocket
inside left front

circumference of skirt = 405 cm

no gathering   gathers

<u>Back View</u>

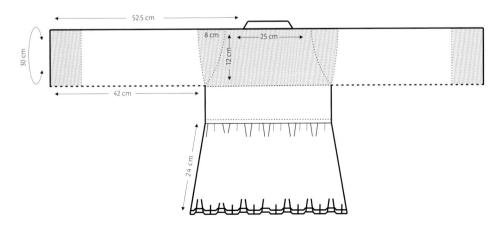

ILLUSTRATION 4.

Woman's dress (*aba*) of tie-dyed
silk from Kachchh, decorated with
embroidery and mirrorwork.

See fig. 4.13.

V&A: Circ. 817-1912

Front View

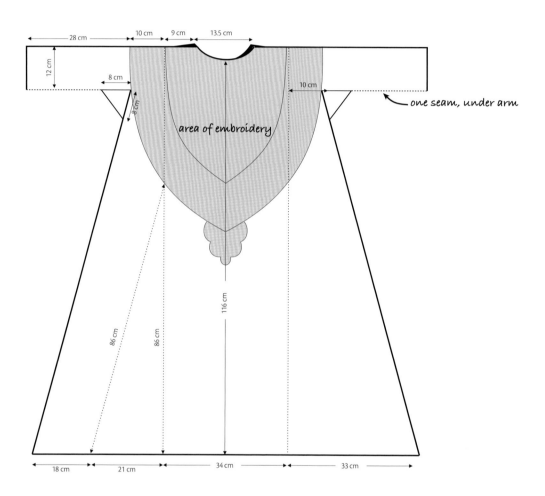

28 cm — 10 cm — 9 cm — 13.5 cm

12 cm

8 cm

10 cm

8 cm

one seam, under arm

area of embroidery

116 cm

86 cm 86 cm

18 cm — 21 cm — 34 cm — 33 cm

Back View

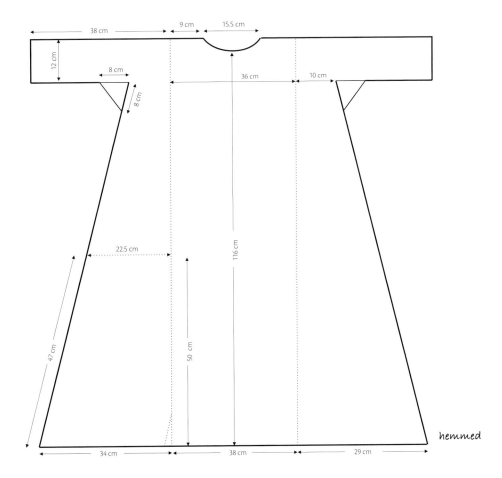

ILLUSTRATION 5. | Girl's blouse of *gajji* silk with cotton gussets under arms, decorated with embroidery and mirrorwork.

A comparable style of garment is illustrated in fig. 3.4.

V&A: IS 26-1957

Front View

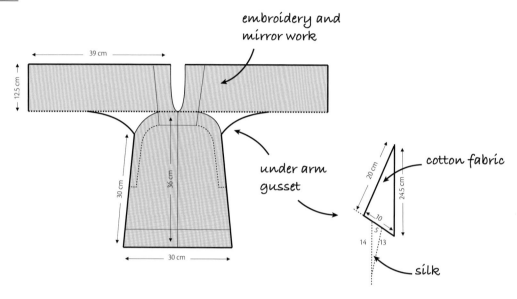

embroidery and mirror work

under arm gusset

cotton fabric

silk

39 cm

12.5 cm

30 cm

36 cm

30 cm

20 cm

24.5 cm

10

5

14   13

Back View

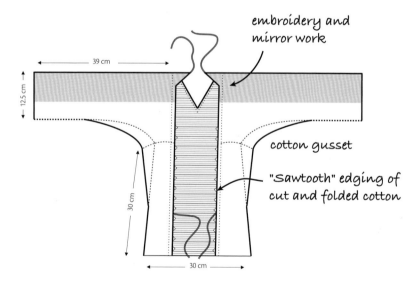

embroidery and mirror work

cotton gusset

"Sawtooth" edging of cut and folded cotton

39 cm

12.5 cm

30 cm

30 cm

ILLUSTRATION 6.

Vagadia Rabari blouse (*kamkho*) of silk (?) decorated with applique, embroidery and mirrorwork. Back of sleeves, lining and gusset are cotton.

A comparable example is illustrated in fig. 5.36.

V&A: IS 143-2007

Front View

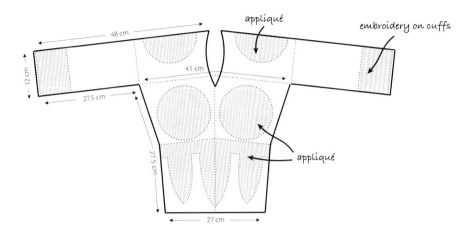

Back View

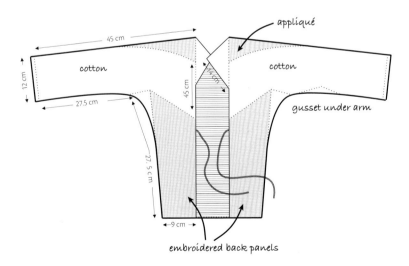

ILLUSTRATION 7.

Dhebaria Rabari blouse (*kanchali*) of tie-dyed *gajji* silk with embroidery and shirt buttons decorating the stomach panel (*pait*) and brocade cuffs.

See fig. 5.44.

V&A: IS 144-2007

Front View

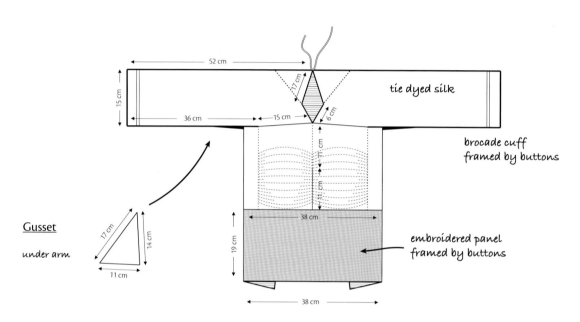

Gusset

under arm

Back View

Neck

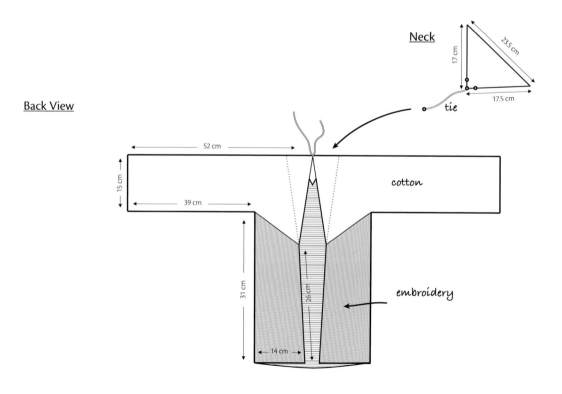

tie dyed silk

brocade cuff framed by buttons

embroidered panel framed by buttons

tie

cotton

embroidery

ILLUSTRATION 8. Short silk blouse decorated with embroidery.

V&A: 34-1893 IS

<u>Front View</u>

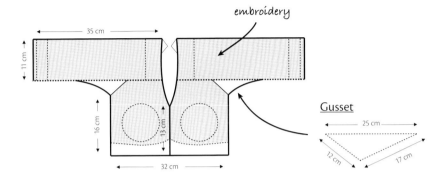

embroidery

35 cm

11 cm

16 cm

13 cm

32 cm

<u>Gusset</u>

25 cm

12 cm

17 cm

<u>Back View</u>

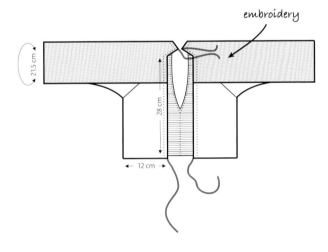

embroidery

21.5 cm

28 cm

12 cm

ILLUSTRATION 9. Meghwal child's tunic of silk with embroidery and mirrorwork.

V&A: IS 33-1957

Front View

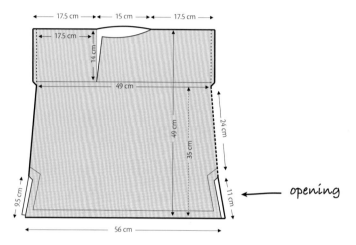

Back View

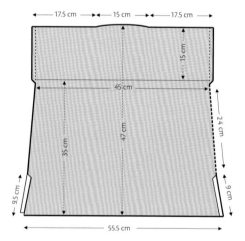

ILLUSTRATION 10.

Trousers (*churidar*) decorated with metalwork embroidery around the ankle cuff.

A comparable style of garment is illustrated in fig. 2.50.

V&A: IS 31-1981

Front View

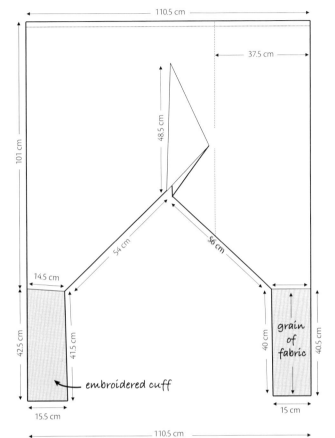

110.5 cm

3cm turnover hand hemmed
to provide channel for drawstring

37.5 cm

48.5 cm

101 cm

54 cm

56 cm

14.5 cm

42.5 cm

41.5 cm

40 cm

grain
of
fabric

40.5 cm

embroidered cuff

Total lenth of leg (outside) = 142

15.5 cm

15 cm

Back View

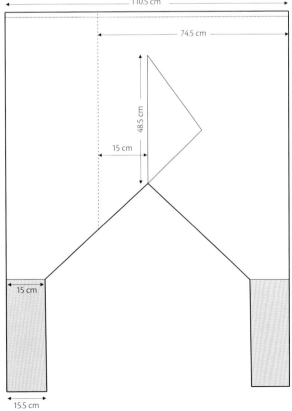

110.5 cm

74.5 cm

48.5 cm

15 cm

15 cm

15.5 cm

Gusset

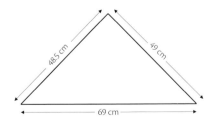

48.5 cm

49 cm

69 cm

ILLUSTRATION 11. Satin pyjama/*salwar* decorated with hand embroidery and mirrorwork. The yoke area is plain; the fabric is embroidered with a spot design from yoke to ankle, ending in a cuff of dense mirrorwork embroidery.

A section of comparable style of garment is illustrated in fig 2.53.

V&A: IM 239-1920

Front View

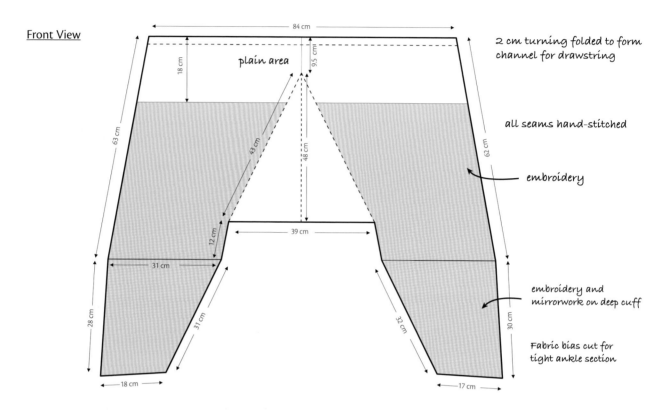

84 cm
2 cm turning folded to form channel for drawstring
18 cm
plain area
9.5 cm
63 cm
all seams hand-stitched
43 cm
48 cm
62 cm
embroidery
12 cm
39 cm
31 cm
28 cm
31 cm
32 cm
embroidery and mirrorwork on deep cuff
30 cm
Fabric bias cut for tight ankle section
18 cm
17 cm

Back View

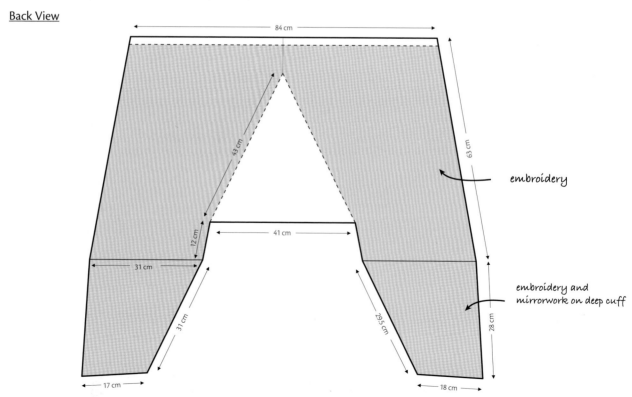

84 cm
43 cm
63 cm
embroidery
12 cm
41 cm
31 cm
embroidery and mirrorwork on deep cuff
31 cm
29.5 cm
28 cm
17 cm
18 cm

ILLUSTRATION 12.

Ahir drawstring trousers (*vajani*) for a child. The cotton ground is covered in hand embroidery and mirrorwork from the yoke, which is plain, to the ankle cuff which ends in several rows of machine stitching.

Comparable examples are illustrated in fig. 2.54.

V&A: IS 147-2007

Front View

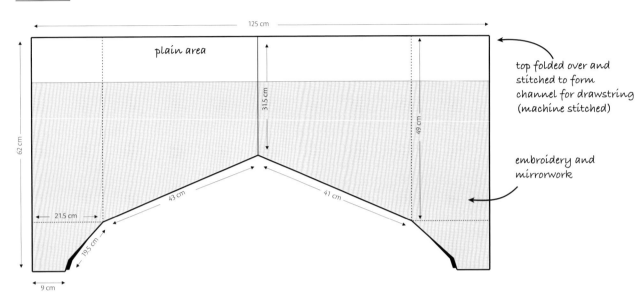

plain area

125 cm

62 cm

31.5 cm

49 cm

21.5 cm

43 cm

41 cm

19.5 cm

9 cm

top folded over and stitched to form channel for drawstring (machine stitched)

embroidery and mirrorwork

Back View

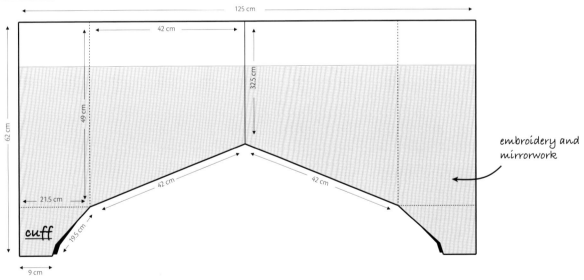

125 cm

42 cm

62 cm

49 cm

32.5 cm

21.5 cm

42 cm

42 cm

19.5 cm

cuff

9 cm

embroidery and mirrorwork

Cuff

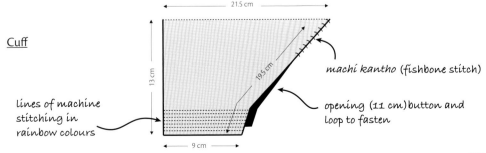

21.5 cm

13 cm

19.5 cm

9 cm

machi kantho (fishbone stitch)

lines of machine stitching in rainbow colours

opening (11 cm) button and loop to fasten

ILLUSTRATION 13.

Wide-legged drawstring trousers (pyjama/*ejar*) of silk.
All seams are stitched by hand.

A comparable part of trousers is illustrated in fig. 2.59.

V&A: 8338/4592

Front View (measurements same on back as front)

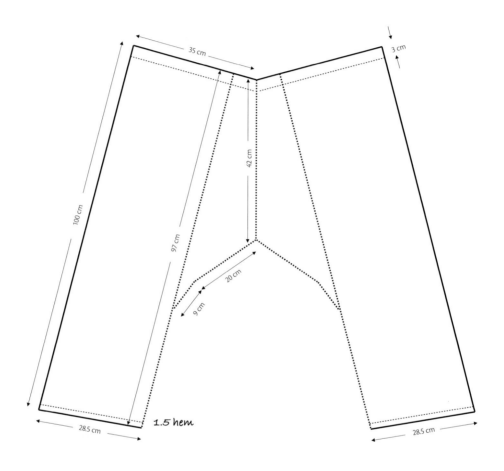

35 cm

3 cm

100 cm

97 cm

42 cm

20 cm

9 cm

1.5 hem

28.5 cm

28.5 cm

Gusset

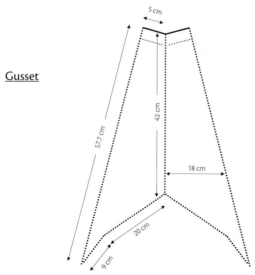

5 cm

57.7 cm

42 cm

18 cm

20 cm

9 cm

ILLUSTRATION 14.

Women's silk salwar with waistband rather than drawstring, decorated with machine stitching at waist and on ankle cuffs.

A comparable garment is illustrated in fig. 3.16.

V&A: IS 22-1995

Front View (measurements same on back as front)

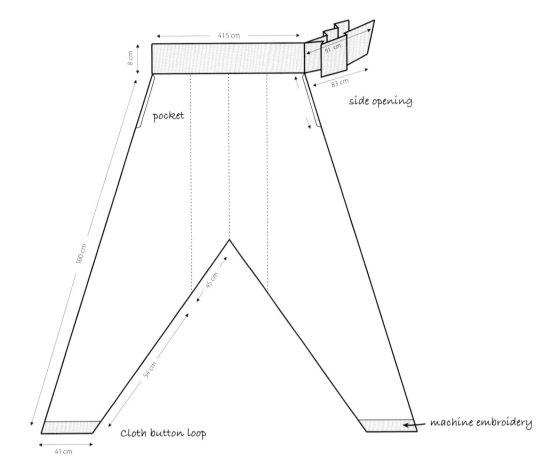

41.5 cm

8 cm

91 cm

83 cm

side opening

pocket

100 cm

45 cm

54 cm

machine embroidery

Cloth button loop

41 cm

ILLUSTRATION 15.

Drawstring skirt of *gajji* silk with Mochi (hook) embroidery from yoke to hem.

See p. 8.

V&A: IM 246-1920

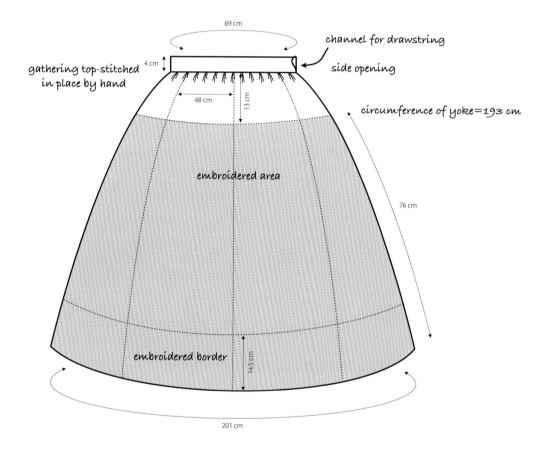

gathering top-stitched in place by hand

69 cm

4 cm

channel for drawstring

side opening

48 cm

13 cm

circumference of yoke=193 cm

embroidered area

76 cm

embroidered border

14.5 cm

201 cm

ILLUSTRATION 16.

Ahir drawstring skirt of handspun handwoven cotton gathered on a yoke and decorated with hand embroidery and mirrorwork from yoke to hem.

A comparable skirt is illustrated in fig. 5.38.

V&A: IS 146-2007

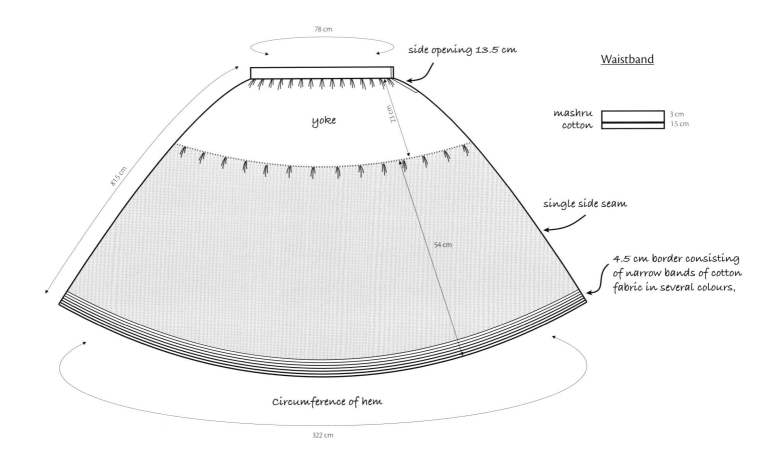

78 cm

side opening 13.5 cm

Waistband

yoke

23 cm

mashru
cotton

3 cm
1.5 cm

81.5 cm

single side seam

54 cm

4.5 cm border consisting
of narrow bands of cotton
fabric in several colours.

Circumference of hem

322 cm

ILLUSTRATION 17. Dhebaria Rabari child's hat (*toplo*) decorated with beadwork and passementerie.

V&A: IS 151-2005

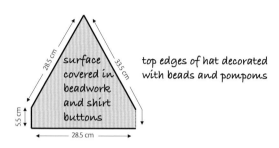

surface covered in beadwork and shirt buttons

28.5 cm   33.5 cm   5.5 cm   28.5 cm

top edges of hat decorated with beads and pompoms

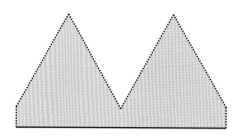

ILLUSTRATION 18. Kanbi child's silk hat (*toplo*) from Kachchh. All-over embroidery in silk. Seams and edges are hand-stitched.

V&A: IS 151-1960

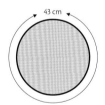

43 cm

11.5 cm   5 cm   12.5 cm

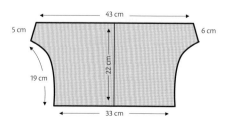

43 cm   5 cm   6 cm   22 cm   19 cm   33 cm

Glossary

Note: *Most of the terms listed are Gujarati; a few are Sanskrit or Hindi, or they are derived from other Asian languages—these are indicated in brackets after the word.*

A

aba, abo: tunic-like dress worn by Muslim women over *ejar* (trousers)

abhla: mirror pieces used in embroidery

abhla bharat: mirrorwork embroidery

Ahir: caste of Hindu pastoralists and farmers who claim to be descendants of Krishna

ajrakh: a resist- and mordant-dyed cotton textile that is block-printed on both sides of the cloth and features the use of indigo and madder. The term is possibly derived from *azrak*, the Arabic for blue.

angarkha (Hindi): a full-skirted, long coat with full sleeves for men. Usually open at the chest and tied in front or to one side with an inner flap.

angavastram (Sanskrit/Hindi): shawl or stole often given as a mark of distinction or merit

angoti: embroidered front panel on a Jat woman's dress (*churi*)

anu: ceremonial departure of a woman after marriage to her conjugal home

ari: embroidery hook, refined version of a cobbler's awl

ari bharat: embroidery executed with an *ari*, worked chiefly in chain stitch

Ashavali: heavy silk textiles with areas of brocade

atariyun: saddle cloth for a camel; usually decorated with appliqué and embroidery by Rabaris

B

badla: flat metallic wire, often silver-gilt, used in brocades and embroidery

bafta (Persian): plain red and blue dyed cotton fabric

baloya: heavy ivory bangles worn by married women

bandhani: tie-dyeing. A resist-dyeing technique whereby a pattern is created by tying small areas of cloth to create a barrier from the dye.

Banushali: caste of Hindu farmers who live mainly in western Kachchh. According to oral history, they are descended from the sun god, Surya.

bhajan: Hindu devotional song

bharat kam: embroidery

Bharwad: caste of Hindu pastoralists (shepherds), living mainly in Saurashtra

bhungri: large dome-shaped earring, gilded or silver and crowning the top of the ear, worn by Vagadia Rabari bridegrooms. Usually worn with two other earrings, *oganiya* and *toriya*.

bhuvo: shaman

bindi: dot. The term is used for the dots in tie-dyed designs, also for the red dot worn on the forehead by Hindu women.

burqa: all-enveloping, often all-black garment worn by some Muslim women

buti: small floral motif

C

chador/chaddar: shawl, wrap or veilcloth

chakla: pair of square embroidered textiles hung on the wall facing the threshold of a home

chandrokhani: tie-dyed silk veilcloth usually black and red worn by Khatri brides

chaupad: ancient board game that is still popular. The board, usually made of cloth, is cruciform and each 'arm' has eight squares. The game is played with counters and many objects and materials have been used for this purpose, including cowrie shells, semi-precious stones, marble, wood and dried animal droppings.

chintz: hand-drawn, mordant- and resist-dyed cotton fabric. Possibly derived from the north Indian word *chint*, meaning to sprinkle or to spray.

Chhipa: caste of textile printers who are said to have come from Rajasthan originally. The name is derived from *chhapana* (Hindi) for printing. See also *rangrez* and *neelgar*.

chinai: lit. 'Chinese'. Also refers to a type of embroidery that was worked in silk by Chinese embroiderers based in Surat, chiefly for Parsi clients.

choli: short blouse worn with a sari

chorni: voluminous, drawstring trousers that are tight from the knee down

chundadi: woman's veilcloth, often tie-dyed

churi: long kaftan-like dress with embroidered front panel worn by Jat women

churidar: trousers that are loose at the top and tight around the calf with gathering at the ankle

D

dabu: mud used as a resist in printing textiles

dadki: quilt

Dalit (Hindi): lit. 'oppressed'. Term for communities formerly known as 'untouchables'.

dandia-ras: popular form of dance performed in a circle using decorated sticks known as *dandia*. The circle of people rotates in time to the music

darji: tailor

desi (Hindi): local, indigenous

dhablo: shoulder cloth; also blanket

dharaniyo: appliqué textile hanging that covers stored quilts

dhoti (Hindi): usually ankle-length man's garment, worn draped and tucked

dupatta (Hindi): scarf usually worn with a *salwar kamiz*

E

ejar: loose trousers worn by Muslim women under tunics known as *aba*

F

farman (Persian): textile cover for imperial (Mughal) correspondence

G

gajji: satin made from imported Chinese silk

ganga-yamuna: type of *kinkhab* that features gold and silver thread. The term derives from two of the great rivers of India, the Ganga and the Yamuna

gara: sari with Chinese embroidery used by Parsi women

ghagra or *ghagro*: heavily gathered drawstring skirt, formerly often made from *khadi*

gharcholu: lit. 'house dress'. Tie-dyed cotton sari or veilcloth worn by brides, particularly among the Hindu and Jain merchant communities of Gujarat

ghunghat: veiling

godiya: decorative ankle band worn by a camel

gorbandh: trapping worn about the neck of a camel

gunthani: wooden needle used in ply-split braiding

gyana baji: games boards painted on cloth that were a forerunner of the modern game of snakes and ladders

H

Haliputra: clan of Muslim cattle herders who live in the Banni area of north Kachchh

hansali: silver necklace, often of twisted silver wire, worn by Jats and other communities in Kachchh

harde: myrobalan (Latin: *Terminalia chebula*). The fruit is a good source of tannin which is used in dyeing

Harijan (Hindi): lit. 'children of god'. Term used by Mahatma Gandhi to describe communities formerly known as 'untouchables'

Hingorja: clan of Muslim cattle herders who live in the Banni area of north Kachchh

I

ikat (Indonesian): resist-dyeing process whereby designs are reserved in the warp or weft threads by tying small bundles of yarn with cotton or other materials to prevent penetration of the dye. The term is derived from *mengikat*, meaning to tie or to bind

J

jala: drawloom

jali: screen of carved wood or stone

jama: man's coat

janoi: 'sacred thread' ceremony that marks the coming of age for Brahmin boys

jari: metallic thread. Flattened gold or silver wire wrapped around a silk core. Synthetic versions made from plastic and rayon are now widely used

Jat: In Gujarat, Muslim herders who live in the north and west of Kachchh. They are divided into three subgroups: Dhanetah, Garasia and Fakirani. According to oral tradition they originally lived in an area called Halaf, somewhere in the region of Iran and Iraq

jhul: trapping for an ox, often decorated with appliqué and embroidery

K

kadla: silver anklets worn by Rabari men and women, and other rural communities

kajal: black cosmetic used to protect and enhance the eyes, also known as *kohl*

kalam: pen

kamiz (Persian): tunic worn by women usually with *salwar* trousers

kamkho: bodice completely covered with embroidery

Kanbi: caste of Hindu farmers

kanchali: embroidered bodice with sleeves

Kanudo: ceremony enacted by Rabaris and others to mark the birth of Krishna. Dialect term for baby Krishna.

kapadu: backless blouse

karkhana: imperial workshop

kediyun: man's smock worn by pastoralists and farmers in Gujarat

khadi: handwoven cloth made from handspun yarn

Khatri: a merchant caste that originated in the Punjab. It has been suggested that their name is a corruption of Kshatriya (warrior caste) and that they are Rajputs. In Gujarat, they are better known as dyers and block-printers.

khesado: black and white checked shoulder cloth used by Rabari men in Kachchh, known as *khes* in Sindh

khurji: small bag made for carrying food and other items by Rabaris. It is usually made from camel hair and goat hair, or wool or cotton, using the technique of ply-split braiding.

kinkhab (Persian): brocade fabric that often features gold or silver thread. Also anglicized as *kincob*.

kors: border of chinai embroidery for saris worn by Parsi women

kurta: knee-length tunic

kusha: kind of grass believed to have sacred properties

kutab: appliqué. The term is probably derived from the English 'cut up'.

L

lac: a red dye made from the insect *coccus lacca*. The term is derived from *lakh* (Hindi/Gujarati) meaning a hundred thousand and is said to refer to the number of insects required for dyeing.

laheriya (Hindi): lit. 'waves', tie-dyed patterns in stripes or zig-zags

laj: lit. 'shame', veiling for modesty.

lungi (Hindi): men's sarong-like garment, often cloth stitched into a tube that is draped and tucked; sometimes hitched up to knee length.

M

maa' (Indonesian): ceremonial cloths believed to possess magical power in Indonesia

maharaja/maharana/maharao: titles accorded to India's princes. From *maha* (Hindi) meaning great and *raja, rana, rao*, or prince. The wife of a prince was referred to as *maharani*.

makhmal (Hindi/Urdu from Arabic): velvet

maldhari: cattle herder from Banni, north Gujarat

mashru (Arabic): lit. 'permitted by Islamic law'. A warp-faced fabric (satin) made with a silk warp and a cotton weft. Developed to circumvent the proscription for Muslim men from wearing pure silk.

mata-ni-pachedi: 'cloth of the Mother Goddess'. Votive textile that is drawn, painted and dyed by Vagharis.

mata-no-chandarvo: 'canopy of the Mother Goddess'. Votive textile that is drawn, painted and dyed by Vagharis.

Meghwal: Dalit community of leatherworkers

mela: fair, usually associated with a religious observance

minakari (Persian): lit. 'enamelling'. The term is sometimes used for *ajrakh* that has been printed and dyed at least twice to achieve particularly deep tones of blue and red.

Mochi: shoemakers' caste, also professional embroiderers

mojdi: handmade leather shoes

moorka: bridle or halter for a camel

mulmul: fine cotton, muslin

Mutwa: clan of Muslim cattle herders who live in the Banni area of north Kachchh

N

naksha (Persian): pattern or design; also drawloom

naksha bandha: skilled draughtsman who transfers designs for weaving from paper to the drawloom

namda: felt rug or floor covering

neelgar: Muslim Chhipas, or *rangrez*, who specialise in indigo dyeing. Term derived from *neel* (Hindi), meaning blue.

Node: clan of Muslim cattle herders who live in the Banni area of north Kachchh

O

odhani (Hindi): large veilcloth that covers the head and wraps the body

ojjal: seclusion of women

P

pachedi: large shawl or blanket worn by Bharwads and other rural communities

pagdi: turban

pallav (Hindi): decorative end panel of a sari

panchanga: lit. 'five limbs'. Calendars used by Hindu astrologers to determine auspicious timings for events and the dates of festivals; painted in pigments on cloth.

panetar: white silk sari with red tie-dyed designs customarily worn under a *gharcholu* by brides from Hindu and Jain merchant castes in Gujarat

pan vel: creeper design, often used as a border pattern in textiles

Parsi: A member of Zoroastrian religion from Persia who fled to Gujarat to escape religious persecution

pasli: ritual of purification and prayer undergone by a bridegroom prior to his wedding

pata: sacred hangings used in Jain temples that feature cosmic diagrams and drawings of pilgrimage sites. Painted in pigment on cloth.

Patel: caste of farmers in Gujarat; they are also associated with the diamond and *jari* trade in Surat and are known for their entrepreneurial flair around the world.

patka: waist sash worn by men, cummerbund

patolu (pl. *patola*): double ikat silk textile dyed with natural colours

pha gujarat (Thai): *saudagiri* prints exported from Gujarat to Thailand

pha surat (Thai): *saudagiri* prints exported from Surat to Thailand

phenta: turban made of glazed printed cotton on a wickerwork base worn by Parsis

phera: part of wedding ceremony in which a Hindu bride and groom circumambulate the sacred flame

phulkari (Hindi/Punjabi): lit. 'flower work'. Style of embroidered veilcloth made by women in the Punjab as part of a dowry. The embroidery was worked chiefly in satin stitch using silk floss and covered much of the ground fabric which was *khadi*, of a red-brown colour, or occasionally indigo blue.

pichhwai: temple hangings of the Vallabhacharya sect that depict Krishna as Shrinathji; their production is particularly associated with Nathadwara in southern Rajasthan.

prasad: sweets, nuts, etc., that have been blessed by a deity, distributed to devotees at religious ceremonies and to wedding guests

purdah (Persian): lit. curtain or veil. Refers to the seclusion of women

pyjama: loose drawstring trousers worn by both men and women

R

Rabari: caste of Hindu pastoral nomads in north-west India. In Gujarat they divide into several subgroups, the names of which mostly reflect the geographical area in which they live. In Kachchh district there are three subgroups: Kachhi, Dhebaria and Vagadia; in Saurashtra district there are seven, including Bhopa, Machhukatha, Jhalawadi, Panchali, Vadhiyara, Gohilwadi and Sorathi; and Patanwadis in north Gujarat.

rangrez: Chhipa printers who converted to Islam. Term is derived from *rang* (Hindi/Gujarati) for colour.

Raisiputra: clan of Muslim cattle herders who live in the Banni area of north Kachchh

roghan: lit. 'resin'. Textiles decorated with a design drawn by hand in a paste made from boiled castor oil and pigments.

rumal: square head-covering worn by men

S

sadla or *sadlo*: half-sari which wraps around the body and over the head; used for veiling face and body.

Salvi: The Salvi family at Patan, belonging to the Jain caste, are renowned for weaving *patola*.

salwar (Persian): loose trousers customarily worn with a *kamiz* and *dupatta* by women

Sameja: clan of Muslim cattle herders who live in the Banni area of north Kachchh

Samma: clan of Muslim cattle herders who live in the Banni area of north Kachchh

sariya: decorative knee band for a camel

saudagiri: block-printed cottons made by Chhipas for export to Thailand between the mid-nineteenth and mid-twentieth century. From *sauda* or 'trade goods' (Persian).

sharam: (lit. shame) used referring to modesty or shyness

sherwani (Hindi): long coat worn by men, usually collarless *shibori*: Japanese technique of resist dyeing

Shrinathji: Krishna in the form of a royal child. Shrinathji is worshipped by followers of the Pushti Marg ('the path of grace'), founded in the fifteenth century by Vallabhacharya. The shrine at Nathadwara in southern Rajasthan is a pilgrimage site.

suf: kind of embroidery featuring triangles worked in fine satin stitch

Sumra: clan of Muslim cattle herders who live in the Banni area of north Kachchh

swadeshi (Hindi): lit. 'of own country', home produce

T

tanchoi: textile featuring silk extra weft decoration on a silk ground of plain or satin weave

tang: decorative camel girth

tek bavaliyo: embroidery design that has alternating mirrors (*tek*) and a motif worked in an interlacing stitch (*bavaliyo*) based on the thorny acacia (*baval*). Made by Rabaris, and others in Kachchh.

tigudi: large embroidered discs, usually 5 or 7 in number, embroidered along the centre seam of a Rabari veilcloth.

tiraz (Arabic): factory or large workshop.

topi/toplo: hat or cap

toran: auspicious hanging with pennants above the threshold of a house

tritik (Malay): resist dyeing technique whereby a pattern is produced by stitching the fabric to reserve it from penetration of the dye.

V

Vaghari: caste who give their original calling as hunting but pursue many occupations in Gujarat, including work as itinerant vegetable sellers, traders in second-hand clothes and embroideries, and tattooists. In Ahmedabad, they are known for making *mata-ni-pachedi* and *mata-no-chandarvo*.

vahana: vehicle of a Hindu deity, usually an animal

vajani: voluminous trousers gathered on a cuff at the ankle worn by males in Kachchh and Saurashtra, often heavily embroidered

varna: Refers to the traditional Hindu social hierarchy delineated in the Vedas, according to which society is divided into four hereditary groups or *varnas*: Brahmins (priests); Kshatriyas (rulers, administrators and soldiers); Vaishyas (merchants); and Shudras (farmers, craftspeople and labourers). Commonly known as the caste system, each *varna* subdivides into numerous subcastes.

vaastu puja: Hindu ritual to purify and bless a house or new building

Veda (Sanskrit): lit. 'sacred knowledge'. Ancient Hindu scriptures, especially four collections called the *Rig Veda*, *Sama Veda*, *Yajur Veda* and *Artharva Veda*. The earliest of these, the *Rig Veda*, is thought to have attained its extant form around 1500-1000 BCE.

Z

zardozi: elaborate designs worked in gold and silver metal threads couched onto satin and velvet with metallic threads.

Bibliography

Allami, Abu' l-Fazl (1989)[1927-49], *The Ain-i-Akbari*, 2 vols. (English translation by H. Blochmann), Delhi: Low Price Publications.

Agrawal, Y. (2003), *Silk Brocades*, New Delhi: Roli Books.

Alkazi, R. (2008)[1983], *Medieval Indian Costume*, New Delhi: Art Heritage.

Ambalal, A. (1987), *Krishna as Shrinathji. Rajasthani Paintings from Nathdvara*, Ahmedabad: Mapin Publishing Pvt Ltd.

Anjaria, J., Minoo Parabia, Gauri Bhatt and Ripal Khamar (1997), *Nature Heals. A Glossary of Selected Indigenous Medicinal Plants of India*, Ahmedabad: Sristi Innovations.

Archambault, M. (n.d.), *Blockprinted Fabrics of Gujarat for Export to Siam: An Encounter with Mr Maneklal T. Gajjar*, no publication details.

Askari, N. and Rosemary Crill (1997), *Colours of the Indus. Costume and Textiles of Pakistan*, London: Merrell Holberton Publishers Ltd in association with the Victoria and Albert Museum.

Balfour-Paul, J. (1998), *Indigo*, London: British Museum Press.

Banerjee, M. and Daniel Miller (2003), *The Sari*, Oxford and New York: Berg.

Barbosa, D. (1918), *Livro de Duarte Barbosa*, translated by M. Longworth Dames, London: Hakluyt Society.

Barnes, R. (1993), *Indian Block-Printed Cotton Fragments in the Kelsey Museum, The University of Michigan*, Ann Arbor: The University of Michigan Press.

_____*Newberry Collection in the Ashmolean Museum, Oxford*, vols. I and II, Oxford: Oxford University Press.

Bauer, M., Bernard Imhasly and Christian Schmidt (n.d.), *Khadi —Textile of India*, no place of publication: Volkart Foundation.

Bayly, C. A. (1986), 'The Origins of *Swadeshi* (Home Industry): Cloth and Indian Society, 1700-1930', in Arjun Appadurai, ed., *The Social Life of Things*, Cambridge: Cambridge University Press.

Bayly, S. (2002)[1999], *Caste, Society and Politics in India. From the 18th Century to the Modern Age*, Cambridge: Cambridge University Press.

Bean, S. (1989), 'Gandhi and *Khadi*, the Fabric of Indian Independence', in Weiner, A. B. and Jane Schneider, eds., *Cloth and Human Experience*, Washington and London: Smithsonian Institution Press.

Beech, S. R., C. A. Farnfield, P. Whorton and J. A. Wilkins, eds., (1986), *Textile Terms and Definitions. Eighth Edition*, Manchester: The Textile Institute.

Behl, B.K. (2005)[1998], *The Ajanta Caves. Ancient Paintings of Buddhist India*, London: Thames and Hudson.

Berinstein, V. 'An Early Jain Embroidery', in Krishna Riboud, ed. (1989), *In Quest of Themes and Skills—Asian Textiles*, Marg, Vol. XL, no. 3.

Bhandari, V. (2004), *Costume, Textiles and Jewellery of India. Traditions in Rajasthan*, New Delhi: Prakash Books India (P) Ltd.

Bilgrami, N. (1990), *Sindh jo Ajrak*, Karachi: Department of Culture and Tourism, Government of Sindh.

Bostock, J. and H.T. Riley, trans., (1857), *The Natural History of Pliny. VI*, London: Henry G. Bohn.

Bühler, A., Eberhard Fischer and Marie-Louise Nabholz (1980), *Indian Tie-Dyed Fabrics*, Ahmedabad: Calico Museum of Textiles.

Bühler, A. and Eberhard Fischer (1979), *The Patola of Gujarat*, 2 vols., Basle: Museum of Ethnography and the Rock Foundation, New York.

Burnard, J. (1994), *Chintz and Cotton. India's Textile Gift to the World*, Kenthurst NSW: Kangaroo Press Ltd.

Burton, R. (1999), *Vision and Accident. The Story of the Victoria and Albert Museum*, London: V&A Publications.

Burton-Page, J., 'Historical Context', in Michell, G. and Snehal Shah (2003)[1988], *Ahmadabad*, Mumbai: Marg Publications.

Campbell, J.M., ed., (1990) [1899], *Muslim and Parsi Castes and Tribes of Gujarat*, Gurgaon: Vintage Books.

Casson, L. (1989), *The Periplus Maris Erythraei*, Princeton: Princeton University Press.

Chakraverty, A. (2002), *The Master Naqshaband of Banaras Brocades*, Chennai: Crafts Council of India.

Chandra, M. (1961), 'Costumes and Textiles in the Sultanate Period', in *Journal of Indian Textile History*, VI.

_____(1973), *Costumes, Textiles, Cosmetics and Coiffure in Ancient and Medieval India*, Delhi: Oriental Publishers.

Chhaya, T.M. (1970), *Rural Pockets in the Urban Structure*, unpublished diploma dissertation, Ahmedabad: School of Architecture.

Cohen, S., 'Textiles, Dress, and Attire as Depicted in the Albums', in Wright, E., ed., (2008), *Muraqqá. Imperial Mughal Albums*, Alexandria, Virginia: Art Services International.

_____(1995), 'A Group of Early Silks. The Tree Motif', in Dhamija, J., ed., *The Woven Silks of India*, Bombay: Marg Publications.

Cohn, B., 'Cloth, Clothes and Colonialism: India in the Nineteenth Century', in Weiner, A. B. and Jane Schneider, eds., (1989), *Cloth and Human Experience*, Washington and London: Smithsonian Institution Press.

Collingwood, P. (1998), *The Techniques of Ply-Split Braiding*, London: Bellew Publishing.

Commissariat, M. S. (1957), *A History of Gujarat with a Survey of its Monuments and Inscriptions, Volume 2, The Mughal Period from 1573 to 1758*, New Delhi and Hyderabad: Orient Longmans.

Crabtree, C. and Pam Stallebrass (2002), *Beadwork. A World Guide*, London: Thames and Hudson.

Crill, R. (2008), *Chintz. Indian Textiles for the West*, London: V&A Publishing.

_____ed., (2006), *Textiles from India. The Global Trade*, Calcutta, London, New York: Seagull Books.

_____(1999), *Indian Embroidery*, London: V&A Publications.

_____(1998), *Indian Ikat Textiles*, London: V&A Publications.

Crill, R. and Steven Cohen (2002), 'Courtly and Urban Textiles', in Barnes, R., Steven Cohen and Rosemary Crill, *Trade Temple and Court. Indian Textiles from the Tapi Collection*, Mumbai: India Book House Pvt Ltd in association with Garden Silk Mills Ltd.

Crooke, W., ed., (1925), *Tavernier's Travels in India*, vols. I and II, trans., Valentine Ball, Oxford: Oxford University Press.

Dalrymple, W. (2007), *The Last Mughal*, London: Bloomsbury Publishing.

Dehejia, V. (2009), *The Body Adorned. Dissolving Boundaries Between Sacred and Profane in India's Art*, New York: Columbia University Press.

Dhamija, J. (2002), *Woven Magic. The Affinity Between Indian and Indonesian Textiles*, Jakarta: Dian Rakyat.

_____ed., (1995), 'Introduction. Woven Silks of India', in *The Woven Silks of India*, Bombay: Marg Publications.

Dhruv, J., 'Untouched: Textile Heirlooms of the Family of the Diwan of Kachchh', in *Embroidery*, vol. 53 (May 2002).

Dumont, L. (1980)[1966], *Homo Hierarchicus. The Caste System and Its Implications*, Chicago and London: University of Chicago Press.

Edwards, E.M. (2010), 'Textiles and Dress Among the Rabari of Kutch', in Simpson, E. and Aparna Kapadia, eds., *The Idea of Gujarat*, London: Orient Blackswan.

_____(2005), 'Contemporary Production and Transmission of Resist-Dyed and Block-Printed Textiles in Kachchh District, Gujarat', *Textile: The Journal of Cloth and Culture*, vol. 3, no. 2.

_____(2005), 'Patterns of Adaptation Among Pastoral Nomads in Gujarat', in *South Asian Studies*, vol. 21.

_____(2003), 'Marriage and Dowry Customs of the Rabari of Kachchh", in Foster, H.B. and Donald C. Johnson, eds., *Wedding Dress Across Cultures*, Oxford and New York: Berg.

_____(2001), 'Textiles and Dress of the Rabari of Kachchh', in *Ars Textrina*.

_____(2001b), 'A Disappearing Craft: Ply-Split Braiding of the Rabari of Kachchh", in Parry, J., Ralph Norman and Ann Norman, eds., *Expanding the Girths*, Oxford: Sagaman.

_____(1998), 'Stitches in Time: The Changing Status of Embroidery Amongst the Rabaris of Kachchh', in *The World of Embroidery*, September, 49 (5).

_____(1996), 'The Vanishing Heritage of the Nomadic Rabaris of Kachchh in North-West India', in *Textiles*, 2.

Elson, V. (1979), *Dowries from Kutch. A Woman's Folk Art Tradition in India*, Los Angeles: University of California Museum of Cultural History.

Enthoven, R.E. (1920), *The Tribes and Castes of Bombay*, vol.1, Bombay: Government of Bombay.

Erikson, J. (1985), *Mata-ni-Pachedi. A Book on the Temple Cloth of the Mother Goddess*, Ahmedabad: National Institute of Design.

Fereday, G. (2003), *Natural Dyes*, London: The British Museum Press.

Field, D. (1996), *In the Street of the Temple Cloth Printers*, Vancouver: Pacific Educational Press.

Fischer, E. and Haku Shah (1970), *Simple Weft Ikat from South Gujarat, India*, Ahmedabad: Calico Museum of Textiles.

Fisher, N., ed., (1993), *Mud, Mirror and Thread. Folk Traditions of Rural India*, Ahmedabad: Mapin Publishing Pvt Ltd.

Forbes Watson, J. (1867), *Textile Manufactures and Costumes of the People of India*, 18 vols., London: Wm. H. Allen and Co.

Foster, W. (1921), *Early Travels in India, 1583-1619*, London: Oxford University Press.

Frater, J. (1995), *Threads of Identity. Embroidery and Adornment of the Nomadic Rabaris*, Ahmedabad: Mapin Publishing Pvt Ltd.

Ghurye, G.S. (1995)[1951], *Indian Costume*, Bombay: Popular Prakashan Pvt Ltd.

Garfield, S. (2000), *Mauve*, London: Faber and Faber.

Gibb, H.A.R., trans., (1997) [1929], *Ibn Battuta. Travels in Asia and Africa, 1325-1354*, New Delhi: Asian Educational Services.

Gillow, J. and Nicholas Barnard (1991), *Traditional Indian Textiles*, London: Thames and Hudson.

Gittinger, M. (1982), *Master Dyers to the World*, Washington D.C.: The Textile Museum.

Goswamy, B.N. (1993), *Indian Costumes*, Ahmedabad: Calico Museum of Textiles.

Greenough, P., 'Nation, Economy and Tradition Displayed. The Indian Crafts Museum, New Delhi', in Carol A. Breckenridge, ed., (1995), *Consuming Modernity: Public Culture in a South Asian World*, Minneapolis and London: University of Minnesota.

Guy, J. (1998), *Woven Cargoes. Indian Textiles in the East*, London: Thames and Hudson.

Hamilton, A. (1930)[1727], *New Account of the East Indies*, 2 vols., London: Argonaut Press.

Hitkari, S.S. (1981), *Ganesha-Sthapana. The Folk Art of Gujarat*, New Delhi: Phulkari Publications.

Irwin, J. (1966), 'Indian Textile Trade in the Seventeenth Century', in John Irwin and Paul Schwartz, eds., (1966), *Studies in Indo-European Textile History*, Ahmedabad: Calico Museum of Textiles.

Irwin, J. (1951), *Indian Embroidery*, London: HMSO.

Irwin, J. and Margaret Hall (1973), *Indian Embroideries. Historic Textiles of India at the Calico Museum*, vol. 2, Ahmedabad: Calico Museum of Textiles.

_____(1971), *Indian Painted and Printed Fabrics. Historic Textiles of India at the Calico Museum*, vol. I, Ahmedabad: Calico Museum of Textiles.

Irwin, J. and Babette Hanish, 'Notes on the Use of the Hook in Indian Embroidery', *The Bulletin of the Needle and Bobbin Club*, vol. 53, nos. 1 and 2 (1970).

Jain, J. (1993), 'The Implicit and the Manifest in Indian Folk Art and Mythology', in Nora Fisher, ed., *Mud, Mirror and Thread. Folk Traditions of Rural India*, Ahmedabad: Mapin Publishing Pvt Ltd in association with Museum of New Mexico Press, Santa Fe.

_____1985), 'Saudagiri Prints. Textiles for Far Off Siam', *The India Magazine*, October 1985.

_____(1980), *Folk Art and Culture of Gujarat. Guide to the Collection of the Shreyas Folk Museum of Gujarat*, Ahmedabad: Bodhi Press.

Johnson, Donald C., 'Pragmatism and Enigmas: The "Panetar" and "Gharcholu" Saris in Gujarati Weddings', in Foster, H.B. and Donald C. Johnson, eds., (2003), *Wedding Dress Across Cultures*, Oxford and New York: Berg.

Kerlogue, F. (2004), *Batik. Design, Style and History*, London: Thames and Hudson.

Kapur Chishti, R. and Rahul Jain (2000), *Handcrafted Indian Textiles*, New Delhi: Roli Books Pvt Ltd.

Kumar, R. (1999), *Costumes and Textiles of Royal India*, London: Christie's Books.

Lalbhai, R. (1995), 'Ashavali Saris of Ahmedabad. Revival of a Technique', in Dhamija, J., ed., *The Woven Silks of India*, Bombay: Marg Publications.

Levey, S. (1998), *Elizabethan Treasures. The Hardwick Hall Textiles*, London: National Trust.

Lynton, L. (2002), *The Sari*. London: Thames and Hudson.

Macauley, G.C., trans., (1890), *Herodotus. The History*, 2 vols., London: Macmillan.

Manucci, N. (1999), *A Pepys of Mogul India (1653-1708)*, New Delhi: Srishti Publishers.

Marshall, J. H. (1973)[1931], *Mohenjo-Daro and the Indus Civilization*, Delhi: Indological Book House.

Masselos, J. (n.d.), 'The Artist as Patron: Women's Embroidery in Gujarat', *Popular Art in Asia: The People as Patrons*. Working Papers No.1, Sydney: The University of Sydney Centre for Asian Studies.

McGowan, A. (2009), *Crafting the Nation in Colonial India*, New York: Palgrave Macmillan.

Michell, G. and Snehal Shah, eds., (2003)[1988], *Ahmadabad*, Mumbai: Marg Publications.

Morrell, A. (1994), *The Techniques of Indian Embroidery*, London: B. T. Batsford Ltd.

Murphy, V. and Rosemary Crill (1991), *Tie-dyed Textiles of India. Tradition and Trade*, London: V&A in association with Mapin Publishing Pvt Ltd.

Nanavati, J.M., M.P. Vora and M.A. Dhaky (1966), *The Embroidery and Bead Work of Kutch and Saurashtra*, Baroda: Government of Gujarat.

Nanda, R. (2002), *Kamaladevi Chattopadhyaya. A Biography*, New Delhi: Oxford University Press.

Ormsby Stoddard, P. (2003), *Ralli Quilts. Traditional Textiles from Pakistan and India*, Atglen, Pennsylvania: Schiffer Publishing Ltd.

Paine, S. (1995), *Embroidered Textiles. Traditional Patterns from Five Continents*, London: Thames and Hudson.

Pandhya, V., 'Hot Scorpions, Sweet Peacocks: Kachchhe Art, Architecture and Action', *Journal of Material Culture*, vol. 3 (1998), no. 1.

Pandya, Y. and Rawal, T., eds., (2002), *The Ahmedabad Chronicle. Imprints of a Millennium*, Ahmedabad: The Vastu Shilpa Foundation.

Parsai, S. (2006), 'Surat as a Centre of the Textile Trade', in Rosemary Crill, ed., *Textiles from India: the Global Trade*, Oxford, New York, Calcutta: Seagull Books.

Pfister, R. (1936), 'Tissus imprimés de l'Inde médiévale', *Revue des Arts Asiatiques*, 10.

_____(1938), *Les Toiles Imprimées de Fostat et l'Hindoustan*, Paris: Les Editions d'Art et d'Histoire.

Postans, M. (2001)[1839], *Cutch; or Random Sketches Taken During a Residence in One of the Northern Provinces of Western India*, New Delhi: Asian Educational Services.

Quick, B. D. and Judith A. Stein (1982), *Ply-Split Camel Girths of West India*, Los Angeles: Museum of Cultural History, University of California.

Rivers, V.Z., 'Kaleidoscopic Images', *The India Magazine*, vol. 13 (May 1993), no. 6.

Sachau, E.C., trans., (1993)[1887], *Alberuni's India*, New Delhi: Low Price Publications.

Sanskriti Kendra (2009), *Sanskriti Museum of Indian Textiles*, New Delhi: Sanskriti Kendra.

Sardar, Z. (1996), 'History of Indian Textiles', in Hatanaka, K., *Textile Arts of India*, San Francisco: Chronicle Books.

Savaijiwala, Y. (2006), *Revival of Saudagiri*, Ahmedabad: Calico Dyeing and Printing Works.

Schwartz, P.R. (1996)[1969], *Printing on Cotton at Ahmedabad, India, in 1678*, Ahmedabad: Calico Museum of Textiles.

Sciama, L.D., 'Gender in the Making, Trading and Uses of Beads: An Introductory Essay', in Sciama, L.D. and Joanne Eicher, eds., (1998), *Beads and Bead Makers. Gender, Material Culture and Meaning*, Oxford and New York: Berg.

Sen, S.N., ed., (1949), *Indian Travels of Thevenot and Careri*, New Delhi: National Archives of India.

Shah, D. (2005), *Masters of the Cloth: Indian Textiles Traded to Distant Shores*, Surat: Garden Silk Mills Ltd.

Shah, H. (n.d.), A Study of the Block Making Techniques of Saudagiri Prints', *Visva-Bharati Quarterly*.

Sharma, D.P. and Madhuri Sharma (2003), *Panorama of Harappan Civilization*, New Delhi: Kaveri Books.

Shukla, P. (2008), *The Grace of Four Moons. Dress, Adornment and the Art of the Body in Modern India*, Bloomington and Indianapolis: Indiana University Press.

Singh, C. (2001) [1979], *Textiles and Costumes from the Maharaja Sawai Man Singh II Museum*, Jaipur: Maharaja Sawai Man Singh II Museum Trust.

Smart, E.S. and Dale C. Gluckman (1989), 'Cloth of Luxury: Velvet in Mughal India', in Krishna Riboud, ed., *In Quest of Themes and Skills—Asian Textiles*, Bombay: Marg Publications.

Smith, J.D. (2005), *The Epic of Pabuji*, New Delhi: Katha.

Srivastava, V.K. (1997), *Religious Renunciation of a Pastoral People*, Delhi: Oxford University Press.

Talwar, K. and Kalyan Krishna (1979), *Indian Pigment Paintings on Cloth*, Ahmedabad: Calico Museum of Textiles.

Tarlo, E., 'The Genesis and Growth of Business Community: A Case Study of the Vaghri Street Traders in Ahmedabad', in Cadene, P. and Denis Vidal, eds., (1997), *Webs of Trade. Dynamics of Business Communities in Western India*, New Delhi: Manohar Publishers.

_____(1996), *Clothing Matters. Dress and Identity in India*, London: Hurst and Co. Ltd.

Temple, R. (1929), *The Itinerary of Ludovico di Varthema of Bologna, 1502-1508*, London: Hakluyt Society.

Templewood, Viscount (1954), *Nine Troubled Years*, London: Collins.

Trivedi, R.K., ed., (1961), *Census of India, Vol VI. Selected Crafts of Gujarat. Bandhani or Tie and Dye Sari of Jamnagar*, Delhi: Government of India.

Varadarajan, L. (1983), *Ajrakh*, Ahmedabad: New Order Book Company.

Varadarajan, L. and Krishna Amin-Patel, (2008), *Of Fibre and Loom. The Indian Tradition*, Ahmedabad and New Delhi: National Institute of Design and Manohar Publishers.

Vogelsang-Eastwood, G. (1990), *The Resist Dyed Textiles from Quseir al-Qadim, Egypt*, Paris: A.E.D.T.A.

Wagoner, P. (1996), ' "Sultan Among Hindu Kings": Dress, Titles and the Islamicization of Hindu Culture at Vijayanagara', in *The Journal of Asian Studies*, vol. 55, no. 4.

Walker, D. (1998), *Flowers Underfoot. Indian Carpets of the Mughal Era*, London: Thames and Hudson.

Watt, G. (1987)[1903], *Indian Art at Delhi*, Delhi: Motilal Banarsidass.

Wheeler, M. (1976)[1968], *The Indus Civilization*, Cambridge: Book Club Associates by arrangement with Cambridge University Press.

Whitcomb, D. S. and Janet H. Johnson (1982), *Quseir al-Qadim 1980*, Malibu: Undena.

Yule, H. and Henri Cordier (1998)[1871], *The Book of Ser Marco Polo*, 2 vols., New Delhi: Munshiram Manoharlal Publishers Pvt Ltd.

Websites consulted

http://www.gardenvareli.com
http://www.ril.com
http://www.kala-raksha.org
http://shrujan.org
http://www.craftrevivalimpact.com
http://www.rajka.com
http://www.bandhej.com
http:www.sewa.org
http://tapicollection.com
http://www.calicomuseum.com

Acknowledgements

I am enormously indebted to many people who have helped me over the years with the research and development of this book. I have enjoyed their warmth, humour and insights and my profound thanks and appreciation go to all those who have collaborated with me along the way.

Two communities in Kachchh district deserve special mention because they have honoured me with their unstinting support for two decades—the Khatris and the Rabaris. My understanding of cloth and dress has been transformed by their expertise and generosity of spirit and I have benefited, too, from their camaraderie and cherish the lasting friendships that have been forged. My heartfelt thanks go to Vanka Kana Rabari and Ramiben, Paba Rabari and family, Kantibhai Ros and family, the staff and students at the Rabari Ashramshala, Anjar, Hirabhai Rabari, Arjanbhai Rabari and family at Kharoi, Arjanbhai and Deviben Rabari and their family at Anjar, Mangalbhai Rabari at Ganeshnagar, the late Mohammad Siddique Khatri and his wife Fatma, Abdulrazzaque and Sakina Khatri, Dr Ismail Khatri and Memuna, Jabbar and Maryam Khatri, and Abduljabbar Khatri at Sidr Craft.

This book has been made possible by the considerable goodwill of craftspeople throughout Gujarat and in other parts of India. They have taken time to discuss their craft, offered me hospitality and in many cases have become good friends. I cherish the time I have spent in workshops throughout the state and I remain in awe of the skills and sense of history that are embodied in the handmade textiles of Gujarat. I am grateful to the following craftspeople for their help: Walaben Rabari, Raniben Rabari, Parmaben Ahir and her daughters, Poopliben, the late Khatri Mohammad Siddique, Abdulrazzaque Khatri, Dr Ismail Khatri, Jabbar Khatri, Abduljabbar Khatri, Husainbhai Khatri, Mansoori Yusuf Umar, Maneklal T. Gajjar, Khatri Ali Mohamed Isha, Khatri Abdul Gafur Daud, Khatri Arab Hasam, Abdulrajak S. Khatri, Khatri Hasam Haroon, Khatri Ibrahim Aboobakar, Umar Ibrahim Khatri, Khatri Abdulla Husen, Vishram Valji Vankar, Shamji Vankar, Bhulabhai Chunilal Chitara, Mohmedsiddique at Kapadvanj, Hari Ballabh and Jugal Kishor Chhipa, Brij Ballabh Udaiwal, R.K. Derawala, Ikramuddin Mohammed Sabir Neelgar, Mahesh Dosaya, Talisetty Mohan, C. Subramanyam, the Salvi family at Patan. I would also like to add to this list three fine tailors; Haribhai Dabhi, Atul Tailor and Valjibhai Darjee who shared their knowledge as well as tea on many occasions.

I have benefited also from the expertise of numerous scholars and the assistance of many institutions, museums and galleries, also non-governmental organisations and businesses. They have not only made material available to me but have been generous with their insights and time as well. My thanks to the following: Dr Abigail McGowan, Professor Anna Dallapiccola, Dr Sonia Ashmore, Professor Jyotindra Jain and Jutta Jain-Neubauer, National Institute of Design, Ahmedabad (Aditi Ranjan and Errol Pires), Anthropological Survey of India (Western Zone), Kachchh Museum (Dr Sadashivan and Umesh Jadia), Calico Museum of Textiles (Giraben Sarabhai and D.S. Mehta), Shreyas Folk Foundation (Leenaben Mangaldas and the late Janaki Dhruv), V&A (especially Rosemary Crill and Liz Miller), Ashmolean Museum (Dr Ruth Barnes), Leicester Museums Service (Emma Martin), Suhas Patel and Ashok Trivedi at Gurjari, Shrujan Trust (Chandaben Shroff and Kirit Dave), Kutch Mahila Vikas Sangathan (Meena Rajput and Pankaj Shah), SEWA (Villoo Mirza and Mona Dave), Craft Revival Trust (Ritu Sethi),

Dastkar (Laila Tyabji), Nazeer Weldingwala and Honeycomb International, Ahmedbhai Shaikh and his brothers at Gamthiwala, Saurashtra Handicraft, Yasin Savaijiwala, Praful and Shilpa Shah and Garden Silk Mills, Archana Shah at Bandhej, Rajshree and Samvit Sarabhai at Rajka, Ashok and Ramesh Chadha at Fabric Ashoka, Charllotte Kwon and Maiwa Handprints Ltd.

Research for this book developed over several years, supported by different grants and also by the institutions at which I have studied and been employed. In this respect I am indebted to the following for their faith in my work: Leverhume Trust (special thanks are due to Jean Cater), University of Manchester (Helen Layland Fund), British Academy, Society for South Asian Studies, De Montfort University, Laura and Luigi Dallapiccola Trust, Nehru Trust, London College of Fashion/University of the Arts London, Victoria and Albert Museum, and Nottingham Trent University. My appreciation and thanks, too, to colleagues and former colleagues at the institutions mentioned who have offered encouragement and sound advice in equal measure. I would also like to acknowledge the support of an inspiring trio of academics under whose influence I completed my PhD at Manchester University and morphed into an academic myself. It was a rare privilege to study with them, great teachers all three, so my appreciation and thanks go to Professor Anne Morrell, Professor John Peter Wild and Professor Tim Ingold.

Many others have been involved in this project in diverse ways, sharing journeys and ideas, making me think and entertaining me along the way, and I am grateful to the following for their support: the late Naranbhai Ahir, Art Book Center Ahmedabad, Nirupam Chhaya, Haresh Dholakia, John Gillow, Hasmukh Gor, Joss Graham, Sue Harris-Fiore, Jenny Hughes, Umang Hutheesing, Umesh Jadia, Rajesh Jethi, Mohmedhusain B. Khatri, Liz Lesquereux, Ranju Mayechha, Sudhaben Mehta, Divyesh Pathak, Jacqui Pestell, the late Ramsinghji Rathod, Jayne Sanderson, Jadavji M. Sathvara, Vinod Solanki, Ayub Wazir. Particular thanks are due to Ritu, Nitin, Yasmin and Tarini Sethi for sharing the delights of the 'City of Djinns' with me and providing a home away from home in New Delhi and also to Yinka Fabusiyi—the best of osteopaths—who straightened me out in all respects as I wrote.

With the task of transforming my research into a book, I was helped immeasurably by a trio of accomplished scholars to whom I am indebted: Dr Abigail McGowan at the University of Vermont, and Liz Miller and Rosemary Crill at the V&A. My sincere appreciation and profound thanks to them for their perceptive reading of draft chapters, timely comments and encouragement. Thanks also to my publishers: Bipin Shah and Vinutha Mallya at Mapin Publishing in Ahmedabad, and Mark Eastment and Anjali Bulley at V&A Publishing who have supported this project through the long years of its realisation. My editor, Carmen Kagal, deserves special mention for her thoroughness and sensitive handling of the text; it is a far better read thanks to her finesse.

I feel tremendously lucky to have been able to live and work in India. As a result of being based in Gujarat, I have been privileged over the past twenty years to enjoy the humour, wisdom and hospitality of the Dhruv clan, my adoptive family in Ahmedabad—I am immensely proud to have joined their ranks. Finally, I would like to pay tribute to the late Janaki Dhruv, a proud Ahmedabadi whose knowledge and passionate enthusiasm for the material culture of Gujarat (and India) was inspiring. I hope this book does justice to her memory.